From the library of
Danny Doyle
Raised on songs and stories

Eleanor
Countess
of Desmond *c. 1545-1638*

WOLFHOUND PRESS – 100th TITLE

For my sister, the 'other' Eleanor!

By the same author

Granuaile: The Life and Times of Grace O'Malley c.1530–1603
(Wolfhound Press 1979; paperback 1983, 1985).
Chieftain to Knight: Tibbot Bourke, 1567 – 1629, First Viscount Mayo
(Wolfhound Press 1983).

Eleanor
Countess
of Desmond *c. 1545-1638*

ANNE CHAMBERS

WOLFHOUND PRESS

First published 1986
WOLFHOUND PRESS
68 Mountjoy Square, Dublin 1.

British Library Cataloguing in Publication Data

Chambers, Anne
    Eleanor, Countess of Desmond (c. 1545–1638)
    1. Desmond, Eleanor Fitzgerald, *Countess of*
    2. Ireland—Nobility—Biography
    3. Ireland—History—1558–1603
    4. Ireland—History—17th century
    I. Title
    941.505'092'4   DA937.5.D/

ISBN 0-86327-190-1

Cover Design: Jan de Fouw.
Typesetting: Design & Art Photosetting Ltd., Dublin.
Printed and bound by Billings & Sons Ltd., England.

Contents

Acknowledgements

I am indebted once again to Dr T. K. Whitaker for his invaluable comments on the first draft.

I wish to thank K. W. Nicholls, U.C.C., for his assistance with the pedigrees. My thanks to Mrs Ogden White, Kiltinan Castle, and the Honorable Desmond FitzGerald, the Knight of Glin, for their practical assistance and hospitality.

To the librarians and staff of the following institutions, National Library of Ireland, Public Record Office of Ireland, British Library, Library of the Tower of London, Library of Hatfield House, Hertfordshire, my appreciation and thanks. And to these, and to the other suppliers of copyright material for reproduction, acknowledged in the relevant captions, my thanks.

To the staff of the Wolfhound Press, to Colm Croker for his excellent editorial work, and to Joan Fanning for her research and secretarial assistance.

Prologue

Out of every corner of the woods and glens they came
creeping forth upon their hands for their legs could
not bear them, they looked like anatomies of death,
they spoke like ghosts, crying out of their graves, they
did eat the dead carrions, happy where they could find
them, yea, and one another soon after, insomuchas
the very carcasses they spared not to scrape out of
their graves and if they found a plot of watercresses or
shamrocks, there they flocked as to a feast for a time,
yet not able long to continue there withal, that in short
space there were none almost left, and a most
populous and plentiful country suddenly left void of
man or beast.

EDMUND SPENSER

Edmund Spenser's horrific account of starvation, cannabalism and decay described the state of the most fertile province of Ireland in 1582. The celebrated poet and civil servant bore witness to the dreadful spectacle that appalled his eyes and compelled his stern Elizabethan heart to cry out in pity. A once fertile province, the size of modern Holland, lay devastated. Lush green pasturelands were torched to a blackened heath, devoid of crops or animals. Famine stalked rampant through the vales and over the gently sloping hills. Among the smouldering remains the skeletal figures of the surviving peasantry foraged in vain. The castles and keeps of the local aristocracy lay in ruins, open to the unrelenting icy rain that hissed in vengeance on the smoking embers. The people were scattered and hid like wild beasts of prey in the fortresses of Munster's rugged mountain ranges and in her great dark forests and wild glens. They peered silently through the bare branches and bracken and waited. They awaited the return of the great overlord, their master to whose house, by traditions as ancient as the vast oak forests that sheltered them, they had given their absolute allegiance. They waited for him to lead them once more into battle in the bloody and futile war that for over three years had raged and ravaged the country.

But the great overlord shared the same fate as his clansmen. Askeaton castle, the mighty pile on the banks of the River Deel in Limerick, the symbol of his family's proud and powerful heritage, lay in ruins. A company of English horse was stabled in the great banqueting hall. Its lord was hunted like a wild animal over the despoiled estates of his Munster kingdom. From the lowly wattle huts of his kern, from the cold mountain caves to the ruined fortresses of his ancestors, through the marshy recesses of the Glen of Aherlow, into the dark forest of Kylemore and across the tortuous mountain passes to the west, Garrett FitzGerald, the fifteenth earl of the ancient and noble House of Desmond, fled for his life.

He had many impediments in his headlong flight for freedom. His once populous army had vanished, decimated more by famine and fear than by actual engagement with the enemy. His erstwhile allies had, one by one, forsaken him. Every friend had become a potential foe as the price on his head increased. His vast inheritance of over a half million acres of land in Munster provided the incentive and the scent to the eager English greyhounds who leaped from the slips in pursuit. But perhaps the greatest impediment to his safety stemmed from the physical disabilities he suffered. His frail body had succumbed to the effects of palsy and the Irish ague, the result of lengthy periods of imprisonment and deprivation, and aggravated by the dampness that oozed up from the marshes and bogs and by the rain that dripped incessantly from the bushes and undergrowth in which he hid or from the sodden thatch of the kern's cabins when he managed a fitful night's respite from the elements and the enemy. Yet despite these overwhelming liabilities, the earl had yet one remaining asset – his countess, Eleanor.

By 1582 Garrett and Eleanor had been married for seventeen years. It had at first sight perhaps seemed an unlikely match—the pale, proud Geraldine widower and the lively young girl from the rival Butler family. But Eleanor had soon proved her worth by bringing to the marriage certain qualities—coolness, prudence, pragmatism, skill in diplomacy, and an instinctive grasp of political realities—which might offset the less balanced traits of character displayed by her husband. For the earl's outlook was rooted firmly in the feudal tradition of a bygone era, from which he derived his jealously guarded status as the virtually absolute ruler of a territory larger than that of any other magnate in either England or Ireland. His pride and vanity and his aristocratic temperament made it impossible for him to come to terms with the challenge of a new age, typified by the Tudor monarchy, with its commitment to progress and reformation, to modernisation and the establishment of strong central government. Such ideals were anathema to the autocratic Earl of Desmond, and were bitterly resented by him as an intolerable affront to his ancient and customary rights, powers and privileges. His diehard attitude set him inevitably on a collision course with the relentless forces of change; and the struggle, if he persisted in it, could have only one outcome. His young wife, with her greater intelligence and political awareness, perceived the likely trend of future events and determined to do everything in her power to safeguard her husband's interests by helping him to adapt to the unfamiliar new power structure in Munster. And even if Garrett himself was doomed to destruction, Eleanor saw it as her duty to ensure the preservation of his earldom intact for his son and heir.

With great skill and courage, the capable and strong-willed countess had set about her difficult task. She had first of all sought to act as a moderating influence on the volatile and headstrong personality of her husband. Where he threatened and raged against his opponents, she counselled caution and diplomacy. Where he engaged in wild schemes or contemplated treasonable conspiracies, she conducted negotiations on his behalf with government officials. Where he took reckless and precipitate action, she moved swiftly to defuse the dangerous situation. On numerous occasions she mitigated the ill effects of his irresponsible and at times irrational behaviour.

Eleanor had also to contend with threats to the peace and stability of Desmond from other quarters. Ruthless Tudor administrators intent on the 'pacification' of Ireland; rapacious English soldiers and government officials; neighbouring lords envious of the earl's vast domain; power-hungry rivals from within his own family—all these desired Garrett's downfall and hoped to profit from the division of his estates. The precarious state of affairs in Munster was further complicated by the deliberate intrusion of a new-fangled ideological dimension arising from recent developments in international politics: on the one hand a group of Catholic zealots were attempting to use Munster as a cockpit in which to launch a great crusade, with papal and continental backing, against the heretical English Queen, while on the other hand the fanatical Puritan officers of the English army were remorselessly determined to stamp out every vestige of papal supremacy. Finally, in contrast to the ultra-modern and largely incomprehensible religious aspect of the Irish political scene in the closing decades of the sixteenth century, there was the age-old problem posed by the multitudes of undisciplined idle swordsmen who surrounded the earl and whose only trade was war and rapine. There was no future for such men in the new Ireland that was slowly and painfully coming into being; the archaic world of these Gaelic and gaelicised clansmen was already doomed, and if their hereditary overlord, the Earl of Desmond, allowed his interests to be identified with theirs, then his fate too was sealed.

Eleanor's efforts, in the face of such opposition, on behalf of her husband and his earldom made many demands on her varied abilities and on her courage. It was she who single-handedly administered the Desmond estates and revenues during Garrett's absence in England. It was she who loyally shared his years of sordid captivity, nursed him through his illnesses, and petitioned for his release. It was she who kept a close watch on the devious activities of his enemies in Munster and on the even more sinister machinations of certain of his own kinsmen and followers. It was she who conducted important negotiations with successive governors and central and provincial administrations. Her concern for the future of Desmond even led her to confront the Queen of England and to maintain contact with her over the years by means of astutely worded diplomatic missives, with the result that the cold hostility initially displayed by the unfriendly sovereign was gradually replaced by a kind of grudging respect for the Irish countess. In her endeavours to save the Desmond inheritance from confiscation and dismemberment, there was no one, English or Irish, who played any significant role in the affairs of Munster with whom she did not come into contact. And now, even after the earl had been proclaimed a traitor and a rebel, she refused to give up hope. Her home had been destroyed, her children scattered, her husband driven out as a hunted fugitive to seek refuge in remote forests and glens. Now once again, as the harsh winter weather penetrated the densely wooded Glen of Aherlow in the early weeks of 1582, she shared the misery and humiliation of his furtive existence—now cowering beneath a thick mass of undergrowth, where the exhausted earl had collapsed, while a scouting party of English soldiers from the garrison at Kilmallock scoured the area for them; now swiftly mounting her horse and decoying the soldiers on a mad chase further and further away from her husband's place of refuge; now wearily returning to nurse the ailing and semi-crippled earl; now composing a letter to the Privy Council; now dashing off northwards to intercede for her husband with the Lord Deputy or one of his officials; now suddenly reappearing with news of the approach of another posse of soldiers; now hurrying with Garrett from one wretched hiding-place to another.

The interest of Eleanor's story perhaps lies not so much in her achievements as in the way it illustrates the clash of two worlds, the old and the new, in Tudor Ireland, and how a woman's valiant attempt to reconcile them was ultimately destined to fail. At another level, the life of Eleanor Butler FitzGerald is a fascinating testimony to her own positive and spirited personality and to her qualities of energy, grit and endurance and her sheer will-power to survive. For she was to outlive Garrett by well over half a century, and the coming years held in store many new and difficult challenges and many strange and surprising twists of fortune.

MAP OF MUNSTER

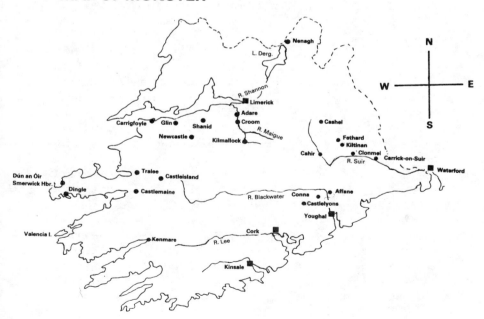

The Arms of the Earls of Desmond. A sixteenth century sculpture of the crest, shield and motto—written 'Shannid-a-bowe' (Shanid Abú)—in the Holy Trinity Church, Fethard, Co Tipperary. (Courtesy of the Knight of Glin).

1

The Baron's Daughter

Sometime let gorgeous Tragedy
In sceptred pall come sweeping by,
Presenting Thebes, or Pelops' line,
Or the tale of Troy divine.

MILTON, 'Il Penseroso'

The Crest of the Barons of Dunboyne.

Eleanor Butler, was born at Kiltinan castle, near Fethard, Co. Tipperary, about the year 1545. She was the second daughter of Edmund Butler, Lord Baron of Dunboyne. Her mother was Cecilia (Síle), daughter of Cormac Oge MacCarthy, Lord of Muskerry, Co. Cork, and widow of Sir Cormac MacCarthy Reagh. Eleanor had eight brothers, James, John, Piers, Richard, William, Thomas, Nicholas and Walter, and three sisters, Ellis, Katherine and Joan.

Kiltinan castle was the principal seat of the family, although at the time of Eleanor's birth her father also possessed the castles of Dangan, Boytonrath, Grange, Ballygellward, Grallagh, Moygarth, Tyrnwyane, Cashel and Fethard, Co. Tipperary. Her father's title of Dunboyne denoted the family's association with Dunboyne, Co. Meath. The connection can be traced back to the Norman invasion of the twelfth century. In 1172 Hugh de Lacy was granted the lordship of Meath, and on his subjugation of the Gaelic clans there he granted the manors of Dunboyne and Moynett to one of his followers, William le Petit. William's line continued until the reign of Henry III, when the sole heiress, Synolda, married Thomas Butler (le Botiller), third son of Theobald Butler, lord of the territory of Ormond in the south. By this marriage Thomas Butler became the Baron of Dunboyne and removed his residence to Co. Meath. The title, however, was not officially sanctioned until 1541, when Eleanor's father was formally created Baron of Dunboyne by royal patent of King Henry VIII.

The Dunboyne Butlers' re-connection with their Munster origin began in the fourteenth century, when Peter, second Lord Dunboyne, married the daughter and heiress of John de Bermingham, Lord of Kiltinan and Knockgraffon, Co. Tipperary. The de Bermingham family had long been settled in Co. Galway, but one of their house had married the daughter of Philip of Worcester, the original grantee of the Kiltinan properties. The de Berminghams maintained their interest in Kiltinan until as late as the mid-fifteenth century, apparently preferring to base their claim not on the feudal law of their ancestors but on the ancient Gaelic code, whereby property was retained by a family's more powerful members without much regard for proximity of blood or inheritance. In view of Peter's marriage, his grandson, Edmund, fourth Lord Dunboyne, staked his claim to Kiltinan by right of his de Bermingham grandmother. But the de Berminghams by 1410 had granted the castle to the third Earl of Ormond's illegitimate son, Thomas Butler, Prior of Kilmainham, in an attempt to circumvent the claims of the Dunboynes. The fourth Earl of Ormond, as overlord of the area, decided that only a duel could cut through the tangled legal web about possession of Kiltinan. Consequently in the spring of 1420 Edmund Bulter of Dunboyne fought a desperate duel to the death with the prior's son, also named Edmund. But Dunboyne was fatally wounded, and the prior's son won a brief respite for his family. The prior's descendants continued to hold Kiltinan until 1452, when the scales of justice were finally balanced. An interest in the property was conveyed to another Edmund Butler of Dunboyne, nephew of the duellist, and the Dunboynes finally entered into their rightful inheritance, albeit one and a half centuries late.

The rock fortress of Kiltinan castle stands in an imposing and picturesque location in the shadow of Slievenamon some miles from Fethard, Co. Tipperary. It is strategically situated above a steep ravine overlooking the Glashawley river, a tributary of the Suir. It commands a fine view over the rich pasturelands of the Suir valley sweeping away to the south and to the Comeragh and Knockmealdown mountains beyond. A remarkable geographical feature associated with Kiltinan is the 'roaring spring' phenomenon. An opening in the rocks leads to an underground river from which a spring emerges; an internal waterfall or cascade is thought by geologists to be responsible for the roaring sound. Described as 'the castle and dwelling-house of the Lord of Dunboyne',[1] it was built at the end of the twelfth century. In Eleanor's time it was a formidable structure of considerable size and comprised a large quadrangular courtyard bounded by four towers, one of which was circular; they were built of

Kiltinan Castle today at Fethard, Co. Tipperary. Eleanor's home. (Courtesy of Mrs Ogden White Photo: Robert Hobby).

limestone and sand mortar and were of a considerable height. The remains of the circular tower can still be seen today; its walls are some seven feet thick. Two of the square towers were subsequently incorporated in the manor house which still occupies the site and which has recently been magnificently restored and renovated by its present owner.

The roadway to Kiltinan castle in Eleanor's time would have swept up to the great arched gateway, flanked on either side by two three-storeyed towers, rising high above the curtain walls which linked the towers to one another. The spacious courtyard was a hive of activity as the guard, servants and labourers of the baron went about their allotted duties for the defence and maintenance of the castle and its inhabitants. High on the wall-walk, inside the parapet, sentries kept a watchful eye on the surrounding countryside. Down in the courtyard water was drawn in iron-bound wooden pails from the underground Glashawley spring. Wood was cut and stacked ready for fetching into the castle for use in the kitchen or to warm the great hall and living quarters. At one end of the courtyard the baron's horses were maintained by the grooms and horseboys, while in an adjoining shed the castle's smith pounded the red-hot iron into shape, pointed the lances and swords and riveted the armour for the baron's cavalry. A fire glowed in the centre of the yard around which armed men hunkered and awaited their master's orders. Through the gateway, carts laden with sacks of barley and wheat, vegetables and poultry, butter and cheese, wood and straw, trundled over the cobblestones, the obligatory payment in kind of the tenants to the lord of the manor.

Inside the castle the narrow corridors and the stone spiral stairway leading to the upper apartments were dark and gloomy. Shafts of light filtered through the defensive slit windows and the musket and archery loops. Dark corridors ran along the inside of the outer walls, with doors leading into various chambers. On the second level an arched opening from the stairway led into the principal chamber of the castle, the great hall. It was a lofty room, running the entire length of the castle. The ceiling was spanned by great oak beams, the walls were lime-washed, and the floor was of limestone slabs polished to a sheen. An impressive carved stone fireplace stood on one side. Light poured into the chamber through wide arched windows which were set in deep embrasures containing stone window seats covered with soft cushions. From the windows there was an all-encompassing view of the rolling Tipperary pasturelands. A massive table, richly carved of solid oak, dominated the top of the room, flanked by two iron candlestands. The walls were dotted with iron brackets to support the big tallow candles used to light the room. Off one end of the great hall was the baron's kitchen, buttery and pantry where the servants prepared the food and drink for his table. When the baron entertained his neighbours and friends or received a visit from his overlord, trestle tables would be set up within the hall to accommodate the visitors.

The bedchambers on the next level were small square rooms, each dominated by a large four-poster bed with a canopy of strong damask or richer velvet. By modern standards, the rooms were spartan. Apart from the bed, the main furnishings consisted of a large box or trunk for linens, a cupboard or press containing a water ewer and basin, and a larger press for clothes. Adjacent to the lord's bedchamber was his private chapel, elaborately decorated with fine plasterwork and with a window of stained or coloured glass. On each floor of the castle there were dark passages and smaller chambers, many used for storage, and various recesses. Life in such sixteenth-century castles was both cramped and chilly. Their primary function was defensive. They had been built in the twelfth century by the Normans to hold the land they had conquered, and in any changes undertaken by their descendants the defensive aspect of their design had been carefully preserved.

In Eleanor's day a medieval village, also of Norman origin, flourished outside the castle walls. The village consisted of a street of cottages and craft workshops, with lanes between the houses leading off into the surrounding countryside. The village craftsmen and workers supplied the castle with their wares and services. A few miles south of the castle stood the important medieval town of Fethard. It had been created an archiepiscopal borough, like Cashel, by letters patent from King John and had been a busy market town for many centuries. In 1553, on petition of the burgesses and commonalty of the town, an important charter ordained that the borough should become a corporate body with the same privileges and liberties as Kilkenny. The charter was subsequently confirmed by James I in 1608.

Together with his administrative and military powers as seneschal of the area, Eleanor's father was a substantial landowner. He received specific rents and services from those who held lands under him. As was the custom, he either leased out land, usually for a period of twenty-one years, for a fixed rent, or let it on a share-cropping basis for the consideration of what was known as the 'third sheaf' or even for as much as a half share of the crop. He in turn provided the tenant

A 16th century bedchamber. Bunratty Castle. (Courtesy of Shannon Development).

with either one-third or a half of the seed. His tenants, especially the more substantial, further sublet the land to others.

Lower in status than the tenanted classes in both the Gaelic and Anglo-Norman lordships was the great mass of the actual land cultivators, herders and labourers, referred to as 'churls'. They did not own land, or even stock, and were not allowed to bear arms. They were therefore totally dependent on their masters and were often treated brutally in both societies.

Together with .the 'third sheaf', the tenants provided obligatory services to the baron, such as the cultivation and harvesting of his crops. The baron counted his wealth, like his Gaelic counterparts, in the size of his cattle herds, but there was a greater emphasis on tillage within his lordship than in Gaelic areas. Crops such as wheat, rye and barley were grown, and some vegetables were cultivated. Pigs and sheep were also kept, and, in common with most lords in the sixteenth century, the baron maintained a stud, Ireland being noted then as now for its 'great breeds of horses'.[2] Falconry and hunting were the main outdoor recreations, while chess, dice and backgammon helped to while away the long winter evenings.

Eleanor's childhood and girlhood were spent mainly at her father's principal castle of Kiltinan. There she grew up in an environment influenced by the two principal traditions that dominated sixteenth-century Ireland: the old Gaelic civilisation, which, after the reversal it had encountered in the twelfth century, had over the succeeding centuries staged a gradual but steady recovery; and the feudal tradition of the Anglo-Norman settlers, which had in the course of time succumbed in varying degrees to the resurgent Gaelic culture. The Butlers were among the original Anglo-Norman invaders, but, like their FitzGerald and de Burgo fellow-conquerors, they had, through proximity with their Gaelic neighbours and their environment and especially through centuries of intermarriage with the Gaelic aristocracy, become gaelicised to some degree. Eleanor's mother was herself a MacCarthy, and she had previously been married to Cormac MacCarthy Reagh, by whom she had one son and four daughters. One of Eleanor's half-sisters had in turn married John Butler of Kilcash, and another became the wife of James FitzGerald of Decies, Co. Waterford. The incidence of intermarriage within those of Anglo-Norman descent and within the Gaelic aristocracy and between both groups was very high by the standards of the time, and most of the great dynastic families of both groups were subsequently blood-related. This feature also led to many incidents of incestuous marriage; for example, Eleanor's father was said to have had a daughter (later married to Séan an tSléibhe O'Carroll) by his own sister who later married Sir Piers Butler of Cahir. Eleanor's uncle Peter Butler was married to Honora, the daughter of James FitzGerald, eleventh Earl of Desmond. Her aunt Joan Butler had married Roland Eustace, Viscount Baltinglass, while another aunt, Ellen, had married David Roche, Viscount Fermoy, thus linking her family with many prominent houses both Gaelic and gaelicised.

The Dunboyne Butlers were a cadet branch of one of the great dynastic families of Ireland, the Butlers of Ormond, over whom the Earl of Ormond was the titular head. The Earls of Ormond enjoyed palatine jurisdiction over their estates in Co. Tipperary, which made them very powerful indeed. This privilege, given them by the Crown, endowed them with the power to establish courts of law, administer justice and appoint court officers, 'thus ensuring that it was they rather than the King who were the ultimate arbitrators'.[3] The Earls of Ormond owed theoretical allegiance to the Crown, but they guarded their independence jealously. While they customarily administered their vast estates by right of feudal law, the indigenous Gaelic law had over the centuries penetrated their territory, and by the middle of the sixteenth century many Gaelic customs and practices were in vogue in Ormond.

The Gaelic legal and social system was distinct to Ireland and had evolved over the centuries from its Celtic origins. It was geared to an agrarian economy and culture where the emphasis was on the outdoor way of life. Gaelic society comprised clans or 'nations' of independent chieftaincies, and was based on the concept of a patrilineal 'descent group forming a definite corporate entity with political and legal functions'.[4] The existence of so many independent entities, each ruled by a chieftain that 'maketh war and peace for himself . . . and obeyeth to no other person . . . except only to such persons as may subdue him by the sword',[5] gave rise to much tribal warfare and unrest. It was also later to irk the pride of the Tudor monarchs, who in the early years of their rule had determinedly extinguished such independent posturings among the English nobility, and who more recently had inflicted a ruthless chastisement on the Anglo-Irish House of Kildare when lords of that house had shown an inclination towards independence.

The clan was the centre-point of the Gaelic system and set it apart from its English counterpart. The leader or chieftain of the clan was elected by the ruling sept, instead of succeeding by right of primogeniture as was the English custom. The tenure of land also differed from the English practice. It was conducted according to a

The Great Hall, Bunratty Castle (Courtesy of
Shannon Development) and inset period
costume illustration of Irish women. (Lucas
de Heere, 16th century).

complicated system of land distribution whereby, on the death of a landholder, the land was shared out among the ruling or landholding members of the clan. The chieftain retained only a life interest in the clan land and could not bequeath it to his son on his death. Although a woman could purchase and own land in her own right, she was prohibited from inheriting land. The wealth of the clan was measured not in the extent of its territory but in the number of cattle it possessed. Cattle were the principal symbol of wealth and often the cause of wars and disputes. The basic unit of value was a young heifer. While cattle denoted the wealth of the clan, the power of the chieftain was measured by the number of his followers. Each chieftain accordingly strove to have as many armed men in his company as he could afford. Similarly, it was important for the chieftain to maintain a large workforce of servants and labourers for the more servile work of tending and protecting the huge cattle herds, tilling the soil, and providing sustenance and accommodation for his band of warriors. The chieftain was also in receipt of certain dues and services exacted, often by force, from the sub-chieftains who held under him. Under various laws he had the right to a wide range of privileges, such as free entertainment and provisions for himself and his extensive household, specific provisions for his horses and hounds, and the right to demand his sub-lords' attendance with a fixed number of armed men whenever he summoned a hosting. The whole system of free entertainment for the lord became known as 'coyne and livery' and was in effect the basis of the Gaelic system of authority. By the middle of the sixteenth century, however, many of these practices had been adopted also by the lords of Anglo-Norman origin.

Fosterage played an important role in Gaelic society, the sons of chieftains being fostered in the household of a dependent chief, who considered it a great privilege and of considerable political importance as a bond between the two families. The system found little favour with the Crown, which had sought to ban it, but it had survived and was widely practised, and in the course of time had penetrated the social mores of Anglo-Norman society in Ireland.

After the Norman invasion the Gaelic chieftains had adopted stone castles as their places of dwelling and protection. There, usually in large banqueting halls attached to the main tower, they held court and entertained lavishly. Every chieftain of note had his 'brehon' or judge who interpreted and administered the law in his territory. He also had a bard (*ollamh dána*), a member of one of the most interesting groups in the professional learned class in Gaelic society, and one who enjoyed a special status in the chief's household. The poet's basic duty was 'the eulogy of the great and glorification of their deeds'.[6] He often used his verses to incite his lord to further violence against an ancient enemy or to a cattle-raid or incursion into a neighbouring territory.

The chieftain had usually three groupings of fighting men in his team. The horsemen were recruited from within the ranks of the ruling sept or the more prosperous elements of the landowning classes. The galloglass (*gallóglaigh*, 'foreign warriors') were the heavy infantry of the chieftain's army, being selected men of great stature and strength, armed with long sword and battle-axe. Originally from Scotland, they had settled in many parts of Ireland, where they had been given tracts of land in payment for their services as a standing army for the Gaelic chieftains and Anglo-Norman lords who could afford them. The Butlers' traditional galloglass had long been the MacSweeneys. The third category of fighting men were the kern (*certhearnigh*); skilled in the use of bows and arrows and darts, they were the lightly armed foot-soldiers of the chieftain's army.

Most of the Anglo-Irish lords and the Gaelic chieftains, despite the Reformation in England, still adhered to the old religion. But Catholicism in Gaelic Ireland differed greatly from that on the continent, and the sweeping reforms of the preceding centuries had by and large failed to be applied in Ireland. A pattern of hereditary clergy had evolved where members of a particular family were traditionally invested with positions of high office in the church. Many of the bishops and clergy were married or maintained concubines. And as a recent historian has remarked, 'In no field of life was Ireland's apartness from the mainstream of Christian European society so marked as in that of marriage. Throughout the medieval period, and down to the end of the old order in 1603, what could be called Celtic secular marriage remained the norm in Ireland and Christian matrimony was no more than the rare exception grafted on to this system.'[7] There was a high incidence of divorce, which was a legal right and could be invoked by either spouse. Plurality of marriages, many within the restricted degrees of consanguinity, and trial marriages were a common feature of sixteenth-century life within both the Gaelic and the gaelicised lordships. Offspring born outside wedlock were not penalised by Gaelic law in their rights of succession or land tenure. Conn Bacach O'Neill, first Earl of Tyrone, stoutly declared that he was a man 'that never refused no child that any woman named to be his'.[8]

Thus Eleanor grew up in a society which, while it adhered in many

Black Tom. Thomas Butler, 10th Earl of Ormond. Engr. by Bartolozzi after Holbein. National Portrait Gallery, London.

ways to its English origins, had also absorbed into its social and political structures many of the trappings of the Gaelic world that surrounded it. While her Gaelic mother would have further strengthened this development in the house of the Dunboyne Butlers, their great overlord, the Earl of Ormond, was then, as in the past, a loyal supporter of the Tudor monarchs, and also the least gaelicised of the Anglo-Norman lords in Ireland. Eleanor's father, together with his brother Peter, had served under the Earl of Ormond in the army of Henry VIII in France. They had been in action at the sieges of Montreuil and Boulogne. After the inexplicable death by poison of the earl in London in 1546 his son and heir Thomas, known as Black Tom, then just fifteen years old, had been brought up in the new Protestant religion and had been reared at court as a friend and classmate for the young future king, Edward VI, and the future queen, Elizabeth I. Black Tom was to remain at court for many years before he entered into his inheritance in Ireland. During his absence Eleanor's father was placed in charge of the Crown forces in Ormond to repel the increasingly frequent raids of the O'Carrolls of Ely. He was appointed Seneschal of the Liberty of Tipperary, an office held by each successive baron since 1295. The duties involved the stewardship of the earl's domains, the exaction and collection of his rents, dues and services, and the administration of his palatine court at Clonmel. Kiltinan bustled with activity during the early years of Eleanor's childhood.

Life for a young girl, the daughter of a nobleman, in the sixteenth century had its set pattern and its share of responsibilities. From the day of her birth Eleanor was groomed as a potential wife for one of the Anglo-Irish lords or Gaelic chieftians who would seek her hand. Provided their credentials and assets were acceptable to her father and an agreement was reached on a suitable dowry, Eleanor would be given in marriage to the most suitable applicant. Political and financial considerations tended to dictate the matrimonial lot of women in the higher echelons of Gaelic and Anglo-Irish society. It was usual for girls to marry at the comparatively early age of fifteen or sixteen. Given in marriage to one of her own class, Eleanor would eventually become chatelaine of her own castle. With the privilege went the responsibility to oversee and administer the domestic and social lifestyle of her lord. The upkeep and maintenance of her husband's castles would be her responsibility. Food and furnishings had to be bought, stored and replaced; servants hired, fired and trained; banquets organised to impress a neighbour or to honour an overlord; household linens, utensils and liveries to be selected and accounted for. The efficient administration of a huge mansion with its servants and retainers had to be undertaken daily. The confidence, poise and presence to entertain and converse diplomatically with both the friends and foes of her husband with charm and courtesy had to be acquired. This involved a political and social awareness not easily mastered. In preparation for her exacting future role, Eleanor's formal education was provided for, and English and Gaelic tutors taught her to converse ably in both English and Irish. She learned to write in both languages, and in later life was to become a prolific letter-writer, able to express herself succinctly and well, with an intelligent turn of phrase and a political insight that denoted a shrewd and comprehending mind. Eleanor was also educated in the more outdoor pursuits. She was an able horsewoman, a skill that was to stand to her many times in the course of her traumatic life.

Gaelic Ireland is often inaccurately depicted as having been a totally male-dominated society where women fulfilled a mainly subservient role, confined to the domestic duties of housekeeping and child-rearing and rarely becoming involved in the political turmoil of the times. On the contrary, there are many examples of women, mainly in the higher orders of both Gaelic and gaelicised society, who became actively and ably involved in politics, not only in a supportive or advisory capacity to their husbands, but also as strong-willed and independent participants in their own right. Eleanor herself in later life was to become a prime example of this little-acknowledged fact.

It was reputed that she was tall in stature, with light brown hair. On special or formal occasions she dressed in the current fashion of the day, in gowns of tafetta, velvet or fine cambric edged with lace, as befitted her station. Her wardrobe might be purchased in Dublin, which tended to follow English fashion, or bought from the travelling merchants, who brought with them the fashions and fabrics of the continent, imported through the ports of Waterford, Cork and Kinsale. The native Irish attire of the time, a linen or fine woollen smock reaching to the ankles, with long wide sleeves falling in folds at either side, over which was worn a sleeveless dress with a laced bodice dyed saffron or russet, might well have been worn by Síle MacCarthy's daughter on less auspicious occasions. The great Irish mantle of warm wool with its thickly fringed collar was worn by the upper classes of both cultures and often proved a welcome and an appropriate addition to both male and female attire, especially when the cold winds blew or as a copious shelter from the prevalent rain and mist.

Travel was a difficult and hazardous undertaking in sixteenth-century Ireland, owing partly to the absence of a developed road system and partly to the constant unsettled state of the country. But journeys, however hazardous, had to be undertaken as business was contracted, military campaigns conducted and social visits made to relations and friends. Such social occasions were marked by great banquets, often lasting many days. The Baron of Dunboyne played host on many such occasions when family, relations, friends and even foes would converge on Kiltinan. In the great hall of the castle the baron's chief steward would conduct each guest to his allotted place in strict order according to social and political status. On the low trestle tables platters of beef, mutton, venison, poultry and game, boiled or spit-roasted, were laid in great joints. Guests helped themselves, cutting with knives and eating with their hands. Wheaten bread and oatcakes were in plentiful supply, as were vegetables such as cabbage, onion, leek and watercress. Wines from France and Spain, imported through Youghal or Waterford, native aqua vitae (*uisge beatha*), ale and mead, 'the dainty drink of nobles',[9] helped to digest the plentiful helpings. Gaelic chieftains in their tight worsted trews and short quilted jackets of fine leather, their hair falling around their shoulders, mingled with the lords of the Pale clad in doublet and hose. The long hall, warmed by a glowing brazier in the centre and lit by the flickering torches in the wall brackets, reverberated with a mixture of English and Gaelic tongues. A bard rose and loudly sang the praises of Eleanor's father and his house, while her mother's MacCarthy origins were equally lauded. A verse extolling the baron's hospitality and the beauty of his wife and daughters followed. Games of cards, dice and backgammon were played, and as the night wore on the bids became more reckless, and many a horse, jewelled dagger, silver plate, herd of cattle or tract of land changed hands. The harp and the pipes were played for the dancers, whose capering shadows loomed in crazy silhouettes on the stone walls.

Eleanor's childhood, however, was not all feasting and revelry. Her early years were disturbed by a bitter feud between her father and her uncle Peter which drove a wedge not only between the brothers but between her father and his overlord, the Earl of Ormond. The feud had its origins in 1524 when Eleanor's grandfather, Sir James Butler, concluded a family settlement of his estate, bequeathing the greater portion to his eldest son, Edmund, Eleanor's father. He also directed that his second son, Peter, was to receive the castle and estate of Grallagh, while Thomas, his youngest son, was to inherit Boytonrath and other lands near Cashel. Edmund was Peter's overlord to whom he owed allegiance and a 'suit and service of six footmen and one horseman'.[10] Despite their initial co-operation, on their return from the wars in France a growing enmity developed between them over possession of the Grallagh estate. Edmund claimed that the estate was entailed on the Barons of Dunboyne and that his father had no right to bequeath it to Peter, who, he contended, had merely a life interest in the property. The quarrel became further aggravated by the personal animosity that arose between Eleanor's mother and Peter's wife Honora, daughter of James FitzGerald, eleventh Earl of Desmond. Their mutual dislike of one another could have stemmed from the ancient animosity between the MacCarthys and the Earls of Desmond. Whether for this reason or for something of a more personal nature, the two ladies goaded their spouses into action against each other, and each plotted for her own husband's triumph over the other. As the feud between the brothers intensified it led to the formation of political affiliations and alliances that were eventually to have repercussions on Eleanor's future.

Her father filed a suit against his brother in the Court of Chancery. But on the advice of his cousin, Black Tom, who had recently entered into his estates and title as Earl of Ormond, Peter refused to appear before the court. Ill-feeling already existed between Eleanor's father and the new Earl of Ormond, largely as a result of an ancient dispute concerning the validity of the palatine rights of the earldom. The earl now considered that Edmund had further rebuffed his authority over him by failing to submit his suit to his palatine court for his judgement. The Court of Chancery found in Edmund's favour and ordered Peter to restore to him the disputed Grallagh estate. Peter, again on the advice of Black Tom, refused to comply with the court order. The dispute continued to rage for many years. The legal battle culminated in attacks and reprisals by both brothers on each other and drove an ever-widening wedge between Edmund and his brother and his overlord, the Earl of Ormond. Eleanor and her family were affected both politically and socially by the baron's estrangement from the House of Ormond. They experienced a sense of isolation as the other tributary lords of Ormond were reluctant to defy their powerful overlord and openly fraternise with the Dunboynes. Few invitations were extended to them to festivities at the earl's court at Clonmel or Kilkenny. The isolation of the Dunboynes left them open to exploitation in the climate of political discord and intrigue which characterised sixteenth-century Munster. In these circumstances it was inevitable that the family would become involved in the intense and long-standing feud between the Houses of Ormond and Desmond.

While the dispute between Eleanor's father and uncle was to continue unabated until their deaths, when Grallagh was finally restored to the Dunboyne estate, it was to pale into insignificance in comparison to the Desmond–Ormond feud which was about to erupt and engulf Eleanor and all Munster in its spreading flames. To understand the reason for the feud and the reckless intensity with which it was pursued in the sixteenth century by the young leaders of both houses, it is necessary to return in time to the twelfth century.

The origin of the Butlers in Ireland can be traced to a certain Norman lord named Hervey who had estates in East Anglia and Lancashire and who was living in 1130. The family had been closely involved in the crusades, and a son of Hervey, Hubert Walter, had been instrumental in raising the enormous ransom demanded by the Emperor Henry VI for the release of King Richard Coeur-de-Lion. The family's loyalty to the English Crown had been well established before their arrival in Ireland. Hubert's brother Theobald was the founder of the family in Ireland, and after the Norman invasion he was created Chief Butler, one of the hereditary offices of state, by King Henry II. He and his descendants were granted the lucrative prisage of wines, which involved the right to one-tenth of the cargo of any wine ship that broke bulk in Ireland. This privilege was held by the family until by an act of parliament in 1810 it was finally restored to the Crown. From this hereditary honour came the family name of Butler.

The Butler lordship in Ireland comprised the northern half of Co. Tipperary, including the disputed overlordship of the old Gaelic kingdom of Ely O'Carroll. Successive Butler lords consolidated their positions over the succeeding decades. They upheld the Crown's interests in the newly conquered territories and were amply rewarded. In 1315 Edward II gave Edmund Butler the castle and manor of Carrickmagriffon and Roscrea and granted him the earldom of Carrick. Edmund's son James married the niece of Edward III, and in 1328 he was created Earl of Ormond and was granted the palatine liberties of Tipperary. In 1392 the third Earl of Ormond acquired the town of Kilkenny, which eventually became the principal seat of the family.

Cheek by jowl with the expanding Butler lordship were the contemporary lordships of two other Anglo-Norman dynasts. To the north-east the FitzGeralds of Kildare had prospered, while to the west the FitzGeralds of Desmond had carved out a vast estate at the expense of the native chieftains. It was perhaps inevitable that the ambitions of these great Anglo-Norman families would conflict as they vied with each other for power, land and royal favours.

The ancestors of the FitzGeralds, or, as they became known, the Geraldines, were also numbered among the Norman conquerors who invaded Ireland. Their background in England, however, differed greatly from that of the Butlers. Their origins were in the wild marcher lands between England and Wales. After the Norman conquest of England their progenitor Gheraldino had been initially granted the lordship of Windsor. From there they had advanced into Celtic Wales, where they had acquired further lands both by military and matrimonial means.

In 1095 Gerald, the grandson of the original Gheraldino, married the beautiful and notorious Princess Nesta, daughter of the King of South Wales, and built Carew castle on the lands granted to him in right of his wife. This Gerald was the progenitor of the Geraldines or FitzGeralds of Ireland. He died in 1135, leaving three sons, Maurice, William and David, afterwards Bishop of St Davids. Together with Nesta's son by her second marriage, Robert FitzStephen, and her illegitimate offspring by a previous liaison with King Henry I, this turbulent brood became a source of constant strife. In the wild border areas along the Welsh marches they conducted private wars of retribution and invasion without the slightest regard for the sovereignty of the English monarch, who in any event was powerless to interfere. It was an able and wily king who could devise the means to rid his kingdom of such independently-minded barons and of such internal discord.

An invitation from the Gaelic King of Leinster, Dermot MacMurrough, provided him with the opportunity. At the forefront of the Norman invasion of Ireland was Maurice, son of Gerald of Wales. In return for his services Maurice was granted land in what is now Co. Kildare and built a strong fortress at Maynooth. The FitzGeralds of Kildare were descended from Maurice's eldest son, Gerald, and they eventually became powerful overlords of the greater part of Leinster. The FitzGeralds of Munster descended from his youngest son Thomas, and they extended the conquest deep into Munster. In 1329 Thomas's great-great-grandson Maurice was created first Earl of Desmond by Edward III, and, similarly to the Earl of Ormond's acquisition of Tipperary, he was granted the county of Kerry as an hereditary palatine liberty. Both he and his successors extended their power until eventually they claimed the overlordship of a vast area which stretched from north Limerick to Youghal and from Dingle in Kerry to the Decies in Waterford.

In the course of time all three houses had, partly by reason of their close association and intermarriage with the neighbouring Gaelic aristocracy and partly because of their isolation from their English origins, became gaelicised. Of the three, the Desmonds could be said to have become the most gaelicised. Despite their English titles and honours, they were, true to their Geraldine tradition, outspoken champions of practical independence from the English Crown. In this they tended to have the moral support of their fellow-Geraldines, the Kildares. In 1345, for example, Maurice of Desmond flaunted his power over the Gaelic and gaelicised lords and convened his own parliament in Callan, Co. Kilkenny. The King hurriedly gathered an army to defeat him before the Crown's authority in Ireland could be usurped by the proud and powerful Geraldine lord. Thereafter the Munster Geraldines tended to withdraw into their remote domains, and in defiance of England gradually became indistinguishable in tongue, dress and custom from their Gaelic neighbours.

Differences arose between them and the neighbouring and less gaelicised family of the Butlers of Ormond, and their quarrels were further heightened when they took different sides in the Wars of the Roses in England, fought between the Houses of York and Lancaster, until finally the antagonism between the Ormonds and the Desmonds became entangled in the wider net of political conflict in England.

The Duke of York was the absentee viceroy of Ireland, but his ambitions soared to more exalted office—to the Crown of England. After his defeat at the battle of Ludford Bridge and his subsequent conviction for treason he was replaced as viceroy of Ireland by the Earl of Ormond. York escaped to Ireland and, aided and abetted by the Geraldines, made plans for the invasion of England. In the event York was killed at the battle of Wakefield in 1460, but his ambitions were later realised by his son, who in 1461 was crowned King Edward IV. One of the first casualties of the Yorkist triumph was the Earl of Ormond, who was promptly executed. His brother and heir, Sir John Butler, in an attempt to revitalise the Lancastrian cause in Ireland, rallied his supporters but was defeated at Pilltown by James, seventh Earl of Desmond. While this incident was, from the Geraldines' point of view, yet another chapter in the Desmond–Ormond feud, the victory was rewarded by a grateful Yorkist King, who had Desmond's son and successor, Thomas, confirmed as chief governor of Ireland in 1463. But despite his apparent Yorkist leanings, the new Earl of Desmond remained independent and gaelicised like his forebears. An anxious King looked on in trepidation as his erstwhile protégé attempted to extend Gaelic law and custom into the English Pale. Soon the normally peaceful Pale was aflame. Desmond was speedily replaced by Sir John Tiptoft, who, without apparent royal order—at least without any that was issued openly—had Desmond beheaded at Drogheda. The effect on the country was instantaneous. Riots and uprisings swept through Munster and Leinster; the dead earl's brother attacked the Pale with a great army and burned and pillaged this sanctuary of English civilisation. The imprisoned Earl of Kildare was released to calm the situation. Tiptoft was recalled, and the King proclaimed his disavowal of the act.

The execution of the earl was the final straw that broke the back of the uneasy alliance between the House of Desmond and the Crown of England. In the succeeding decades the Geraldines of Desmond withdrew from all contact with the Crown and its administration in Dublin. They turned their backs on their English origins in favour of their adopted Gaelic world that welcomed them as the premier buffer between it and the English Crown. Their great rivals, the Earls of Ormond, continued to hold for the Crown and many of the succeeding earls spent much of their time at the English court. Now in the second half of the sixteenth century the long-standing feud and the political divergences of both houses had come to rest in the hot, reckless hands of young Black Tom of Ormond and Garrett FitzGerald of Desmond, each eager to uphold the honour of his house by the destruction of the other.

Secure in Kiltinan, surrounded by her large family, Eleanor took little notice of the gathering storm-clouds. Her main preoccupation was that of any young eligible woman: she patiently plied her needle or read her verse and waited and wondered about her marriage prospects. What dashing lord or handsome chieftain would come to Kiltinan to seek her hand? Or would she instead become the prize in some political or financial deal, a sop to placate some ageing, lascivious noble? Fate was often known to deal a cruel hand in the matrimonial stakes. But whatever her thoughts, little could she have realised how inextricably her future would become entangled in the Ormond–Desmond feud and its repercussions which would hurl her into the very eye of the impending storm.

2
The Feud

Two households, both alike in dignity,
In fair Verona, where we lay our scene,
From ancient grudge break to new mutiny,
Where civil blood makes civil hands unclean.

SHAKESPEARE, *Romeo and Juliet*, I, i

In 1558 the daughter of Anne Boleyn and Henry VIII ascended the throne of England. Deemed illegitimate by some of her subjects, God's appointed sovereign majesty by others, the twenty-six-year-old, slight, pale-faced woman determinedly grasped the sceptre of state, aware of the doubts and of the awesome task that she faced. Her inherited kingdom had floundered like a rudderless galleon since the death of her father over a decade earlier. She had inherited a throne 'humiliated in war, paralysed by ineptitude and sinking into spiritual and financial bankruptcy'.[1] With a great sense of destiny, this autocratic, vain woman embarked on a life's mission to protect and defend her legacy, the kingdom of England, which was to become her substitute lover, husband and child, and to prove that she had indeed 'the heart and stomach of a king'.

Part of Elizabeth's legacy was Ireland, which yet remained, despite the best efforts of her wily father, a country without political cohesion or racial homogeneity; an island in close and dangerous proximity to England but which her cartographers had not yet accurately mapped; a country which in its present state was the antithesis of everything that the sovereign Elizabeth and her renaissance age represented. Gaelic Ireland seemed barbarously medieval by the standards of renaissance England and continental Europe. Its outmoded political, social and religious structures, its dogged rebellious attitude to the 'civilising' attempts of the English Crown, its intertribal dissension and its consistent lack of common

Principal Lordships in Tudor Ireland.

purpose made it a potential attraction to England's foreign enemies. In 1558 Ireland, with her myriad of independent lords and chieftains, confronted Elizabeth with a similar problem to that which had faced her grandfather Henry VII in England many decades previously. At that time the great English feudal lords had also strained at the royal bit before being short-reined into submission and into the admission that their royal overlord was invested with a God-given temporal and spiritual power over them. The Tudors demanded, and had received, the total loyalty and acquiescence of their feudal barons in England. Now it was the turn of the independent chieftains and lords of Ireland to proffer a similar obeisance. But the Gaelic lords were to prove reluctant to relinquish the powers and privileges enjoyed by them for centuries by right of Gaelic custom and law. Elizabeth was not to have her way in Ireland without a protracted, expensive and bitter struggle.

Elizabeth's supposedly liege lords in Ireland were a mixed bunch. In Leinster the Earls of Kildare, the Leinster Geraldines, had, during the reigns of Henry VII and Henry VIII, reached the pinnacle of their power. Henry VIII feared their potential as an alternative to the Crown in Ireland and their inherited Geraldine tendencies towards independence. Their star finally fell when a hot-blooded young scion, Silken Thomas, son of the ninth earl, convulsed the House of Kildare into a hasty rebellion and provided Henry with the excuse he had long awaited. The rebellion led to the execution in 1537 at Tyburn of Silken Thomas and his five uncles, and to the demise of the Kildares as an alternative power to the English monarch in Ireland. Henry hurriedly had himself confirmed 'King of Ireland' before any Anglo-Irish lord or Gaelic chieftain could snatch the title from him.

In Ormond the Butlers, after years of eclipse by the Kildares, had re-emerged as the champions of the Crown in Ireland. Now with Black Tom, his Boleyn connections and his close personal relationship with the young queen, a new chapter of Ormond supremacy in Ireland was about to begin. Black Tom's loyalty to and friendship with Elizabeth was to last to the end of her long reign. She referred to him as her 'black husband', which gave rise to much speculation that, while not her husband in the legal sense, Black Tom had been awarded the pleasure of the royal bedchamber. He was twenty-seven years of age at the time of Elizabeth's accession to the throne. As his nickname suggests and as is evident from his portrait, he was a black-haired, dark-skinned, tall, well-set, elegantly attired courtier, handsome and charming, but also cruel and ruthless when the necessity arose. He was the veritable renaissance man, modern and confident in outlook

Queen Elizabeth 1.

and action. Just as his loyal ancestry, Boleyn connections and personal ability had struck Elizabeth's sensibility, so his startling good looks and charm had touched a chord in her heart. Black Tom was and would continue to be her favourite Irish noble, a fact which she made no effort to hide but preferred to flaunt by means of the personal and political favouritism which she showed towards him. In 1559 she appointed him to the office of Lord Treasurer, and he became closely identified with the Sussex faction at the royal court.

In 1558 also, Black Tom's neighbour and adversary, Garrett (Gerald), son of James FitzJohn FitzGerald, became the fifteenth Earl of Desmond. He was the antithesis of Black Tom, especially in Elizabeth's eyes. His ancestry made him politically less acceptable to her, and from a physical point of view the delicate, pale, vain, melancholic, temperamental Geraldine aroused no passion in her Tudor heart. Henry VII had desired that Garrett, like Black Tom, should have the benefit of an English upbringing and education and attend at court with his son Edward. But Garrett's father, in the wake of the execution of his kinsmen, the Geraldine Kildares, saw little reason to entrust his son to the care and attention of the Tudor court. Consequently Garrett was reared and educated in the hard school of Gaelic Ireland. He was fostered with the O'Moriartys in Kerry and was subjected to the rigorous physical training demanded by the Gaelic system for mastering the skills and techniques required of a warrior, a leader and a ruler. But he also aspired to more learned ways and was given to the composition of verse. Lest his literary and general melancholic disposition should arouse any doubts as to his physical ability to succeed his father to the earldom, and in accordance with the Gaelic custom which ordained that 'every heir or young chieftain of a tribe was obliged in honour to give a public specimen of his valour before he was owned or declared governor or leader of his people', Garrett led his followers 'to make a desperate incursion upon some neighbour or other that they were in feud with; and they were obliged to bring by open force the cattle they found in the lands they attacked or die in the attempt.'[2] The MacCarthy clans of Carbery and Muskerry were singled out for assault by the young Geraldine lord in order to demonstrate his prowess. Not only did the clans pay the price of Garrett's initiation in the customary penalties of cattle and booty, but to emphasise his abilities he captured and imprisoned Lord Muskerry's son for good measure. Such was the tough school of Gaelic custom, which traced its origins back to the legendary Celtic world with its cattle-raids and warrior chiefs, in which the son and heir of the Earl of Desmond was reared.

But Garrett's succession to the earldom was fraught with controversy. It had originated when Maurice, the son of the twelfth Earl of Desmond, married his own first cousin, by whom he had a son called James. A nephew of the twelfth earl named James FitzJohn, Garrett's father, disputed the right of James to succeed his father on the grounds of consanguinity. The matter was settled, not by law but by the sword, when James was murdered by James FitzJohn's brother. But James FitzJohn then found his own way to the earldom disputed on the grounds of his equally prohibited marriage to his own grand-niece, the daughter of Maurice Roche, Lord Fermoy, by whom he had a son known as Sir Thomas Roe FitzGerald. Yielding to pressure from his sub-chiefs and lords who feared yet another bloody succession dispute, James FitzJohn divorced his first wife and married Mór O'Carroll, the daughter of the lord of Ely O'Carroll, by whom he had Garrett, his heir, born in 1532, John, later known as Sir John of Desmond, and five daughters. By a later marriage to Ellen, daughter of Donal MacCarthy More, he had another son called James 'Sussex' FitzGerald. Upon Garrett's succession to the earldom in November 1558, Thomas Roe, the disinherited son, unsuccessfuly appealed his case in the English court.

Garrett's father had been a vigorous supporter of the House of Kildare and had become one of the principal activists in the league formed to protect and reinstate the only surviving member of the Kildare dynasty, but after the disbandment of the league he had submitted to the Crown. He was subsequently created Lord Treasurer and governor of Munster. He had, by his fourth and final marriage to Katherine Butler, the second daughter of the eighth Earl of Ormond, and by various marriage alliances between other members of the Butler and Desmond families, mitigated somewhat the endemic rivalry and rancour that had existed between the two families and thereby brought a brief period of peace to the troubled province. Well might the annalists, with a sense of impending doom, mourn his death in 1558. 'The loss of this good man', they recorded, 'was woeful to his country, for there was no need to watch cattle or close doors from Dúnchaoin [Dunquin] to the green-bordered meeting of the three waters [i.e. the rivers Suir, Barrow and Nore].'[3] The scene was now set for the enactment of a drama that had all the ingredients of a tragedy of Shakespearean proportions. With the fate and fortune of the two great aristocratic dynasties lying in the hands of two young and untried heirs, Ireland waited with bated breath for the storm to break.

But the young Desmond heir had already aroused his rival's

personal enmity by his sensational marriage in 1550 to Black Tom's mother, Joan, the Dowager Countess of Ormond. Garrett, scarcely twenty years old, had thus become Black Tom's step-father. Joan, twenty years Garrett's senior, was the daughter of James FitzGerald, the eleventh Earl of Desmond, and was thus Garrett's second cousin. On the death of Black Tom's father, Joan had subsequently briefly married at the Crown's insistence the Lord Justice, Sir Francis Bryan. But it was alleged that Joan had fallen for the pale melancholic heir to the Desmond dynasty even before her marriage to Bryan. And Garrett was obviously attracted to his older cousin. The prospect of such a marriage gave rise to considerable speculation and anxiety in various quarters. It was recorded, for example, that great 'displeasure' had arisen 'between Lady Ormond and Lady Desmond re the Countess of Ormond's practice to marry with the heir of Desmond'.[4] The English administration too was appalled at the potential consequences of the union. Black Tom was still a minor, and the government feared that the gaelicised Desmond heir would bring 'the uncyville and Yrishe'[5] customs of his house to bear on the loyal House of Ormond. Consequently the Crown had intervened, and Joan was summarily 'sent for into Inglande and bestowed as wife to Sir Francis Bryan'.[6] Bryan died in February 1550, and even at his funeral, which was attended by Garrett, 'the Countess of Ormond's practice to marry with the heir of Desmond'[7] was common knowledge. The Lord Chancellor urged the countess to show some restraint, and reluctantly Joan promised him 'upon hir honor that she wolde lyve sole for one yeore'.[8] But in affairs of the heart promises are made to be broken, and by May 1550 Joan and Garrett had married.

The marriage was the sensation of the day, and at Kiltinan Eleanor's family too must have heard of the unlikely union which had become the butt of many crude jokes and was the principal topic of conversation from the courtyard fire to the great hall. But initially the marriage had a stabilising effect on the young heir of Desmond. Under Joan's quiet influence, her young husband, on the death of his father in November 1558, assumed the earldom despite the claim of his dispossessed half-brother. Her concern that Garrett should be confirmed in his doubtful title by the Crown bore fruit when he agreed to undertake the journey to London, where 'with a willing mind and intention',[9] the new earl made his submission in style before the new queen, 'he being well attended on by one hundred prime gentlemen, waytering and attending upon him'.[10] This impressive show, however, cut little ice with Elizabeth who, with her calculating Tudor eyes, coldly surveyed the proud Geraldine peacock who flaunted his power before his sovereign, and mentally made a note to clip the wings of so overbearing and so dangerous a subject. Elizabeth knew the controversy that surrounded his title, but, as her own title to the throne was held equally in doubt, for the moment she smiled frostily at the swaggering lord and graciously confirmed him in his title and estates.

Garrett's inheritance comprised over a half a million acres extending 110 miles. Rents forthcoming from the estate amounted to over £7,000 per annum, 'a prodigious revenue in these times and perhaps greater than any other subject in Her Majesty's dominion'.[11] Together with their feudal rents, successive earls, as they had gradually adopted and submitted themselves to Gaelic law, also claimed its privileges. Garrett was entitled to the traditional tributes and payments known as 'cuttings and spendings' from the many Gaelic chieftains and lords who held under him. These tributes varied widely both in content and extent. When, for example, the earl travelled through the territory of an underlord, the expenses he incurred for food, drink and lodgings were borne by the underlord. He received specific dues in kind from the territories under his control, varying from wood and candles to drink and cattle. He 'cessed' or quartered his armed followers, his horses and his hunting hounds on the country. The earl and his family were entitled to 'cuddy' (*cuid oíche*) or entertainment for the night at the houses of the gentry within his lordship. If he did not avail in person of the cuddy, the equivalent cost in meat, flour, whiskey, honey, or a money payment was forwarded to his castle in lieu. If the payments and tributes due to the earl were not readily forthcoming, they were likely to be extracted by force. To judge from the many complaints made against him by his dependent lords, Garrett was wont to exact at times more than his due. Foremost among the privileges pertaining to the earldom under Gaelic law was the highly prized right of the 'rising out' whereby the earl, when he raised his standard, whether in rebellion or against a neighbour, was entitled to receive the support in arms of every member of his house and every dweller upon his lands. It was claimed that 'no less than fifty lords and barons paid them [the Earls of Desmond] tribute and were ever ready to march under their banner'.[12] Such power, if vested in a lord hostile to the Crown, posed a grave threat, and as her reign progressed Elizabeth had every reason to fear it and to seek strenuously to extinguish it. The Earl of Desmond claimed jurisdiction over some of the most powerful chieftains and lords in Munster. His power was centred in Co. Limerick and Co. Kerry and parts of Co. Cork, but his influence extended over a much wider area. He claimed a disputed overlordship of the three MacCarthy clans: MacCarthy More, MacCarthy Muskerry and MacCarthy Reagh. In northern Kerry the FitzMaurices, kinsmen and hereditary marshals to the earls, often resisted his claim of jurisdiction over them. The Barry septs of Co. Cork, the Knight of Kerry, the Knight of Glin and the White Knight, together with the FitzGeralds of Imokilly in Co. Cork, the earls' hereditary seneschals, were all allied to the House of Desmond.

Together with his vast acres, he had also inherited many castles and manors, the principal ones being Askeaton, Newcastle and Shanid in Co. Limerick, and Tarbert, Castleisland, Castlemaine and Dingle in Co. Kerry. Garrett's principal residence was Askeaton castle, a great Norman pile built in 1199 and situated on an island on the River Deel. A sixteenth-century account described it as

> the one great castle built of square plan, a chief house of
> the Earl of Desmond, having at each angle of the same a
> round tower, with various places and chambers in each
> tower. And there is at the south corner, on the western
> side at the south part, a high square tower or peel, built
> for defence, within the walls, and also there were within
> the walls of the said castle many buildings, namely a large
> hall, a large room, and an excellent chamber, one garden
> and, in the same, two fishponds. And outside the walls,
> and near them, are divers orchards and gardens.[13]

The castle, perched on its rock plateau, commanded a fine view east and south to where the dark forest of Kylemore stretched for miles into the distance towards the Galtee and Ballyhoura mountains.

The earl claimed overlordship of the port town of Youghal and had an annual chief rent there of £71 6s 8d, together with administrative privileges within the town. He was also in receipt of the 'custom and cocket of Kinsale'.[14] His extensive household comprised a secretary, lawyers versed in both Gaelic and English law, a personal physician who held in payment for his service 'a ploughland free for his service and a tenement in Youghall',[15] constables who guarded the earl's other residences in his absence, a seneschal, a marshal, a standing army of galloglass, a large company of bards and rhymers, countless retainers, servants, tradesmen, labourers and hangers-on. The entire earldom in reality was divided into 'highly localised units, each unit with its own castle or town house'.[16] To conquer the lordship presented major difficulties because 'victory was not symbolised by the capture of any one town or castle but was the result of encroachment and penetration until every castle had been destroyed or yielded up'.[17] The earls tended to rule their palatinate by an amalgam of Gaelic and English laws, and brehons or Gaelic judges were employed to arbitrate in disputes. Gaelic customs of dress, language and law flourished, and the earls guarded jealously their palatine rights conferred by the Crown, while they just as assiduously sought to preserve the wide-ranging privileges granted them by Gaelic custom. In effect they sought and acquired the best of both worlds.

The first years of Garrett's marriage passed without major incident as Joan exerted her influence on her son and young husband and kept them out of reach of each other. Garrett busied himself within his lordship to establish his authority over his liege lords and chieftains, to exact the customary dues and tributes, and to punish recalcitrant lords who thought to question his right or to deny him his dues. His aversion to any interference in the affairs of his lordship extended also to the Crown. English officials and administrators who arrived in Munster gaped in disbelief at the existence of this relic of a feudal state, operated by an autocratic, gaelicised earl who refused to acknowledge not only their presence but the authority of their sovereign mistress. When a confrontation over succession arose among the O'Briens of Thomond, Garrett backed the Gaelic contender for office, thus demonstrating his preference for the Gaelic system and leaving Elizabeth in no doubts as to where his loyalties lay.

In 1560 Joan's restraining hand seemed to weaken when a disagreement arose between Garrett and Black Tom over payment of her marriage settlement. Garrett claimed the rent from the manors of Clonmel, Kilsheelin and Kilfeacle as Joan's dowry, but Black Tom refused to pay. Garrett then attempted to extract the rents by force, and Black Tom responded by invading Garrett's lands. Garrett retaliated by denying Black Tom passage through his territories to collect his right of prisage at Youghal and Kinsale. Recourse to law would have been the practical way to resolve the dispute, but where the Ormond–Desmond feud was concerned, good sense did not enter into the question. The galloglass were mustered, the liegemen summoned to arms, and the place of battle, Bohermore, Co. Tipperary, selected. But the annals record as the 'two great hosts had come front to front and face to face, the great God sent an angel of peace to them, so that concord was established between the hosts'.[18] The 'angel of peace' referred to was Joan, who for fourteen days, as her son and husband faced each other in open hostility, traversed the drawn battle-lines and eventually succeeded in effecting a reconciliation and persuading them to seek mediation by the law. In the event Elizabeth ordered them both to her presence. Black Tom obeyed the summons immediately, but Garrett made vague excuses and declined to appear at the English court. He complained to the Queen that Ormond had refused to honour his promise of marriage to one of his sisters, and that Black Tom should consequently forfeit the substantial marriage bond of £4,000. A personal letter to Garrett from the Queen demanding his presence in London went unanswered for a month. Joan cajoled and counselled, and reluctantly he acquiesced. In 1562, accompanied by an even more impressive retinue than previously, he presented himself before Elizabeth and her Privy Council. 'Being charged before the Council with openly defying the law in Ireland, he answered contumaciously, and when called to order, refused to apologise.'[19] Elizabeth swore in her harsh voice and spat with anger, as was her wont, at the impudence of her subordinate vassal and committed him into custody. She afterwards wrote to soothe the anxious Joan and in a friendly tone explained that 'a little gentle imprisonment'[20] would do her vain young husband the world of good. But evil tongues and court gossip whispered in Garrett's ear that it was Joan who was responsible for his detention so that her son could be further favoured by the Queen. Garrett listened and wrote impulsively to reprimand his wife. Joan implored the Queen's secretary to inform her husband as to her innocence in the matter, declaring with a certain pathos that she had continually sought for 'them both to be perfect friends, as two whom I love as myself'.[21]

But Garrett's confinement had the desired effect. Denied his freedom and hard-pressed for money, he swallowed his pride and in 1563 signed a treaty with Elizabeth. He promised to pay his dues to the Crown, to maintain English law and order within Desmond, to abolish Gaelic law and practice there, and to prohibit the unrestricted movement of bards and rhymers. In 1564, after a further imposed stay in custody in Dublin on his return from England, he was finally reunited with his lordship and his wife. Joan, however, did not long survive her husband's return. On 2 January 1565, worn out, perhaps, by the constant pressure of keeping her husband and her son from each other's throats, Joan died and was buried in Askeaton abbey. That Joan loved Garrett, and loved him deeply, cannot be disputed. Joan Butler FitzGerald was not a silly middle-aged matron who sought to prolong her youth by an amorous dalliance with the pale, poetic warrior earl. 'By birth she was among the noblest women of the realm, by inheritance one of the richest ... admired for her maturity and intellect',[22] a confidante of Elizabeth, a healer of old wounds. With the death of Garrett's first countess there died also the prospect of peace in Munster.

Askeaton Castle and Abbey in the 16th century (*Pacata Hibernia*).

3

The Lady of Desmond

How hight that Amazon (says Artegall)?
    And where, and how far hence does she abide?
Her name (quoth he) they Radigund doe call,
    A princess of great power and greater pride.

SPENSER, *The Faerie Queene*, III

It is perhaps a quirk of fate that, despite the ongoing feud, it should be a Butler that the Earl of Desmond chose for his new countess. On the surface it might appear that the earl was seeking, by virtue of such a marriage alliance, to heal old wounds and to re-establish the connections with the House of Ormond which had been severed by Joan's death. But the reverse was in fact more likely, as both the manner and choice of his future bride could only antagonise Garrett's rival. For Joan Butler was no sooner laid to rest than her husband began a frantic courtship of Black Tom's kinswoman, Eleanor Butler, the daughter of his out-of-favour liegeman, the Baron of Dunboyne.

Eleanor was about nineteen years old and well within marriageable age. Her father had doubtless received many proposals for her hand, but either the suitors had proved unsuitable or the marriage settlements unsatisfactory, for by 1565, despite her good looks and connections, Eleanor was still unmarried. Her father's dispute with his brother still raged on, with Black Tom ranged firmly on the side of her uncle. Relations between the Baron of Dunboyne and his powerful overlord remained strained. The Earl of Desmond's choice of Eleanor could be said to have been politically motivated to exploit the differences between Black Tom and his subordinate baron. From the evidence of their subsequent relationship, however, it is more likely that the impulsive earl fell head over heels in love with the baron's daughter. They had had many opportunities to meet through the connections that already existed between their families. Eleanor's half-brother, Donal-na-Píopaidhe MacCarthy Reagh, the nephew of the Lord of Carbery, had married the daughter of the earl's half-brother. Garrett's sister was married to Edmund Butler, Black Tom's brother. Their most recent meeting might well have been at Askeaton, at the funeral of the late countess. There Eleanor had perhaps fallen for the aristocratic earl, his pale sensitive face starkly contrasted by the black velvet of his mourning apparel. Like everybody else throughout Munster, she had heard the speculation and gossip about his unlikely union with the middle-aged Dowager Countess of Ormond. She had also been aware, however, of the improvement the marriage had wrought on the vain, wayward earl. While contemporary accounts, generally written by his adversaries, accuse Garrett of being weak, coarse, vain, hypersensitive and void of judgement, there is no doubt that he was attractive to women, particularly to strong-willed women. To them he appeared a handsome noble, of a pensive nature, totally misunderstood; someone to be protected from both himself and his adversaries. 'Behind him Desmond left no cool-eyed observers; he moved through his age enveloped in rumours and turmoil, and if his actions repelled some, the riddle of his personality irresistibly drew others.'[1] Joan Butler had been a mature and intelligent woman. Eleanor Butler was also to prove herself of a similar intelligent stamp, and both were irresistibly drawn to Garrett.

Garrett himself, once his infatuation with Eleanor had taken hold of him, lost no time in appearing at Kiltinan castle as he commenced his somewhat ill-timed courtship. From the window seat of her chamber Eleanor watched for her future husband, his fine silk cloak billowing behind as he recklessly galloped up the narrow road to Kiltinan. The entire Dunboyne household was thrown into disarray as the impatient earl conducted his courtship at the same hectic pace as he was wont to gallop his horses. There is little doubt that Eleanor returned his advances with eagerness. Her knight had arrived, albeit from an unexpected quarter. Eleanor's intelligence and beauty had a powerful impact upon the complex personality of her suitor, that strange mixture of poet and warrior. His love for Eleanor and his penchant for verse perhaps inspired his only composition to have survived, aptly entitled 'Against Blame of Women':

> Speak not ill of womankind,
> 'Tis no wisdom if you do.
> You that fault in women find,
> I would not be praised of you.

Sweetly speaking, witty, clear,
  Tribe most lovely to my mind,
Blame of such I hate to hear.
  Speak not ill of womankind.

Bloody treason, murderous act,
  Not by women were designed,
Bells o'erthrown nor churches sacked.
  Speak not ill of womankind.

Bishop, king upon his throne,
  Primate skilled to loose and bind,
Spring of women every one!
  Speak not ill of womankind.

For a brave young fellow long
  Hearts of women oft have pined.
Who would dare their love to wrong?
  Speak not ill of womankind.

Paunchy greybeards never more
  Hope to please a woman's mind.
Poor young chieftains they adore!
  Speak not ill of womankind.[2]

Eleanor and Garrett were married, possibly at Kiltinan, in late January 1565. The storm-clouds which were then gathering on the horizon would prevent the sun from shining for long on their union. For Eleanor was destined to become involved in a grim episode of history which would culminate in appalling personal tragedy and loss. Her endurance and intelligence alone would enable her to withstand the onslaught and survive.

The earl and his new countess began their married life together at Askeaton castle. Eleanor had a substantial dowry from her father, and Garrett, for his part, endowed her with the castle and town of Bridgesford, Co. Tipperary, as part of her jointure. To judge by their later correspondence, Eleanor, despite their traumatic life together, was devoted to Garrett, who in turn proved a loving and caring husband to her to the end. Her marriage brought her into the new environment of her husband's lordship, which was markedly different from what she had been used to at Kiltinan. It was necessary to adjust to life in the more gaelicised and robust Desmond household, to walk a diplomatic tight-rope with the Desmond clans and followers who despised the very name of Butler.

Garrett brought her on a tour of his vast lordship. His many underlords received her with the hospitality and deference due the Earl of Desmond's countess. She viewed the great Desmond castles of Askeaton, Newcastle, Castlemaine, Shanid and the rest with a new bride's eye to future adjustments and refurbishment. For the moment she was content to accompany her lord and his ever-present large retinue on a tour of inspection of his estates as he received the rents, services, homage and entertainment that befitted his station, while in the meantime she enjoyed the festivities and pleasures of her brief honeymoon.

But political developments in Ireland waited for no such pleasant dalliances, not even for the great Earl of Desmond, whose turbulent and impulsive spirit was at all times easily provoked, particularly over any matter connected with his feud with the House of Ormond. Eleanor was about to witness at first hand the intensity with which the two rivals were willing to pursue their differences. This time the row was sparked off by Garrett's claim to rents from Sir Maurice FitzGerald, Lord of Decies, in Waterford. Decies was originally part of the Desmond estate, but Sir Maurice now claimed to hold it by feudal tenure of the Crown. Garrett, however, insisted on his right of overlordship of Decies, which, he proclaimed, 'is and always hathe beene a member of the house of Desmonde and in the rule and governance of the saide Earle and his ancestors'.[3] Sir Maurice appealed to the Earl of Ormond for protection. Black Tom readily agreed. Garrett thereupon summoned a hosting. His dependent lords and clansmen flocked to his standard and welcomed another chance to avenge themselves on their Butler enemies. The intensity of their hatred, nurtured for generations, doubtless surprised and dismayed Eleanor as she watched the Desmond forces mass before Askeaton. The mail-coated MacSheehy galloglass with their massive battle-axes slung over their shoulders formed the vanguard, as they would in battle when their ferocious strength and inborn hunger for slaughter would be unleashed on their opposing counterparts, the MacSweeneys. The lightly armed kern with their short Irish bows, targets and swords milled impatiently around the gateway. Inside the courtyard the horses attended by horseboys awaited their masters, who emerged from the castle clad in protective helmets, mail-shirts and jackets of quilted leather. Each carried a sword and dagger in his belt and a long spear. Garrett himself took command of this hot-blooded and impatient force. As he swung into the saddle, his standard was raised and the ancient war-cry of the Desmond Geraldines erupted in a deep-throated roar. Amid shouts of 'Shanid abú!' Garrett, fifteenth Earl of Desmond, led his hereditary army to war against the hereditary enemy.

A cattle raid—an attack by gaelic kern on a homestead. (Pl. II *The Image of Ireland*, John Derricke, 1581).

Eleanor watched her husband and his soldiers disappear from view, enveloped in the long woollen cloaks which would serve both as shelter and bed during the duration of the campaign. This was her first parting from Garrett, and she experienced a great sense of loneliness and an even greater sense of fear for his safety. She was also uneasily conscious of her own vulnerability in her isolation in a still alien lordship. But the loneliness and fear would of necessity pass. Her training and education had conditioned her to accept the inevitability of her husband's involvement, like that of his contemporaries, in the unending litany of feuds, disputes, raids and rebellions, the hallmarks of the volatile country and society to which they all belonged. She busied herself in the administration of her husband's estates in his absence. Her inexperience and her Butler origins might well have made her task more difficult, but Eleanor Butler FitzGerald proved to be no pushover when it came to asserting her rights. From the moment of her husband's departure she determinedly set about establishing her position and authority in Desmond.

The years of skirmishing and verbal warfare between Garrett and Black Tom finally ended on 1 February 1565 at the ford of Affane near Lismore. This time no 'angel of peace' appeared. The rents of Decies were forgotten as, faced by the Ormond forces, Garrett put spurs to his horse and personally led the charge against the ancient enemy. A brief but fiercely fought battle ensued until Garrett, in a sharp encounter with Sir Edmund Butler, was 'stryken doune by shott of hagbut throughe his leg and woundid dangerously in iii severall places of his body, besides divers bruses'.[4] Some three hundred of his men fell in battle, while others who tried to swim to safety were hacked to pieces by the Ormond galloglass along the banks of the Blackwater. Garrett was taken prisoner by an exultant Black Tom. As he was being carried shoulder-high on a litter from the battlefield by his enemies, they taunted him by asking: 'Where now the great Earl of Desmond?', to which Garrett haughtily replied: 'Where he belongs, on the backs of the Butlers.'[5] Brave words indeed. But for Garrett and Eleanor, Affane was to result in humiliation, imprisonment, loss of prestige, physical and mental deprivation, and the start of the slippery slope to rebellion and ruin.

The Queen was incensed at the entire episode and angrily ordered both earls to her presence. From Elizabeth's point of view, the Affane incident was an insult to her dignity and sovereignty as Queen, two attributes jealously guarded by the Tudors. Affane was the last battle to be fought between two private armies in these islands, and as such it accomplished little but to provoke the Queen's anger. A recent historian, in commenting on the episode, has stated that 'It was impossible for a reforming government to ignore this assumption by nominal loyalists of a right to settle a family dispute by an appeal to arms.'[6] The two offending dynasts were to be vehemently put straight on the matter by an irate sovereign. Meanwhile, however, Black Tom was extacting his personal revenge on his vanquished enemy. For six weeks he had Garrett incarcerated in his jail at Clonmel until the Lord Justice ordered both himself and his prisoner to Waterford. Black Tom, fearful that he might be adjudged of equal guilt in the affair by the Crown, was determined that the Earl of Desmond should be seen in public as the defeated and discredited villain of the piece, while he himself should be recognised as the aggrieved but victorious party. He consequently had Garrett bound in chains and paraded him through Waterford 'with sounding of trumpett and gunne shott, in suche tryumphant sort as though he were an open enemye or traytours rebell ... the whole inhabitants of the cyttie staring and wondering and diversly speking thereon to his shame and dishonour'.[7] The jeers and catcalls of the citizens rang in his ears as he was led, sick, stumbling and dishevelled, through the streets. It was a bitter humiliation for the proud Geraldine earl.

Eleanor probably witnessed her husband's disgrace. News of the defeat of Affane and of Garrett's capture by the Butlers had been brought to Askeaton by the defeated Desmond clansmen. Eleanor immediately set out for Clonmel to see him. She found him in great agony from the wound in his thigh, which was never to be fully healed. Together they discussed the likely outcome, and Eleanor soothed his feverish ramblings and bitter outbursts against the Butlers. He entrusted to her the administration of his estates in his absence. He was conducted to England to answer, with Black Tom, in person to the Queen for their presumptuous and precipitate action. To add to his discomfort, Garrett, it was recorded, suffered greatly from sea-sickness on the trip. Consequently it was a haggard and ragged shadow of the vain, swaggering noble of their former meeting who was carried on a litter into the royal presence to answer for his crime. Garrett expected little mercy and even less justice from the angry Queen, who by now was well versed in Black Tom's version of events.

But now, as if history repeated itself, the affair took on a more complicated aspect as the Ormond–Desmond feud once again became entangled within a wider political court intrigue then rife between the Sussex and Leicester factions. Robert Dudley, the Earl of

Leicester, had emerged as the Queen's favourite. There was some trepidation in the Sussex camp, as her admiration of him ran to such lengths as to encourage speculation that she had at last found herself a prospective husband. Sussex defended Ormond and lauded his loyalty and the loyal tradition of his house. He berated the Earl of Desmond, accused him of treason and of being an oppressor of his neighbours. Leicester, with the backing of Sir Henry Sidney, favoured Desmond, and they cautiously indicated that his claim over Decies was no more than an assertion of a right enjoyed by the Earls of Desmond for generations. While Elizabeth was critical of the conduct of both adversaries at Affane, she reserved the sharper edge of her tongue for Garrett. Both earls were forced to enter into recognisances for £20,000 and to abide henceforth by the Queen's law. In an attempt to bridle Garrett's influence in Munster, the MacCathy More, over whom he claimed supremacy, was created the Earl of Clancar. Temporarily chastened, but undoubtedly relieved, towards the end of 1565 Garrett was permitted to depart for Ireland, while Black Tom chose to remain at court.

He returned to Eleanor not yet fully recovered from the wounds received at Affane, and bearing also the mental scars of his further alienation from the Crown. Eleanor listened as he bitterly complained about the humiliation he had endured in the English court and the dismissive way Elizabeth had received his case against Ormond. He had been cold-shouldered and snubbed, while his rival, Black Tom, equally culpable, had received affection and respect from Elizabeth and her officials. Even the Leicester–Sidney faction, Garrett protested, had merely used him as a pawn in their political schemes and court intrigues. Eleanor soothed the ruffled pride of her aggrieved husband. She urged him to maintain his relationship, however tentative, with the faction of Leicester and Sidney as a means to bypass the antagonistic, ambitious petty officials in the administration in Ireland. And initially he seemed likely to take her advice and pursue a more loyal course. He refused to be drawn into a confederacy with the restless Ulster chieftain, Shane O'Neill of Tyrone. On the contrary, he journeyed to Drogheda to meet Sidney, recently reappointed as chief governor of Ireland, and offered him his services in the campaign against O'Neill. However, the Geraldine and Butler feud simmered on. Factions from each side raided and counter-raided the territory of the other. Both lordships were in a constant state of disorder. In the continued absence of Black Tom, his brothers contributed to the chaos in Ormond by their intemperate treatment of the dependent lords, tenants and town citizens. The feud between

Eleanor's father and uncle continued unabated. After his ineffectual foray into Ulster against Shane O'Neill, Sidney turned south to attempt to cool the seething cauldron of lawlessness and malpractice which by now seemed to be on the point of boiling over and plunging all Munster into total ruin. He first took in hand the feud between the Baron of Dunboyne and his brother. He promptly had them both, together with their quarrelsome wives and Eleanor's eldest brother James, committed to Dublin Castle. He next moved against Black Tom's brothers and had them detained for trial at Clonmel. Sidney then turned his attention to the vast sprawling territory of the Earl of Desmond. Reports and rumours as to the state of the unbridled lawlessness of Garrett's estates had reached Sidney's ears. Stories of the earl's tyranny and the excesses of his rule, and the intolerable exactions he demanded from those over whom he claimed suzerainty, greatly disturbed Sidney's legalistic English mind. But neither Sidney nor the Queen ever comprehended the determination and intensity with which the earl guarded the hereditary powers and privileges of his position, nor the fervour with which his adherents accepted his overlordship, which bound him to them as much as them to him.

For just as the Tudors claimed divine right to receive total loyalty and exert total authority, so did Garrett FitzGerald, fifteenth earl of Desmond, claim by ancient Gaelic and feudal laws his right to the loyalty and the obligatory dues of his tributary lords. Garrett's estate exceeded that of any other lord either in Ireland or England. His income both in money and in kind was immense, yet he paid not a penny to the Crown either in tax or cess. He used the revenue to subsidise his private army which he used to enforce Geraldine law. He brooked no interference in the administration of his estates. He meted out a harsh and summary justice based on the Gaelic principle that the strong must naturally overcome the weak. He was proud, even vainglorious, but in this he was a typical product of a society that expected such traits in a leader. He was an autocratic dictator and a true aristocrat, having been reared to expect homage, power and wealth. The Crown administrators and officials sent to dislodge him from his lofty perch he considered as mere lackeys and underlings to be contemptuously dismissed. He was an absolute ruler by right, and this he intended to remain.

Eleanor presided over his unruly household and received the lords, chieftains, emissaries and spies who brought news of the happenings in Ulster, Ormond, Dublin, London and the continent. Friars and priests came ashore at Youghal and Kinsale and beat a path to Askeaton to give tidings of the great religious crusade against the 'heretic queen' then sweeping the continent. But the real news was that which related to Desmond and its immediate enemies. The wider political developments, with their religious undertones, did not concern the gaelicised earl. Smarting yet at his treatment by Elizabeth and needled into action by his ambitious brother John and his wild captains, like a Celtic warrior he led his raiding parties at will. What Eleanor thought of his reckless behaviour is open to conjecture. The wild excesses of her husband and his followers seemed undoubtedly bound to invite the attention of the Crown. There is evidence to show that she attempted to restrain her husband's more outrageous undertakings and was more apt than he to see through the ill-advised plots of his brother. But for Garrett there was little choice but to play the Gaelic chieftain, to keep his competitors at bay and still the wagging tongues that, on any signs of weakness on his part, might reopen the controversy surrounding his succession and right to the earldom. Gaelic Munster demanded that he be an active leader, to the forefront in every dispute. To retain his position in the Gaelic world, the pale, melancholic poet-chieftain had, of necessity, constantly to demonstrate his strength as proof of his ability to rule and to be consequently accepted as fit to wield absolute power in Munster and to receive the allegiance and support of his dependent lords.

Eleanor could hardly fail to observe the state of lawlessness that existed within her husband's lordship and Garrett's unwillingness or inability to curb it. The number of his followers was legion and legendary. All the footloose and landless swordsmen of Munster flocked to his table and followed in his wake. The contrast between the administrations of Black Tom and her husband was, in some aspects, remarkable. Black Tom assiduously flaunted his loyalty before Elizabeth and her government while he still retained within his lordship many of the old practices for which the Queen berated the Earl of Desmond. He had, however, made noticeable efforts to administer his estates by the English system, while not necessarily forgoing any of his traditional dues and privileges under the Gaelic system. By his outward show of allegiance and his more circumspect and pragmatic administration of his lordship, Black Tom, in contrast to Garrett, presented to Elizabeth's admiring eyes the commendable image of a loyal and anglicised Irish earl. Garrett, by his very nature and inability to adapt and play the politician, appeared the antithesis. Eventually Elizabeth decided that something should be done about the situation in Desmond. In July 1566 she ordered Sidney to bestir himself and find out

> why such rebells and offenders as be under the rule of the
> Earle of Desmond and his brother John … have not ben
> apprehendid by them or why the said Earle or his brother
> … have not ben charged and made answerable thereto
> being to be committed to prisons as they ought to be.[8]

The Queen could not forget that Sidney had favoured the Earl of
Desmond at court, and she was suspicious that he might deal
leniently with him at the expense of her protégé Black Tom. 'Of which
two persons,' she reminded Sidney, 'without any private respect of
either of them, it is … most easiest to judge which of them aught to
recyve favor and countenance.'[9]

With the royal accusation of favouritism ringing in his ear, Sidney
hurried to Youghal to confront the object of the Queen's anger. But
Sidney well realised that his policies for the reform of the great feudal
lordships of Ireland must bring him into conflict not only with the
Earl of Desmond but with the Earl of Ormond too. For Sidney planned
to establish a militarily backed presidency in Munster which would in
effect 'undermine the power of the feudal lords by depriving them of
their palatinate jurisdiction, by prohibiting the maintenance of
private armies and by truncating their power'.[10] The loyal Earl of
Ormond would be affected as much as the disloyal Earl of Desmond.
But Black Tom was at the seat of power and had access to the Queen,
who in any event had been less than enthusiastic for Sidney's
proposals as they would necessitate further expense. When Sidney
suggested Sir Warham St Leger for the post, the Queen, prompted by
Black Tom, gave full vent to her disapproval. 'Wee did mislyke in
deede to see you so addicted to the favour of thearle of Desmond',
she fumed, 'as to the place St Leger the president of that Counsell,
whose inward preferrid friendship towards the Earle of Desmond was
notorious.' 'And', she added, echoing Black Tom's sentiments, 'the old
inimitye that St Leger's father bore to the Earle of Ormond's father,
whome he brought to his end heere in England by prosequuting of
him so as we assure you nether needid We the information of the
Earle of Ormond to disallow St Leger to be president.'[11] Sidney
appeared astounded at the Queen's vehement prejudice, but he had
little alternative but to let the presidency issue rest for the moment.
Ormond's objection to St Leger masked his fear of the power and
status of a president *per se* and its likely effects in curbing his own
absolute authority in Ormond.

Eleanor and Garrett were at Youghal, where Eleanor had been

Departure of Sir Henry Sidney from Dublin Castle (Pl. VI *The Image of Ireland*, John Derricke, 1581). *Inset*: portrait of Sidney by Lucas de Heere (NPG London).

recently delivered of her first child, a girl whom they christened Margaret. Spies daily brought to Garrett news of Sidney's progress through his territory, and as Sidney drew closer to Youghal his sense of grievance at the Lord Deputy's unsolicited intrusion increased. He called for a 'rising out' of his tributary underlords and armed followers and vowed that Sidney should be made to realise just who was master in Munster. As he rode through the Munster countryside, Sidney reported the waste and untended state of Garrett's domain to the Queen:

> Like as I never was in a more pleasant country in all my life, so never saw I a more waste and desolate land ... and there heard I such lamentable cries and doleful complaints made by that small remain of poor people which yet are left, who (hardly escaping the fury of the sword and fire of their outrageous neighbours, or the famine which the same, or their extortious lords, hath driven them unto, either by taking their goods from them or by sending the same, by their extort taking of coyne and livery) make demonstration of the miserable estate of that country. Besides this, such horrible and lamentable spectacles there are to behold as the burning of villages, the ruin of churches, the wasting of such as have been good towns and castles, yea, the view of the bones and skulls of your dead subjects, who, partly by murder, partly by famine, have died in the fields, as in troth hardly any Christian with dry eyes could behold.[12]

Early in 1567 Sidney confronted Garrett at Youghal, where the earl made little attempt to hide his displeasure at the Lord Deputy's presence in Munster. Sidney immediately ordered an investigation into Garrett's long-standing dispute with Black Tom over possession of Kilsheelin castle. The investigation duly found in favour of the Earl of Ormond. The decision provoked Garrett into a passionate tirade, in Sidney's presence, against the Crown. He swore that no English sovereign should ever have jurisdiction within his territory and 'that he would never disperse with the old state of his family, but would have five gallowglasses where he had formerly had one'.[13] Sidney brushed aside the earl's intemperate outburst and with some sympathy attempted to excuse it to the Queen on the grounds of her preference for the Earl of Ormond, which he had warned her would make Garrett 'grow desperate for that he cannot have his causes ended between the

Earl of Ormond and him, in which matters I suppose each doth the other wrong'.[14] But mindful of his duty as a loyal servant of the Crown, Sidney also pointed out that if Garrett did rebel and was defeated, his lands could be subsequently confiscated and 'thereby the Queen to be made mistress of a great part of the realm'.[15] This was the first time that the idea of confiscation of the Desmond estates was, albeit hypothetically, propounded. But as Garrett continued rashly to flaunt his independent stance, and as the attention of land-hungry speculators in England became fixed on the vast acres ruled by an irresponsible and disloyal subject, Sidney's idea was to gather momentum.

Garrett now sought to put his threats into action. Sidney had attempted to clip his wings still further by sending invitations to the earl's dependent lords to make their submissions to him personally and independently of their overlord. Garrett acted promptly to counter this move, and soon messengers were bringing him word that the traditional Desmond allies had answered his call to arms and that a thousand armed men were mustered to await his orders. Sidney's force in Munster numbered only two hundred. Garrett saw that the odds were in his favour and attempted to leave Youghal to assume control of his army. Sidney forestalled him and in March 1567 committed the irate earl under guard to his house in Youghal. Eleanor lay in bed still recuperating after the birth of her child. Her husband's rash and irresponsible behaviour must have made her fear greatly for the consequences. She had urged him to curb his intemperate conduct towards the only potential English ally he had. But he could not be restrained and became even more incensed as he watched his tributary lords troop in, one by one, to submit to Sidney. The Lord Deputy listened as they recited long lists of complaints against Garrett, whose overbearing treatment 'so injured and exacted upon by him as in effect they are or were become his thrals or slaves'.[16] Sidney was appalled at the state of events in the lordship and ordered Garrett to accompany him on his journey to Limerick. Eleanor remained at Youghal, later returning to Askeaton. As Sidney moved towards Limerick with his small force, with Garrett reluctantly in tow, he received reports that the earl's army intended to attack. Sidney retaliated by placing the earl under arrest, and with this insurance he was able to pass without hindrance through the Desmond heartland to Limerick. From there the proud Earl of Desmond was brought captive in Sidney's train as he moved at a leisurely pace through Limerick, Galway, Athlone and back to Dublin. There he was confined to prison, branded by Sidney as 'a man void of judgement to govern and will to be ruled'.[17]

News of her husband's imprisonment was relayed to Eleanor at Askeaton. She feared greatly the effects of this new humiliation on his mental and physical well-being. His brother, Sir John, to whom Sidney had conveyed the overlordship of the Desmond estates in the earl's absence, was sent to Dublin to seek terms for his brother's release. But shortly after his arrival there he found himself sharing the same cell as Garrett. Shades of the fate meted out by Henry VIII to the House of Kildare crossed Eleanor's mind. Was Henry's daughter about to order a similar chastisement of the House of Desmond? All Ireland awaited the fate of the earl and wondered in awe at the bold seizure of such a powerful lord. Even Elizabeth appeared somewhat aghast at the temerity of her Lord Deputy in seizing Desmond on his own ground with such a small army. In Munster there was little reaction to the imprisonment of the earl except from his kinsman, the Knight of Glin, who took the field with his son Thomas. They were eventually captured and condemned to death. By a legal loophole the Knight escaped his fate, but his son was hanged, drawn and quartered in Limerick. 'There is a tradition that his mother was present at his execution, seized his head when he was beheaded and drank his blood and collected for burial at Lislaughtin abbey the parts of his dismembered body in a linen sheet.'[18]

Meanwhile Garrett languished with Sir John in Dublin Castle and complained bitterly to Sidney about the treachery of his capture. Sidney sought to establish the Queen's pleasure about the fate of his troublesome prisoner. But Ormond had the Queen's ear in England, and in September 1567 Elizabeth ordered that the earl and his brother should be transferred to the Tower of London. Eleanor's worst fears were realised. She hurried to Dublin and received permission to visit her husband. There was no indication of what lay in store in London. But they both realised that his absence from Desmond was bound to be exploited by his enemies both from within and without. The old Gaelic dictum 'A lordship without a lord is a dead lordship'[19] was very much a reality in gaelicised Desmond. Few could be trusted there. Officials and officers in the Crown's pay were casting envious eyes on Desmond and were reckoning up the potential of the earl's estates as a means of revenue both for themselves and their royal mistress. Garrett's step-brother, Thomas Roe FitzGerald, the disinherited contender for the earldom, waited in the wings to reassert his claim by whatever law offered him the opportunity. His cousin, James FitzMaurice FitzGerald, was the most able and likely contender for his place in his absence. But he too would have to be watched lest the unexpected promotion to power made him unduly ambitious. Eleanor alone could be completely trusted, and once again Garrett entrusted to her the administration of his estates. He urged her to write regularly to him with details of her stewardship and to be vigilant in collecting his rents and dues. For in the grand Geraldine manner Garrett insisted on being escorted to his London prison by a princely retinue of followers. He intended to hold court in the traditional style of his house, even though Elizabeth intended his palace to be a dungeon. But there were no multitudes of willing peasants in London to provide the earl with the means for this vain display. The rents and dues from his estates must pay for his self-indulgent and expensive tastes. Eleanor returned to Munster to begin the unenviable and daunting task of holding the fort in her husband's absence. The earl and Sir John, accompanied by a hundred followers, were sent to London in December. Sir John fell ill during the voyage, and there was 'much ado to get him to Lichfield', where their escort reported they were 'thus constrained to tarry there to see what he will do tomorrow, when if there be any health in him they will travel towardes London'.[20] They eventually reached the capital, where they were lodged under honourable confinement in the Tower. The terms of their custody permitted them access to their followers who daily flocked to the Tower. From the drab cells of the prison Garrett, while his money lasted, kept 'open house' and a hospitable table for his dependants and generally held court as if he were at home in the great hall of Askeaton.

While Garrett kept up a brave show in England, Eleanor was left to bear the responsibility of funding her husband's extravagances and to oversee and safeguard his interests in Munster. As she had anticipated, the vacant earldom unleashed the unquiet ambitions of Garrett's relations. In order to foment unrest within Desmond, rumours of his death were circulated, and there was little Eleanor could immediately do to stem them; the borders of her husband's territory were far-flung, and communications were primitive. The rumours provided the basis for the main contenders to throw their hats into the ring and attempt to revive their claims to the earldom. Garrett's step-brother, Thomas Roe, 'taking advantage of his brother's misfortunes ... took upon him to command in chiefe the Earledome of Desmond'.[21] It was rumoured that Thomas Roe was supported in his bid for power by the Earl of Ormond. But Thomas Roe was stopped in his tracks as James FitzMaurice FitzGerald, proclaiming that his own interest in the vacancy was merely to preserve his cousin's rights, 'leapes into the lists, challenging any man that durst presume to question the Earle's right'.[22] But Eleanor viewed the motives of both contenders with suspicion. Their bid to usurp her husband's position seemed likely to split the lordship apart as both prepared to implement their claims by force. She acted swiftly to pre-empt their plans and summoned a hosting of Garrett's loyal retainers and galloglass. Like an avenging eagle, she swooped on the two claimants and took them into custody until she could establish Garrett's will in the matter. After some time he wrote his instructions from the Tower and appointed James FitzMaurice FitzGerald to assume the position of captain in Desmond during his absence. He further urged his dependent lords 'to aid the countess and James FitzMaurice in collecting rents and in keeping the peace'.[23] But Eleanor's suspicions about FitzMaurice's motives were unappeased. Garrett had been absent for almost six months, and his volatile sub-lords and chieftains were in need of an overlord to protect and direct them. As the situation stood, any contender with even the vaguest claim to the overlordship, but with sufficient strength to enforce it, could usurp Garrett's position. Her husband was far removed from the real situation and was willing to place too much trust in his cousin. Eleanor was by no means sure that FitzMaurice's motives were as unselfish as he loudly proclaimed. Until her suspicions could be allayed Eleanor decided to keep FitzMaurice and Thomas Roe under lock and key. She had also to contend with the prying advances of the Crown Commissioners of Munster, established to protect the Queen's interests in the province. They too sought to take advantage of her husband's absence and to extend their power into his lordship. She had thus to keep the Crown Commissioners at bay, while at the same time restraining the ambitions of Thomas Roe and James FitzMaurice. In addition, she was under constant pressure from the Commissioners to deliver her prisoners into their custody. But Eleanor well realised that such action on her part would achieve little but to incur the wrath of their respective followers and lead to even greater disorder within the lordship under her care. She knew that she had to avoid giving way to such demands; and to do this she had to play for time.

The Commissioners summoned her to meet them at Waterford, but she fobbed them off, pleading the unsettled and poor state of her husband's country and her own deprivation. 'I can scant abyde in one house past two dayes and two nights,' she wrote, 'though it be wynter, but trudging and travaylinge by day and ptly. by night from place to place meaninge to appease the fury of their lewd attempts the best I can.'[24] She had set out in January 1568, in the depths of a severe winter, to attempt to quell the rumours of her husband's death, to appease the anxiety of his dependent lords, and to determine their views on the proposed appointment of James FitzMaurice FitzGerald as the earl's temporary replacement. On her journey she tried to collect the rents due to her husband, but, as she informed the Commissioners (no doubt in order to dispel any hopes they might have of securing a share of the revenue for the Crown), the state of the country was so poor that she 'could not find in my harte to take up myne owne dutys of the inhabitants there'.[25] But the Commissioners insisted on a meeting to discuss the situation in Desmond and urged her by return messenger 'to lett us understand yor determinate answear whether yo will come to us or we to yo in any convenient place'.[26] They further ordered her to deliver her prisoners to the Crown and to ensure that all the tributary lords of Desmond submit to the Commissioners. But Desmond's sub-lords indicated to the Commissioners that, following the abduction and imprisonment of the earl, they would not come freely to the Commissioners unless under the protection of the countess, whom they acknowledged as the earl's only representative. Despite the ulterior ambitious motives of FitzMaurice and Thomas Roe, Eleanor was loath to hand them over to the Crown. Desmond needed a strong lord at the helm, especially at this decisive time. She subsequently extracted pledges and securities for Thomas Roe's release and loyalty from the Munster lords Roche and Power and endorsed Garrett's choice of James FitzMaurice to act in a caretaker capacity until his return. She then ordered their release, pretending to the irate Commissioners that it had been perpetrated 'by the rude people the erle's captens of galloglasses, constables and other of the countrey'.[27] With her husband's lordship for the moment under control and in relative peace, Eleanor now set out, escorted by Hugh Lacy, the Bishop of Limerick, to keep her long-postponed appointment with the Crown Commissioners at Cork. She reassured them that she would not seek to impede the extension of English law into Desmond, though she qualified her promise by stressing that it applied only 'as far as my good will may thereunto extend'.[28]

During 1568 Eleanor maintained a steady flow of correspondence with her imprisoned husband. From the Tower Garrett wrote urging her to be vigilant in his interests in Munster and to endeavour to collect his rents, of which he was now in dire need. The Queen had reduced her allowance for his upkeep, considering it altogether contrary to her parsimonious mind that such an unfaithful subject, together with his overbearing retinue, should be maintained at her expense. His health had begun to deteriorate in the damp, unhealthy confines of the prison, while he became withdrawn and silent as he brooded long hours over the humiliation and injustice of his detention. His thoughts were constantly on Munster, and Eleanor received one letter rebuking her, uncharacteristically, for her apparent tardiness in sending him news from home. Otherwise the tenor of his letters to her was warm and loving; they were generally addressed to 'the Right honourable and my veray lovinge wife dame Elinor Countesse of Desmond in Ireland',[29] according her all the respect and affection pertaining to her position as his countess and wife. In his letters he frequently sent his commendations to Eleanor's mother, the Baroness of Dunboyne, who, on the death of her husband in 1567 after their release from Dublin Castle, had continued to be harassed at Kiltinan by Peter Butler and his Ormond supporters. The heir of Dunboyne, Eleanor's brother James, was yet a minor and had been sent to England to further his education at Cambridge. In a letter to his step-brother, whom he addressed as Mr Thomas of Desmond', Garrett instructed him in his behaviour towards Eleanor:

> This shalbe to desire you not to fayle as my trust is no less in you, to be vearie kindlie towardes my Ladie my wif, and that she maie not slacke nor perceive the contrarie but your good will and yt you and everie of yours, as you tender my good will and advoid my displeasure.[30]

His friend and seneschal, John FitzEdmund of Imokilly, he instructed to aid and protect Eleanor in all things.

Conditions in the Tower continued to worsen. Elizabeth had put a stop to the carnival atmosphere of his confinement, and Garrett found himself lodged 'without furniture and left to suffer from the cold'.[31] His vexation was exacerbated when he was compelled to appear before endless inquisitions to answer for his conduct within his own lordship. As usual, there were plenty of paid spies and informers ready to talk. He was accused of providing meat and drink to proclaimed traitors in Munster. Disdainfully he explained the Gaelic custom of liberal hospitality, but denied that he had aided any treasonable acts. Proudly reasserting the inherited powers conferred on him by right of the palatine status of his lordship, he loudly proclaimed before his inquisitors that he had sole authority to rule and to administer justice there without regard to the Queen's sheriffs, judges or administrators. His judges could scarcely comprehend such seemingly outlandish claims which harked back to the bygone age of the independent barons of feudal England, long since moulded into loyal subjects of the Crown by successive Tudor monarchs. That such a political dinosaur as the Earl of Desmond could still exist, even in

Ireland, was beyond the comprehension of the Elizabethan mind. Evidence of raids on his neighbours, of the great disorder of his lordship and of intrigue with O'Neill against the Crown was produced against him. The whisper of treason began to circulate. Visions of the executioner's block, of Tyburn and the jeering mob flashed before his mind. The pale ghosts of his Kildare kinsmen came to haunt him in his lonely cell. Not willing to place his head entirely in the lion's mouth, in July 1568 he made a complete submission to the Privy Council at Howard House. The submission reads as follows:

> I, Garrett, Earl of Desmond, knowing myself to have offended the Queen's laws and to stand in great peril of life and forfeiture of all my lands and goods; and besides knowing myself to be in danger of forfeiting £20,000 wherein I stand bound to Her Majesty by recognisance: therefore, to obtain her favour, I submit myself to her mercy and clemency, and do offer to Her Majesty all my possessions, thereof to take into her hands so much as she thinks convenient and to dispose of the same for benefit of the realm of Ireland, at her pleasure and I grant and promise that within days after her pleasure shall be signified to me, what castles, lands or liberties she shall think good to take, I will make assurance thereof to Her Majesty, her heirs and successors.[32]

The Queen had the imperious Geraldine where she wanted him, on his knees, and 'so far as the law went, Elizabeth now had Munster at her mercy, but she kept fast hold on her prisoners until time should declare how far the law coincided with the facts'.[33] Garrett had saved his neck from the block, but at a terrible cost to both his pride and his pocket. His fate hung on a thread, for, despite his submission, he was still in prison, destitute, ill and friendless. His only hope depended on his wife's ability to counter the intrigue, greed and double-dealing directed from every quarter against his patrimony. The outlook in the summer of 1568 looked as grim as the cold grey stones of his prison cell.

But now a new threat to the stability of Munster emerged and for a time seemed likely to spawn the unlikeliest of alliances between the rival Houses of Desmond and Ormond. While Sidney's plan to establish a presidency in Munster had been forestalled by the machinations of the Earl of Ormond, he had also raised the idea of colonisation as a means to extend the Crown's authority in the province, and his proposals on this subject were examined with interest by the English government. He envisaged the establishment of English settlements 'as oases of civility in a desert of barbarians'.[34] Lands confiscated by the rebellion of their Irish owners, or land held by tenure that could be proved faulty or uncertain, would provide the means for the establishment of the proposed settlements. The Queen looked favourably on the proposal as a less expensive method of conquest and in keeping with the mood of discovery and colonisation then in vogue among English financial entrepreneurs and intrepid, land-hungry adventurers. The settling of the disorderly areas of Ireland with English farmers, yeomen, artisans and soldiers and the establishment of English shire practices therein seemed practical and augured well for a more stable and less expensive administration in Ireland. Elizabeth's domestic and foreign problems had intensified. Scotland, in complicity with the ever-scheming Mary Stuart and her French Catholic allies, threatened revolt. 'The life-and-death wrestle between the Reformation and the unreformed Church had already settled into a permanent struggle between England and Spain.'[35] While the struggle was as yet to be fought 'unofficially' by Elizabeth's privateers who plundered Spanish treasure ships as they returned from the Americas, Munster, with its unstable political situation, unreformed religion and strategically situated harbours like Youghal, Kinsale and Dingle, could provide Spain with backdoor access to England.

The colonisation project was greeted with enthusiasm in England. First into the fray, with a dubious claim originating from the Norman conquest some centuries earlier, came Sir Peter Carew of Devon, an enterprising Elizabethan soldier and adventurer. Carew claimed lands in Cork, Kerry, Waterford, Meath, and also the barony of Idrone, the property of the Earl of Ormond's brother, Sir Edmund Butler. The ire of the loyal Butlers was unleashed as Sidney had the claim confirmed by the Irish Privy Council. On the strength of Carew's initial success, scores of enthusiastic English adventurers, including Sir Richard Grenville, Sir Humphrey Gilbert and Sir Warham St Leger, set their sights on the rich land of Munster in a mission of plunder on the grand scale. To the majority of these pirate-adventurers, Ireland was as remote and unknown as the far-off Americas, peopled by a race as alien as the Red Indians, governed by savage chiefs and mysterious brehons, an ideal terrain for the ambitions and energies of restless young men in search of wealth and adventure. To add to the growing anxiety among both Gaelic and gaelicised landowners in Ireland, Sidney, on his return to Ireland, had failed to bring with him the Earl of Desmond. Fear spread among the aristocracy—even into the loyal House of Ormond, where the earl's brother declared 'that no man of Irish descent could be safe'[36] from the seizure of either his land or his person. Sidney convened a parliament in 1569 which was primarily 'used to promote the policy of conquest'[37] and which thereby caused futher unrest. Shane O'Neill, recently murdered, was deemed 'attainted, the name of O'Neill extinguished and the Queen entitled to Tyrone';[38] thus was sounded a clear warning to every lord and chieftain 'that there could be but one sovereignty in Ireland'[39] and that possession of their lordships was no guarantee of legality of tenure by English law.

The first wave of adventurers landed in Munster and laid instant claim to lands and castles in the vicinity of Cork, possessions of the Earl of Desmond and MacCarthy More. James FitzMaurice FitzGerald seized his chance to exploit these developments in Munster. He convened a conference of Geraldine leaders and informed them that 'their chief and his brother were condemned to death or at least to perpetual imprisonment'.[40] Garrett's continued confinement, the uncertainty over land titles, the threatened colonisation, combined with the unlikelihood of Elizabeth being reconciled with the papacy, gave James FitzMaurice the opportunity he sought to extend and broaden the basis of the local struggle over land and lordship and to assimilate it into the wider international religious and political crusade against Elizabeth. To seek international recognition and material assistance for his new-found cause, FitzMaurice sent Maurice FitzGibbon, papal appointee to the see of Cashel, to King Philip of Spain. FitzMaurice next sought to make common cause with the estranged brothers of the Earl of Ormond, smarting under Sidney's chastisement and Carew's threat to their lands. The brothers agreed to become involved, though they maintained that they would not make war against the Crown but 'against those that banish Ireland and mean conquest'.[41] The prospect of an alliance between the usually loyal House of Ormond and the rebel House of Desmond aided by foreign enemy intervention sent shivers of apprehension down Elizabeth's spine. She ordered Black Tom to resume his responsibilities in Ormond, but gave no such commission to the still captive Earl of Desmond.

Eleanor observed the unfolding events and wondered at the unnatural alliance being forged between FitzMaurice and the Ormond Butlers. They were no friends of her own family, and even less of the Desmonds. They had lately terrorised her mother and plundered her late father's estates. She was suspicious of FitzMaurice's real intentions as he promoted his religious crusade and sought to influence her husband's tributary lords to fight in it. The question of religion mattered little in Munster, and she saw in FitzMaurice's use of it merely a means to subvert her husband's authority and positon. She feared the undoubted leadership abilities of FitzMaurice. In the continued absence of their overlord, and with the constant threat of colonisation and encroachment by the Crown, the loyalty of her husband's followers might waver. Caught in a dilemma between the Queen's reluctance to release her husband and the unfolding ambitions and designs of FitzMaurice, she could do little but await developments and keep alive the receding memory of her husband among his people.

Robert Dudley, Earl of Leicester.

Robert Devereux, 2nd Earl of Essex.

Walter Devereux, 1st Earl of Essex.

Sir Francis Walsingham, Secretary of State.

Hampton Court Palace, scene of Eleanor's first meeting with Queen Elizabeth I.

4
Exile

We have been here much molested with the erle of Desmond's wief . . . pretending that she hath not brought with her wherewith to mayntayne her owne charge nor the charge of her husbande . . .

Queen Elizabeth to Sir Henry Sidney, 17 April 1570

James FitzMaurice FitzGerald raised his crusading banner over an uncomprehending Munster and with fire and sword swept through the province with all the avenging fury of a convert hell-bent on doing the Lord's work. In Ormond his confederates, the Butler brothers, plundered and raided the countryside on the less lofty but nonetheless bloody mission of defence of their land. Confronted by the 4,500 men of this diversely motivated force, the newly settled English planters and their families fled for their lives and cowered for safety behind the high protective walls of Cork, Kinsale and Youghal. Leaving a trail of corpses, looted and burnt-out houses and hovels, bare fields and thousands of cattle stampeded into the wilderness, FitzMaurice arrived before the gates of Cork on 15 July 1569 and ordered the mayor to 'destroy out of the town all the Huguenots with the first wind'.[1]

Sidney proclaimed the Butler brothers and FitzMaurice as traitors, and Carew commenced a campaign of indiscriminate slaughter in Ormond. News of the atrocities spread. In Connaught the Earls of Clanrickard and Thomond bestirred themselves into action and united with their Geraldine and Butler counterparts to defend their land. In Leinster the Earl of Kildare waited uncertain but wavered in the direction of his Geraldine kinsmen. Black Tom prepared to return to Ormond and made no secret that 'anti-Geraldine though he was, if the lands of the ancient owners were to be seized by strangers, then he would make common cause with his countrymen'.[2] The situation was rapidly getting out of hand. The Queen made Sidney her scapegoat.

She berated him for tarring Black Tom's brothers with the same brush of rebellion as FitzMaurice despite their participation with him in besieging Kilkenny. Upon the arrival of their brother at Rosslare in August, however, they deserted FitzMaurice and, spurning Sidney, submitted instead to Black Tom. Shortly afterwards Carew's colonisation schemes in Ormond were abandoned. Sidney was ordered by the Queen to leave the Butlers to their own devices and to concentrate his efforts against FitzMaurice.

At Sidney's approach, FitzMaurice fell back from Cork and sought shelter deep inside the Kerry mountains. For a second time in a matter of months Munster was subjected to a baptism of slaughter and rapine as Sidney retaliated with the same ferocity as FitzMaurice had shown to the planters. The Earls of Clanrickard and Thomond promptly submitted, together with many of the confederates. Deserted by his erstwhile allies, FitzMaurice established his camp within the inaccessible fastness of the Glen of Aherlow. His first attempt to promote a religious confederacy, linked to international developments, had failed. But he had sufficient political awareness to realise that the question of religion had not as yet penetrated as a political issue in Ireland, itself as yet 'merely a pawn in the great game of European diplomacy'.[3] He could afford to lie low, consolidate his position and formulate his plans for raising the banner of crusade another day.

But FitzMaurice's hasty action and Sidney's reprisals had focused the attention of the Crown on the lordship of the Earl of Desmond. Eleanor soundly cursed the ill-advised revolt which had presented the Crown with the opportunity it had sought to establish garrisons in the abandoned castles of Garrett's tributary chieftains who had followed FitzMaurice. The countryside bore the scars of the revolt and, as Eleanor testified, 'was utterly distroid and wasted by the unhappie rebellion of James Fitzmorrish'.[4] She found it impossible to collect the rents and dues owed to her husband, and whatever meagre sums were forthcoming were summarily expropriated by the Crown to redeem the expenses incurred in suppressing the revolt. Oblivious to the state of affairs within his lordship, Garrett begged her to come personally to him with as much money as she could obtain for the relief of himself and Sir John, both of whom, he told her, 'greatly lack apparel and other necessities and especially money'.[5] Their situation in prison had deteriorated to the level of common felons. But there was little that she could do to relieve their condition. She wrote to inform Garrett of the desperate conditions prevailing in Desmond which had prevented her from collecting 'no p^te of yor rents or other duties that maye enable me to repaire toward you'.[6] She held FitzMaurice responsible for the destruction and voiced her suspicions about his true motives, which she saw as being 'to bring you yf he could in further displeasor but also usurpe all yo[r] enheritance to himself'.[7] The ostensible religious overtones of FitzMaurice's revolt cut little ice with Eleanor. The misery and depression which she suffered at this time is evident in a letter to Garrett in which she confided: 'I pray God send us joyfull meeting or me shorte dep[ture] out of this world. — Yo[r] loving miserable wief Ellynor Desmond.'[8]

She sought permission from Sidney to go to her husband and moved to Kinsale in anticipation of his reply. Whether out of a sense of genuine sympathy for her plight, or in the hope of using her as a means to secure the release of the earl (a better alternative from the Lord Deputy's point of view than to continue to contend with the more dangerous aspirations of his deputy FitzMaurice), Sidney secured her a pass into England. Accompanied by her husband's lawyer and friend, Morris Sheehan, who throughout the traumatic years that were to follow was seldom far from her side, and a small company of servants, Eleanor arrived in Bristol in the early weeks of 1570. From there they journeyed down the long bleak road to London.

It was her first visit to the great city, but as she made her way through the maze of narrow bustling streets, flanked by the wooden-fronted houses, taverns and shops, there was little time to wonder or admire. Hers was a mission fraught with danger and uncertainty. Her means were meagre, and the awesome task that confronted her, to effect her husband's release, would take every ounce of her energy, ability and resources. She had to move the mind of a resolute, autocratic queen whose known antipathy towards her husband seemed as unyielding as the hard grey stone of his tower prison. She was conducted through the grim, dark corridors of the infamous prison, and as the heavy iron-bound door closed with a shuddering bang behind her she was reunited with a husband whom she scarcely recognised.

They had been apart for eighteen months, and time had greatly changed Garrett's appearance. The once handsome, proud, richly attired noble was no more. In his place stood a trembling, gaunt and shabby figure who with red-rimmed eyes cried out his welcome and his fear. The reality of their awful dilemma was perhaps temporarily banished as for a moment a beam of happiness and joy shone on their reunion and briefly lighted their gloomy surroundings. Through the prison bars they may have looked down together on the slow-moving muddied waters of the Thames, flanked by a jumble of dingy riverside buildings, and thought perhaps of Askeaton and the rushing Deel and the green pasturelands of Limerick. Eleanor related to him the latest tidings from Munster and the changes that had occurred in Desmond during his absence. They knew that it was now of the utmost urgency that Garrett should find a way out of the Tower and back to Ireland if he was to salvage what remained of his lordship. But with Munster subdued, there seemed even less likelihood that the Queen would see any reason to restore him. If, however, Munster was to relapse into disorder, then the heavy cost of restoring peace and the Queen's known aversion to paying the piper, allied to Sidney's advice that the vacant Desmond lordship was the source of internal discord and a temptation to England's enemies, might well have the effect of making Garrett's restoration seem the lesser of two evils. Consequently FitzMaurice had to be encouraged in his religious rebellion and foreign intrigues. But before Garrett's return to Ireland could be contemplated, Eleanor first set about securing his release from the Tower.

From both financial necessity and a desire to be with her husband, Eleanor took up residence in the Tower. The ancient stronghold, situated in the south-east corner of the old city of London, on the north bank of the Thames, was founded about 1066 by William the Conqueror. It was initially constructed as an enclosure within the surviving Roman city walls. Within this enclosure the imposing White Tower was erected. Over succeeding centuries the site developed with the addition of a series of smaller towers connected by curtain walls and surrounded by a moat. Eventually by the sixteenth century the Tower complex was to encompass some twenty-three individual towers, a chapel, and various lodgings, gardens and walks. Henry VIII was the last monarch to occupy part of it as a residence, and it gradually came to be used more as a prison to lodge important political prisoners. One of its towers, the Beauchamp Tower, had a tragic association with the FitzGeralds. It was in the apartments of this tower, following in the tradition of former inmates, that Silken Thomas, to pass away the days leading up to his execution, started to carve his name in the brick wall. The inscription, still visible, was abruptly cut short, however, at 'THOMAS FITG' as the executioner at Tyburn interrupted the doomed engraver. Like his kinsman, the Earl of Desmond had also been allotted an apartment in one of the towers. The degree of comfort which might be introduced into the cold, damp, cheerless rooms depended on one's own means or the generosity and influence of one's friends outside. Garrett's distinct lack of both meant that there were for him few comforts to ease the agony of the long dreary days.

From the Tower Eleanor daily sallied forth to Whitehall or Westminster, or further afield to Greenwich and Richmond, wherever Elizabeth and her court were in residence, to seek her husband's release. From the fringes of the court circles and cliques she importuned, bribed and cajoled the influential and corrupt in her endeavour to obtain access to the Queen. She endured humiliation and defeat as backs were firmly turned and doors slammed in her face. Her lack of means was reflected in her meagre and threadbare wardrobe. The powdered, coifed and bejewelled court ladies, and their equally elegantly attired male counterparts, would have little truck with the down-at-heel countess from Ireland. The powerful Ormond faction spied on her every move as she picked her way through the spider-like web of intrigue and double-dealing on the long and perilous road to the Queen. A cash handout here, a promise of land there, it was a costly mission which soon absorbed her slim resources, and no further income could be expected from the Desmond estates. In desperation Garrett wrote directly to Elizabeth's chief secretary, Sir William Cecil, explaining that as 'verie extreme necessitie' had prohibited Eleanor from continuing 'her sute for my delyverance into the cyttie of Londone', he was appealing to Cecil 'to have rememberance the futherance of her sute'.[9] On foot of her husband's message, Eleanor redoubled her efforts, and eventually her persistence was rewarded. In May 1570 she was officially informed that Elizabeth had, albeit reluctantly, agreed to grant her an audience. The audience was held at Hampton Court. The ill-feeling that the Queen bore her husband was not concealed at the meeting, and was indeed extended to Eleanor herself. She realised that her petition to the unfriendly, short-tempered Queen must be couched in humble and repentant tones. With cold, calculating eyes the older Queen looked down upon the younger countess who knelt before her and listened to her plea for sustenance for herself and her husband and for his release from the Tower. Eleanor promised in return to steer her husband on a path of loyalty and obedience to the Queen and to her laws. Elizabeth appeared unmoved by her request, and her attitude was reflected in the atmosphere of her court, where little friendship or support was accorded to the Irish countess. It was dangerous to appear sympathetic to the wife of a rebel, personally out of favour with the Queen and presently awaiting his fate in the most dreaded prison in the land. A friendly look or a quick word of consolation or encouragement to his wife could be misinterpreted. Elizabeth's impenetrable face gave little indication of the likely outcome of the meeting, and Eleanor withdrew from the royal presence and returned to Garrett in the Tower to wait on events.

London in Eleanor's time.

A state prisoner's apartment in the Tower of London, 16th century, with inset the carved signature (unfinished) of Silken Thomas, kinsman of the Earl of Desmond.

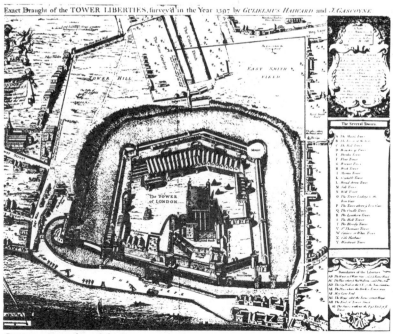

Contemporary plan of the Tower.

They had not long to wait. In a letter that bristled with indignation and impatience at Eleanor's dogged persistence and her penury, Elizabeth informed Sidney that

> We have been here much molested with the erle of Desmond's wief who pretending that she hath not brought with her wherewith to mayntayne her owne charge nor the charge of her husbande and on the other parte we have been at no smale charges with him and his synce his comying over.[10]

As ever, the cost factor involved in the maintenance, however frugally, of the Desmonds was Elizabeth's preoccupation. To rid herself of the burden, she acceded to Eleanor's request and ordered their removal from the Tower into the custody of Sidney's protégé, Sir Warham St Leger, on whom she also dumped the cost of their maintenance. Eleanor, Garrett, Sir John and fourteen servants were subsequently transferred from the Tower and lodged at Leeds castle, on the country estate of St Leger in Kent.

Garrett and Eleanor were well acquainted with their jailer. St Leger held a fee farm from the Earl in Desmond at a rent of 53s—4d per annum—and at the time of Carew's speculative sortie into Munster had obtained additional land west of Cork city, in recompense, it would appear, for having given financial assistance to Garrett during his period of captivity in the Tower. St Leger's known antagonism to the Earl of Ormond and his friendship with the Sidney faction at court had initially drawn Garrett to him. St Leger, anxious to expand his estate in Munster, had provided his destitute landlord with money, but at a price. In any event, Eleanor had accomplished the first step towards achieving her husband's total freedom and repatriation. And after the long months of captivity in the Tower, the relative freedom of Leeds castle and the fresh summer air of the Kentish countryside must have acted as a tonic to the physical and mental well-being of the Desmonds.

For a few short months of the summer of 1570 they enjoyed partial liberty in unfamiliar but pleasant surroundings. But the financial burden of their upkeep became apparent later in the year as St Leger's resources began to feel the strain. In October 1570 he complained of the dire straits of both himself and his prisoners. He begged the Privy Council for 'a warrant for receipt of money for their diet, otherwise', he threatened, 'I shall be constrayned to bring them to court, being not able, by my greate losses sustayned in Ireland, to beare the chardges thereof any longer'.[11] The earl and his family, St Leger complained to the Council, had not 'any thing of their owne to relieve them selfes withal, having your honn^rs not so muche as to buy them a pair of shooes, nor have not had since their cominge in to my chardge and stand in despair to have any thing out of their owne country'.[12] No rents were being forwarded to Garrett from his estates in Ireland; he and his retinue were totally dependent for their food, clothing, shelter and necessities of life on their reluctant custodian. Garrett in captivity had cost Elizabeth more than when unrestrained in Desmond. Yet Elizabeth was still not prepared, particularly now that she had successfully transferred the actual burden of his upkeep to an out-of-favour servant, to risk sending the earl back to Ireland, even in view of the potential financial benefit which she stood to receive from the revenue raised on his estates. St Leger's protest of impoverishment fell on deaf ears, and the straitened conditions which he and his aristocratic charges endured were suffered to continue.

In December 1570 the long-postponed decision to appoint a president in Munster was reached, and the Queen nominated Sir John Perrot to the office with instructions to seize 'the castle of the Earl of Desmond in Kerry [i.e. Castlemaine] ... for the use of the Lord President and Council and also to seize the Liberty of Kerry which Desmond claimed as a palatine'.[13] By the establishment of a presidency and the negation of the Earl of Desmond's hereditary palatine rights in Kerry, the Crown sought to undermine the power exerted by the earl by right of Gaelic law over the tributary lords of Desmond and to institute English law and administration in its stead. The choice of Perrot as President and the 'vigorous career of law enforcement and the discouragement of Gaelic institutions'[14] that he was about to pursue put him firmly on a collision course with the House of Desmond. Sir John Perrot, the supposed illegitimate son of Henry VIII, was a bluff, energetic, gallant if somewhat imprudent Elizabethan knight. He had been educated with the Earl of Ormond at court, and initially showed little enthusiasm for his new appointment in Ireland.

Rumours of the new regime in Munster, and of the Crown's intention to render him powerless, filtered through to the Earl of Desmond, adding to the torment that afflicted his mind. In his captivity in England it was to be expected that the distracted earl would champ at the bit that restrained him from his patrimony. St Leger had by now been forced to move himself and his destitute charges to his town house at Southwark, across the river from the Tower, a grim reminder to the Desmonds of their vulnerable circumstances. The house was unfashionably located 'east of London Bridge beside a depot for municipal building materials. The house had once been a friary in the country, but grown up about it was Bankside, a rowdy neighbourhood of breweries, brothels, the Clink Prison and the Paris Garden bear pits.'[15] It was a dark, damp building, far too cramped for the two large households which were compelled to reside there in varying degrees of poverty and despair. The fog, damp and stench of the Thames seeped through every chink and hole in its timber-faced façade, while the cries, shouts and curses of the squalid tenement area that surrounded it permeated to further disturb and harass its inhabitants.

Eleanor, to outward appearances at least, bravely soldiered on. She was now pregnant, and the misery and unhealthiness of her surroundings must have added greatly to her discomfort. Garrett's health, reprieved by their brief sojourn in Kent, had succumbed again to the unwholesome environment and inadequate nourishment. The bills for the attendance of physicians and for pills and potions for their ailments mounted. In desperation St Leger again beseeched the Privy Council for some relief and even offered to go to prison to free himself from the responsibility and cost of his imposed guests. Too ragged to be seen by her peers in public, and in dread of the low dockland society that surrounded her, Eleanor was forced to remain cooped up within St Leger's house and was very ill throughout the entire duration of her confinement. Eventually through the good offices of Sir William Cecil a sum of £130 was sent for their relief, which, according to St Leger, 'hath ben ymployed uppon necessary apparel and phisick, they having been all very sick, the lady his wife yet so, and his lordship and Sr John but lately recovered. Their health cannot be long,' he warned, 'being pent upp in so little a rome altogether.'[16] St Leger once again pleaded that he might 'be delivered of them, whereby I may bend myself towarde Ireland to seek to recover some p^te of my losses'.[17] The rich pasturelands of his prisoner beckoned the jailer.

In the stifling, deprived environment of their dockland home Eleanor was delivered of a son in June 1571, whom they called James. The birth of a son and heir to the great Desmond dynasty should have been an occasion of great jubilation and festivity but for the circumstances of the infant's birth and the dark shadow that hung over the fate of his father and of his inheritance. In their drab surroundings Eleanor and Garrett briefly celebrated the joyful event. News of the birth was less joyfully communicated to the royal court, where the continuation of the 'cankered' rebellious Desmond line was hardly considered an event for celebration. Nor was the birth of a son and heir to the Desmond title and estate welcomed by all the Desmond party at Southwark. A rift had grown, over the months, between Eleanor and Sir John. The Desmond historian Russell later concluded that after Eleanor 'had become the mother of that young son the Ld. James, Sr John of Desmond was out of all hopes to enjoy or inherite the Earledome after his brother's death; whereas before the birth of that child he conceived otherwise'.[18] But the strain of their long captivity, destitute condition, frequent illness and close confinement had even before this begun to jar on the relationship between Garrett and his brother. Their frequent arguments merely intensified when Eleanor had borne the earl a son. From later evidence it would appear that Sir John had anticipated that Garrett's frail health would succumb under the harsh conditions of his long imprisonment, and that he himself would then succeed to the earldom. He had not foreseen that Eleanor would first choose to leave Ireland to be with Garrett, or that Garrett would withstand the rigours of prison and father a son.

Eleanor, for her part, viewed Sir John with deep suspicion, and the rift that had emerged between them in London was never to be healed. She suspected that he had evil intentions towards her new-born son, whom she guarded like a lioness. The safeguarding of the infant's inheritance was to become her sole aim. Oblivious to the intrigue and danger that surrounded him, the young Desmond heir, sickly from birth, fought for a life which was to prove as unfortunate as the circumstances of his birth.

Shortly after the birth of his son it came to the earl's attention that his brother had offered, in return for his own freedom, to accept a commission to suppress James FitzMaurice. And it appeared that he had convinced Sir John Perrot, who in August 1571 advised the Privy Council that Sir John should be returned to rule in Munster instead of his brother. The earl protested to the Privy Council that if permission was thus granted to Sir John, it would only serve to undermine his own position in Munster and, as he phrased it, 'geve me occasion to thinke that your honnours do either suspect my trewe and loyall service towards my soveraigne Lady the Queene or els do judge me unhable to geve them the overthrowe'.[19] The rebels, the earl maintained, 'who besedes that they are traytours to her Matie so have they bene utter enemyes and spoylers of all my patrymony'.[20] which to a degree was true. In the event, however, Sir John's proposal, even with the endorsement of Perrot, did not find favour with the new Lord Deputy, Sir William Fitzwilliam, who bluntly advised Chief Secretary Burghley (the former Sir William Cecil): 'God keep both Sir John of Desmond and base money out of Ireland.'[21]

Letter from Garrett FitzGerald, 15th Earl of Desmond, 1571, to Queen Elizabeth I.

The birth of his son in captivity and destitution, his wife's protracted illness, his uncertainty about the state of his inheritance in Ireland, and, above all, the Queen's negative response to his continued pleas for repatriation—all these factors drove Garrett to acts of sheer recklessness in his desperate desire for freedom. Throwing all caution to the winds, he began openly to abuse the semi-free status that had been allowed him. St Leger complained that he was no longer able to control the earl, who he claimed 'refused to go down to Kent with him and in his absence had rashly ranged into sundry parts of London'[22] outside the confines of his allotted parole. St Leger 'prayed to be delivered of him or to have command to keep him prisoner without liberty'.[23] Garrett had been granted the liberty of Southwark, Bankside and the marshes west of Lambeth Palace. Tormented by his obsession to return to Munster, he roamed the narrow streets and alleys and hung around the seedy riverside taverns as he desperately sought some scheme for his deliverance. He listened to the chimerical plans and projects offered by the waterfront confidence tricksters and rogues who filled his head with wild plans of escape but who, with the earl's deposit of gold in their grasping hands, simply slunk away and disappeared among the milling dockside crowds.

Whispers of the frantic attempts by the Earl of Desmond to effect his escape back to Ireland reached the court and reverberated abroad and became entangled in the more complex political web of international intrigue. The St Bartholomew's Day massacre of some 4,000 Huguenots in Paris, masterminded by the Catholic Queen, Catherine de Medici, and her son Charles IX, coupled with the excommunication of Elizabeth by the Pope, had finally polarised the European power struggle of England, Spain and France into a religous conflict. In Ireland the initial attempt by FitzMaurice to 'use religion as a catalyst to make a common cause of local grievances'[24] now appeared a more serious threat in the light of international developments, and his cause now attracted the attention of Elizabeth's enemies on the continent. Papal emissaries were despatched to Ireland to make contact with FitzMaurice. Sir John Perrot intercepted Edmund O'Donnell with letters to the Geraldine leader from Pope Gregory XIII. Agents from Rome had also infiltrated England to bestir the remnants of the Catholic aristocracy there.

Garrett, in his daily prowls along the Thames dockside, was watched lest he should be contacted by the papal or Spanish conspirators. Both Eleanor and Garrett had secretly written to encourge FitzMaurice in his revolt as a means to obtain their freedom and reinstatement in Desmond. Some of their letters had been intercepted by Perrot, who protested against any intention of allowing the Earl of Desmond to return to Munster and recommended to Elizabeth that he should be indefinitely restrained in London. Garrett and Eleanor also wrote to the Earl of Leicester to inform him of their plight in London and of the miserable condition of the Desmond estate in Munster. To further exploit the prevailing court factions, their trusted confidant, Morris Sheehan, was sent to Leicester armed with details of their version of the Desmond–Ormond dispute over the lordship of Decies and the ownership of Kilfeakle and Kilsheelin, which, as Garrett informed Leicester, 'are wrongfully witholden from him by the saide Erle of Ormonde'.[25] Not to be outdone in subterfuge the same Earl of Ormond arrived in London and invited Garrett to dine with him. Black Tom made sympathetic noises about the exile's miserable plight, and, lulled into a false sense of security, he readily accepted Black Tom's offer of help. But it would appear that the Earl of Ormond and his court cronies, as part of their vendetta against their opposite camp at court, and also in the hope of augmenting their personal fortunes out of Garrett's vast estates in Munster, had set a trap for the unsuspecting captive, who unwittingly found himself implicated in a more sinister political plot of international dimensions.

Shortly after the meeting with Ormond a Captain Martin Frobisher introduced himself to Garrett as he brooded over his continuing misfortunes in a dingy Bankside tavern. Frobisher offered to effect the earl's escape to Ireland for a suitable fee together with the island of Valentia. Garrett eagerly agreed to the proposal and, elated at the prospect of freedom and encouraged by Frobisher, talked loosely and wildly of treason, foreign schemes, intrigues and rebellion. Frobisher was one of Elizabeth's most loyal sea-dogs, and his masters hoped that Garrett would implicate himself, St Leger and even Sidney in his outburst, details of which were duly reported to the government.

But before Garrett could be apprehended, a series of rapid events in the international political arena intervened to have him finally restored to his lordship. Elizabeth's change of heart sprang from her fear—and Eleanor's hope—that the dangerous and unstable situation that was fast developing in Munster would get out of hand. For, exhorted by promises from the papal and Spanish courts, James FitzMaurice FitzGerald had emerged from his retreat and raised the banner of crusade aloft once more in Munster. The Lord President, Sir John Perrot, despite his initial resolve to wipe out the rebels and to eradicate all semblance of Gaelic law and custom in the province, was by 1572 forced to admit that he was merely whistling into the wind. Despite the severity of his rule, the rebellion still raged on and

Munster was more ruinous and desolate than when he took up office. Well might Perrot wonder, as he wearily led his surviving hungry, underpaid soldiers through the wastelands of Munster in search of FitzMaurice, what it took to conquer such a wild land and such headstrong lords. There were no words of encouragement from the Queen, only impatience at his apparent lack of success against FitzMaurice and incredulity that the bogs and marshes of Munster could so relentlessly soak up her precious revenue. Gradually Perrot was forced to adopt some of the Gaelic customs which he sought to destroy. He learned the advantage of the Gaelic method of warfare, of ambushes by small numbers of lightly armed soldiers, and came to adopt Gaelic rather than English military dress as being more suitable for the climate and terrain of Ireland.

Perrot's war with FitzMaurice had developed into a personal vendetta, and this was turned to advantage by his enemy when, with characteristic rashness, Perrot allowed himself to be drawn into a well-planned trap, from which he had barely escaped with his life. The Lord President's pride had been dented and his energy sapped by the unceasing, unrewarding campaign against an elusive enemy. He resolved to resort to the Celtic method of single combat in an attempt to bring the inconclusive war with FitzMaurice to an end. FitzMaurice accepted his challenge, but insisted on the use of Gaelic weapons, the sword and dart, and stipulated that both combatants should wear Gaelic attire. At the appointed time and place the President duly arrived, sporting his short pleated tunic, tight worsted Gaelic trews and a leather quilted jerkin. Thus arrayed for battle, the former champion of the Queen's tiltyard waited for his Gaelic adversary. The hours passed, but FitzMaurice failed to appear. Finally his bard approached and spoke his master's message to the waiting Perrot:

> If I should kill Sir John Perrot, the Queen of England can send another President unto this province; but if he do kill me, there is none other to succeed me or to command as I do, therefore I will not willingly fight with him, and so tell him from me.[26]

All Munster soon knew about Perrot's humiliation, and when the news reached the Queen only the restraining hand of Burghley deterred her from recalling him. Perrot redoubled his efforts against FitzMaurice and vowed 'to hunt the fox out of his hole'.[27] He drove FitzMaurice back into the Kerry mountains and took the strategic Desmond fortress of Castlemaine, but the elusive FitzMaurice still evaded him. Then, in February 1573, FitzMaurice rather unexpectedly submitted to the Lord President, who pardoned him, maintaining that like 'a second St Paul'[28] he had seen the error of his ways. But FitzMaurice was merely playing for time as he waited for developments to unfold on the continent that would enable him to resume his crusade in Ireland.

From Eleanor and Garrett's point of view, FitzMaurice's rebellion had accomplished the objective for which they had hoped and plotted. The rebellion had made it impossible for the colonisation process started by Carew to make headway in Garrett's lordship during his absence. It had demonstrated to the Crown that the earl's removal had not produced the results anticipated, namely the extension of English law and custom throughout Desmond and thereby the curtailment of his power and privileges there. His removal merely exchanged one Gaelic leader for a far more dangerous and able one. Elizabeth had seen no improvement in her finances resulting from her imprisonment of the Earl of Desmond. On the contrary, she had to dig even deeper into her pocket to support her prisoner and his retinue in England, while at the same time endeavouring to suppress an expensive rebellion within his territory. It was to be hoped that the wayward earl and his countess had learned their lesson; and now that the earl had an heir, it might be expected that he would conform to ensure his son's succession to his estates and title. Elizabeth signified her intention to open negotiations to rid herself of her tiresome prisoners, and, after much discussion, terms for their release were agreed. Garrett undertook to be

> answerable to the laws, ordinances and statutes of the realm, as the Earles of Kildare and Ormond are, and shall assist the Queen's ministers in Munster to serve and execute and process writs and the levying of her rents, customs, subsidies, services and duties.[29]

He also promised to apprehend all known malefactors within his territory, to renounce all foreign jurisdictions, and to put down the remaining vestiges of FitzMaurice's rebellion. He agreed to the suspension of his palatine liberties in Kerry, pending an investigation as to their legality, and to the forfeiture of such castles in his lordship recently seized by Perrot for as long as the Crown deemed it necessary for the public good. In theory Garrett effectively signed away the hereditary powers and privileges of his earldom and part of the property enjoyed by the House of Desmond for centuries: in practice, however, the Crown had yet to prove conclusively its ability to impose its authority and to hold that which had been forfeited. But in the spring of 1573, after an exile and imprisonment lasting six years, freedom meant everything to the Earl of Desmond: freedom from humiliation, squalor, fear and poverty. For Eleanor, cooped up with her child in St Leger's house, still weak from the ordeal of the birth, from undernourishment and the unhealthy atmosphere of her surroundings, the prospect of freedom and return to Munster went to her head like potent wine.

Shortly before their departure for Ireland they were ordered to appear before the Queen. Still unable to conceal her personal dislike of Garrett, Elizabeth concentrated her attention upon Sir John, to whom 'she gave a privy nip, that as he hath a good wit, so he should hereafter use it wele'.[30] The Queen seemed better disposed to Eleanor than at their previous meeting and, knowing Eleanor's ability to control her husband's rash nature, urged her to direct him on a more loyal and law-abiding course. The Queen perceived the ragged condition of the Desmonds and in a rare display of generosity towards their plight ordered presents 'of some silks for apparel and some money in reward'[31] for them. Garrett boldly asked that the Earl of Ormond should also be returned to his lordship—as a means, he maintained, to deter rebels driven out of Desmond from automatically seeking refuge in Ormond. For Garrett could not let the opportunity pass to remind Elizabeth that there were others in Ireland, of equal status, who had, despite their proclaimed loyalty, harboured rebellious subjects and relations within their lordships but whom she had not thought fit to punish as he had been. Moreover, he would prefer to have his enemy in sight in Munster than at court in London, where the crafty Black Tom could more effectively intrigue against him. The cold eyes of the Queen flashed dangerously at his suggestion.

Before they set out on their journey Eleanor had to endure a final heart-rending deprivation. It was decided that her infant son, scarcely two years old, should be left in care in England. There is no evidence to suggest that the child was demanded by the Crown as a hostage for his father's future loyalty. On the contrary, the evidence points to the fact that he was presented to the Queen by his parents on their own initiative. He was taken into the care of their mentor, the Earl of Leicester, who stated in a later letter to Garrett and Eleanor that

> Yo[r] Ls request for the presentinge of yo[r] sonne to Her Ma[tie] I have also accomplished. Her Highness accepteth of him and taketh yo[r] offer of him in very good p[te] as I

have signefied by lres to my Lady yor wife and by cause
he is yet to younge to be brought hither, Her Matie hath
taken ordre for his plasinge until he shal be fit to be
removed.[32]

The child had been sickly from birth, and Eleanor may well have
considered that the long and arduous journey to Ireland might
compound the infant's ill-health. It was, however, more likely that the
decision to leave their child in England sprang from fears for his
safety from Garrett's relatives and competitors in Munster. The rift
between Eleanor and Sir John of Desmond had continued to widen.
The unsettled state of her husband's lordship and the uncertainty of
their future there were hardly conducive to the safety and health of
the heir to the earldom of Desmond. Under the patronage and care of
the powerful and friendly Earl of Leicester, his life and future might be
better assured.

Despite despatches from the President of Munster, who
unceasingly advised the Queen against Garrett's restoration, the
Desmonds were permitted to depart for Ireland. They were to be
conducted there under the charge of the newly appointed
vice-treasurer, Sir Edward Fitton. Rumours of Perrot's aversion to their
return reached them in London; and suspecting that Fitton and the
Lord President were in league together, Garrett, Eleanor and Sir John
made a dash across England and Wales for Beaumaris in search of a
quick passage to Ireland. But Fitton caught up with his fugitive
captives, and eventually the entire party set sail for Dublin. They
landed at White Friars in Dublin on 25 March 1573 after an exile of
almost six years.

Signature of Eleanor's son, James, 16th Earl of Desmond.

5

A Troubled Homecoming

> There went he and the Countess towards Loughgure, where a nombre of the freeholders of the Countie of Lymerick met hym. He and his wiefe put on Irishe rayment and made proclamation that no deputie nor constable nor sheriff should practise their office in his countrey.
>
> Justice Nicholas Walshe to Lord Deputy Fitzwilliam,
> 24 November 1573

The joy of liberty was short-lived, and the nightmare of captivity was to continue. No sooner had Garrett, Eleanor and Sir John disembarked at the walls of Dublin than they were promptly taken to Dublin Castle where they were held in 'easy restraint'[1] at the behest of the Lord President of Munster, Sir John Perrot. Perrot had long resisted the Earl of Desmond's restoration and, as he doused the final embers of rebellion in Munster, saw even less reason for the earl's return. He proposed to interview him to determine whether reports of his reformation were true. Eleanor, while not personally held in custody, remained initially with Garrett in Dublin. They were permitted daily access to the city and were obliged once again to incur much expense as they strove to maintain themselves in some state conducive to their rank and position. But Eleanor's main preoccupation was to pacify and control her husband. Garrett was incensed at his further detention at the behest of petty officialdom. He accused the Crown officials in Dublin and in London of a breach of faith. What right had they to restrain him, the Earl of Desmond, set at liberty by the Queen? Garrett's aristocratic temperament and lack of political cunning were exposed, and he made wild threats and treasonable outbursts against the Crown. Eleanor realised how much he had suffered, both physically and mentally, and just how near to breaking-point he was being pushed. Despite her pleas for caution, he was not sufficiently politic to control his sense of outrage before the sneering faces of the petty Castle officials, who reported every word and goaded him into even more damning utterances. He could not be restrained even in the presence of Perrot, who contemptuously reported 'that Desmond was devoid of reason and that nothing could be done with him'.[2] Perrot urged the Queen to have him speedily returned to England, as he considered him 'more fit to keep Bedlam than to rule a newly reformed country'.[3]

Garrett's brother, Sir John, played his cards more cautiously, and with a promise to uphold English law in his terrritory was allowed to depart for Munster. Eleanor became suspicious at the ease with which he obtained his release from Perrot, who had previously indicated to the Queen his readiness to accept Sir John as leader of the Geraldines in Munster in preference to Garrett. To thwart Sir John's ambitions in this regard, Eleanor decided to accompany him to Munster. Lack of money and the collection of the overdue rents of his estates were used as the excuse to explain Eleanor's sudden departure. 'Such rentes and duties as were owing in my country', Garrett complained to the Irish Privy Council, 'were taken up by suche as tooke little cause to heere in what beggered estate I lyde there in Dublin.'[4]

Eleanor found Munster in relative peace and slowly recovering from the ravages wrought by the rebellion of FitzMaurice and Perrot's subsequent reprisals. As Askeaton loomed into view, despite her undoubted fatigue, she must have felt a warming sense of homecoming after her long and bitter exile. Her daughters awaited to be reunited with her. As news of her arrival spread, Garrett's tributary lords and dependent clansmen came to her to seek news of their overlord and give an account of themselves during his absence. She listened as they complained of the erosion of their powers and privileges by the encroachment of Perrot's administration into their domain. The return to power of their overlord was the only remaining hope by which they might in turn have their traditional rights restored. Their anxiety about the fate of their overlord sprang more from this consideration than from a sense of affection or loyalty. In July the news of Perrot's sudden departure from Ireland, due, it was claimed, to ill-health, spurred the Munster lords into action to bring about Garrett's release. Glin castle was seized and the surrounding countryside plundered. James FitzMaurice intensified negotiations with Spain and Rome to revitalise interest in his religious crusade. At the same time he divorced his wife on the grounds that she had conducted an amorous correspondence with his erstwhile ally, Edward Butler. He promptly remarried O'Connor Kerry's widow and thereby gained access to the strategic O'Connor castle of

Carraigafoyle on the Shannon. Munster was in a restless state once more.

In Dublin the Council began an investigation into the legality of Garrett's privilege of palatine rights in Kerry and adjudged it to be void. There was henceforth to be but one legal palatinate in Ireland, the Earl of Ormond's palatinate of Tipperary. The Crown's preference for one earl over the other was thus blatantly continued. Eleanor kept her husband in touch with developments in Munster and redoubled her efforts to secure his release.

But Garrett also received intelligence from England to the effect that the dreaded nightmare, his return to captivity there, was being actively propounded by Perrot. As the Crown had failed to honour the terms of his release, Garrett considered himself free from whatever promises he had made at court. Meanwhile in Munster Eleanor was speedily co-ordinating plans to effect his escape from Dublin.

On a chilly morning in early November 1573 the Earl of Desmond informed the Mayor of Dublin, in whose custody he had been placed, of his intention to join in a hunting party to the city environs. This was customary, according to the terms of Garret's detention, which stipulated that he must return to the mayor's custody by evening. But at Grangegorman Garrett gave the hunting party the slip and, accompanied by the faithful Morris Sheehan, rode south through the territory of his kinsman Kildare without hindrance. There they were met by Rory Oge O'More and Piers Grace, two prominent rebel leaders, who, with a guard of 'some hundred kerne and shot of the Moores',[5] escorted him safely through the midlands to Béal an Droichid where Eleanor awaited her husband. Together they hurried towards Limerick.

News of the Earl of Desmond's dramatic escape spread rapidly, and, as if awaiting the return of a messiah, his followers flocked to Limerick to see him at the Geraldine lake fortress of Lough Gur. The crowds had already assembled as the earl and countess rode down towards the lake shore. With a great cheer of welcome which vibrated over the still waters, they surged forward to greet their overlord. For many of the wildly cheering clansmen the reappearance of their almost forgotten lord was like a resurrection from the dead. As he climbed stiffly down from his horse, the misery of his long years of imprisonment was etched on his haggard features and his threadbare hose and worn shoes. It was an emotive and highly charged meeting between the earl and his loyal Desmond retainers and clansmen. Later, as was subsequently reported to the Lord Deputy, the earl 'and his wiefe put on Irishe rayment and made proclamation that no deputie nor constable nor sheriff should practise their office in his countrey'.[6] Symbolically donning the clothes and speaking the words expected of a Gaelic warrior chieftain, the proud Geraldine lord appeared triumphantly before his people, and all the pent-up anger, frustration and humiliation which he had endured at the hands of the Crown spilled forth. This was his hour of glory, the destiny of which he had dreamed and from which he had drawn solace and comfort in the long, dark nights in his Tower cell and in the destitute lodgings in Southwark. The traditional retainers, dependants, galloglass and kern of his house pressed excitedly around him, their roars of welcome acting as a stimulus to his long-suppressed ego. Vain and dangerous threats against the Crown and rash promises of a return to Gaelic ways gushed forth incautiously as the earl basked in the adulation of his supporters, 'knowing no God, no prince but the earl, no law but his behests'.[7] With exultant cheers, the Earl of Desmond and his countess were escorted home to Askeaton.

Eleanor must have heard, with some misgivings, the indiscreet outbursts of her husband and perhaps wished that he had spoken with more restraint. She understood that it had been an emotional reunion for him and that it was natural that he should vent his spleen on the Crown which had broken faith with him on many occasions. His health had suffered considerably from his enforced detention, and the doubts of his Gaelic followers as to his fitness to receive and command their allegiance had to be assuaged. There were many competitors waiting in the wings should he fail. On the other hand, Eleanor well realised that, partly as a result of the events that had occurred in Munster during his exile, and partly because of the recent developments on the international front and their possible effects in Ireland, a return to the old ways would be firmly resisted by the Crown. The Crown had established a foothold in Garrett's lordship which it intended not only to maintain but to extend.

To maintain one's position one had to adapt to the changing political parameters of the day. Eleanor had first-hand knowledge of English law, administration and life. She had personally experienced its power, its commitment to progress and modernisation (in comparison to the indigenous Irish culture), its renaissance philosophy of inquiry and change, its unity of purpose, its lust for exploration and exploitation, and above all its determination to succeed. The Earl of Desmond, as leader and protector of the Gaelic cause, was doomed; but the Earl of Desmond, if only he had sufficient foresight to adapt to the changing circumstances relentlessly being promoted by the Tudor political machine in

Ireland, could not only survive but retain and extend his power like his neighbour Ormond. Perhaps it was Eleanor's acute perception that influenced Garrett to write to placate the irate Queen and the indignant Lord Deputy regarding his flight from custody in Dublin. It may have been Eleanor's idea too that she should be blamed as the cause of her husband's unlawful escape so as to mask the real reason. Garrett excused his unauthorised departure to Munster as having resulted from his concern for Eleanor, 'in whose care in myne absence, having no thing els to lyve upon ... did pricke so deeply that I camme away without your lycence with intent faithfully to serve her ma^tie as becommeth a true subject'.[8] With tongue in cheek, Garrett assured Lord Deputy Fitzwilliam that 'if I thought my staye there [in Dublin] had ben ane way a further cause to your highness service, I would [be] well contented to end my lyfe there in captyvitie'.[9] For the moment there was little Fitzwilliam could do but grit his teeth at the insolence and audacity of the earl.

Garrett's fiery speeches to his supporters brought immediate and predictable results. Castlemaine and Castlemartyr, which had taken Sir John Perrot so long to capture, were seized. Garrett ordered the strongholds of Glin and Castletown to be razed to the ground, and he granted Glin, Carraigafoyle and Tarbert to his cousin James FitzMaurice. Rumours of foreign-based conspiracies circulated, and a servant in the Earl of Desmond's livery was reported to have been sighted at the Spanish court. The earl revelled in his freedom and power. His dramatic escape from Dublin had enhanced his prestige among the Gaelic and gaelicised grandees. O'Neill and Clanrickard anxiously sought an alliance. To those on friendly terms Garrett loudly declared that 'he would rather have an old mantle in Munster than a torn silk gown in England'.[10] With less likely allies, such as the redoubtable Butler brothers, he was more circumspect: he stoutly professed his loyalty to Elizabeth but his independence of her administration in Dublin—for fear, he claimed, of being subjected again to the extremities he had suffered in the past. To emphasise his argument, 'he exhibited the patched and pieced hose and shoes which he had been forced to wear continually in England'.[11] The Butlers were unimpressed and refused to be drawn into another Geraldine conspiracy. Defence of their lands was one thing, but intrigue with alien powers against the Crown was another matter entirely. Like bees to a honey-pot, however, the idle swordsmen of Munster swarmed to Garrett's gates. Soon his army numbered over a thousand, all of whom had to be fed, clothed and maintained at his country's and people's expense.

The Lord Deputy, Sir William Fitzwilliam, could do little to curb the earl's increasing power in Munster. Lack of money and poor co-ordination of resources and manpower in his administration had resulted in turmoil in every province. In Connaught the restless sons of the Earl of Clanrickard, Elizabeth's 'impudent imps', plundered unchecked throughout Galway. Turlough Luineach, chief of the O'Neills in Ulster, was known to be plotting with the Scots and the Spanish. In Leinster the O'Mores raided at will through King's County and Queen's County, and even the Pale was subjected to attacks. In Ormond the palatinate of Black Tom, absent yet again in London, was said to be as disturbed and wasted as Desmond. The Lord Deputy and his vice-treasurer, Sir Edward Fitton, were at each other's throats and could not agree on tactics to quell the maelstrom. Finally Fitzwilliam, at the end of his tether, begged the Queen to relieve him of his post in Ireland. With her administration and military commitments in Ireland stretched beyond their limits, Elizabeth outwardly was compelled to pursue a policy of reconciliation towards the Earl of Desmond. She despatched warrants to Dublin which formally but belatedly granted the self-liberated earl his freedom. She urged him to make his peace with the Lord Deputy and to disperse his private army, which far outnumbered the Crown forces in Munster. But the earl now reckoned that he negotiated from a position of strength and, flushed by his reception and successes in Munster, replied that if the Queen would remove her garrison from nearby Kilmallock, he would then find little need to maintain so large an army.

In an attempt to breach the widening gulf between the Earl of Desmond and her administration in Ireland, Elizabeth consented that Edward FitzGerald, the brother of the Earl of Kildare, should be sent to negotiate with his imperious kinsman. But Garrett proved reluctant to negotiate with anybody. Eleanor, fearful that the ever-widening gap between the Queen and her husband should become an unbridgeable chasm, urged him to at least hear what FitzGerald had to offer. While he awaited Garrett's decision FitzGerald stayed at Eleanor's old home, Kiltinan castle. As floods on the Shannon prevented Garrett from a planned rendezvous with the Earl of Clanrickard, he reluctantly acceded to Eleanor's request to meet the Queen's emissary instead. Eleanor was pregnant and unable to accompany him. The earl set out with Sir John of Desmond, James FitzMaurice and Andrew Skiddy, the judge of the palatinate of Kerry, to meet FitzGerald at Clonmel. FitzGerald assured the earl that the Queen did not seek to dispossess him but merely wished to be assured of his loyalty and his compliance with the promises he had made to her in England. Garrett flatly refused to go to Dublin, but indicated his willingness to parley with the Lord Deputy on the borders of his own territory. He refused to hand over Castlemaine and Castlemartyr to Captain Bouchier, the English constable at Kilmallock, but slyly offered them to FitzGerald, who he knew had no commission to accept them and no means of holding them. Beyond this, as FitzGerald reported back to the Queen, Desmond would not be moved. Elizabeth had little option but to pardon him, which she did reluctantly on condition that 'he would restore such castles as either we were possessed of before the time of his escape or any other that we should like to be delivered into our hands'.[12] Once back in the safety of Askeaton, however, he flatly refused to forfeit any of his fortresses. Elizabeth thundered against her luckless Lord Deputy as Garrett claimed a moral victory over the Crown, a thing abhorrent to Elizabeth's Tudor sense of sovereignty. 'We think ourselves touched in honour', she raged, 'that the earl may have cause to think that we should now seek upon him a thing very unfitting for the place and quality we hold.'[13]

Eleanor noted how Garrett's moral victory over the Crown had further enhanced his standing among his peers. With increased rumours of alliances and intrigues, domestic and foreign, her husband was becoming identified as the principal motivator of a wider conspiracy of opposition to English rule in Ireland, whereas in fact his real motivation was still the retention of his individual powers and estates in Munster. Eleanor was well aware of her husband's unsuitability and incapacity to adopt the mantle of leadership of a unified Gaelic alliance against England. Garrett was not endowed with the strength, charisma or commitment necessary to mould the highly individualistic tendencies of the Gaelic and gaelicised lords into an effective, organised and patriotic alliance, where personal ambition for power and status would have to be abandoned for a common cause. But Gaelic society was, as it had always tended to be, fragmented and divided and as yet unable to spawn and succour a national alliance. Every lord sought independence of his neighbour as much as of the Crown. It would require the services of a ruthless, powerful leader, driven by a vision of nationhood to control and unite his independently-minded peers into a national opposition to the English Crown. Garrett FitzGerald, fifteenth Earl of Desmond, was no such visionary.

Eleanor's personal objective was to make her husband secure in his title and estates. But to attain that seemingly realistic and understandable ambition, she realised that the must contend and come to terms with the changing political scene in Ireland, as

England relentlessly endeavoured to assert control over her wayward neighbour. The Tudors, and particularly Elizabeth, were adamant that Ireland's autocratic lords, whose independent tendencies she viewed just as much as an affront to her sovereignty as a threat to England's security, must be brought into line. The lords in turn could either conform and accept the new political parameters by affirming their loyalty to the Crown and submitting to the required measure of English law, thereby retaining the degree of power and privilege allowed them by that law, or they could rebel and risk losing everything. Garrett's temperament and character would in any event make a painful transition inevitable. But there were other forces, more sinister in their motivation and more clandestine in their operation, from within the Desmond family itself, that sought to make that transition even more difficult. To Eleanor these powerful rival interests were as devious and dangerous as the enterprising and ruthless agents of the Crown in Ireland who also sought her husband's downfall; both groups cast envious eyes on his estates and plotted for his alienation from the Crown and eventual destruction. It was therefore vitally important to convince the Crown that her husband would require time and persuasion to make the transition from a sovereign lord in his own right to a loyal and dependent earl of the realm.

Eleanor actively sought to gain that time and wrote frequently to the Lord Deputy to assure him of her husband's loyalty. Initially her letters would seem to have had the desired effect, and Fitzwilliam and his army remained in Dublin. Garrett meanwhile ruminated over his position in Munster while his liegemen ran riot throughout the province. James FitzMaurice captured Captain Bouchier and kept him prisoner, while Garrett's galloglass, the MacSheehys, seized the Mayor of Limerick. Hundreds of kern and wild clansmen continued to flock to Askeaton and looked to their indecisive overlord to provide them with work for their weapons and food for their bellies. Wild reports reached Dublin and London that Desmond had now at his disposal an army of 3,000 men-at-arms, that he had captured Kilmallock and Cork, and that he intended to deliver Valentia Island to the King of Spain, with whom he was said to be in constant intrigue. It was also said that he intended 'to purge the country of the name of England'[14] and that he would listen to no counsel but that of the rebel James FitzMaurice.

Under pressure from all sides, Garrett brooded over his position. In the great oak-beamed hall of Askeaton the earl listened as the Desmond bard O'Daly solemnly intoned the valorous deeds of his ancestors. The bard recited a litany of treachery and deceit perpetrated against the House of Desmond by successive English monarchs. Words of exhortation flowed from his lips as he listed the heroic tales of Nesta's sons and the first Geraldines. Low, deep-throated growls erupted from the bearded chieftains, seated at the trestle tables which stretched in rows down the full length of the hall, as O'Daly bewailed the cruel fate meted out to the earl's kinsmen, the Kildares, at Tyburn. The assembly was brought to its feet as the bardic recitation reached its climax with the late treacherous imprisonment and exile of the present earl and the subsequent attempts of the English to usurp his power and patrimony. 'Shanid abú!' cried the bard, and in the emotionally charged atmosphere the wooden drinking-cups overflowing with the heady wine of Spain were raised as lord, chieftain, constable and captain saluted their pale, brooding overlord seated impassively at the top of the hall. 'Shanid abú!'—their answering roar of allegiance seemed to lift the great beams overhead from their stone corbels and fly south over the dark mass of Kylemore to strike terror into the heart of any faint-hearted or doubting inhabitant of Munster. Beside her husband, Eleanor looked in fear at the upraised faces and frantic eyes of his supporters, who in their wild homage to her husband also demanded their age-old right to his leadership in the defence of their Gaelic world. Even in the stifling and charged heat of the overcrowded hall, Eleanor might well have shivered.

As reports of the lawlessness in Munster continued to reach her, Elizabeth angrily berated Fitzwilliam for his apparent unwillingness to move against the Earl of Desmond, whom the Queen considered to be the source of the latest disorder. Fitzwilliam attributed his inaction to Eleanor's stalling intercession on her husband's behalf. 'The Countess with her contynuall impertinancie', Fitzwilliam complained, 'and constant assercions of his conformitie made me to hope he wolde in tyme prove so conformiable as she reported him.'[15] Eleanor's action had been successful in staying Fitzwilliam's hand against Desmond, but Fitzwilliam was about to be pushed aside in favour of Elizabeth's new favourite, the dashing extrovert, Walter Devereux, Earl of Essex. Essex had come to Ireland in August 1573 with the vain hope of conquering Ulster for his royal mistress. But the Ulster chieftains, as Essex found to his cost, did not part easily with their territories. Their strenuous resistance, together with the insubordinate conduct of his demoralised soldiery, whose fear and hatred of Irish warfare and irregular pay made them desert in hundreds, had tarnished somewhat the gilded image of Gloriana's shining knight. Essex sought to make amends. The seemingly impossible task of reconciling the Earl of Desmond with the Crown seemed an appropriate challenge. Essex wrote to Garrett, seeking a meeting with the reluctant earl and urging him to free himself from 'ill counsellors who hiss you on to that which is evil'.[16] Echoing Eleanor's fears, Essex advised Garrett:

> My lord, consider well of this and look into the case
> deeply and give care unto the sound and faithful counsel
> of your friends and stop the ears from hearkening unto
> them which seek by their wicked counsel to destroy
> yourself and to overthrow your house.[17]

He wrote in similar vein to Eleanor and urged her to use her influence to persuade her husband to meet him. Eleanor's counsel prevailed, and Garrett agreed to hold discussions with Essex at Waterford. He was accompanied by Eleanor, James FitzMaurice and some sixty horsemen. On 1 July 1574 they halted at a bridge some three miles outside the city, where they were met by the Earl of Kildare. They refused to enter Waterford without a safe protection, which they promptly received; it was for twenty days' duration. Garrett brought Eleanor only with him as the one person whom he could absolutely trust and whom Essex had no hesitation in accepting at the conference table. Accompanied by the Earl of Kildare, they rode into Waterford and were received by Essex at his rooms in the city. After a series of friendly meetings, on the advice and under the personal protection of both earls, Garrett and Eleanor agreed to go to Dublin, where Garrett's case was again to be examined before the Council there.

Despite Essex's friendship and protection, the journey to Dublin must have been a difficult and fearful one for the Desmonds. Eleanor might well have wondered whether the faith she had—and had induced Garrett to have—in Essex would be vindicated. Her husband's dread of further imprisonment had become an obsession. The nightmare of Dublin Castle, the Tower and Southwark was still a vivid, raw reality. Could a sense of honour and good faith exist in their present circumstances? Would Essex keep his word? Eleanor had placed her trust and her husband's life and liberty in his hands. But unknown to her or to Essex, the Council in Dublin had lately received a stinging missive from the Queen, who demanded immediate action against the Earl of Desmond. In her anger she ordered Fitzwilliam 'to proclaim him traitor and to proceed against him with all celerity'.[18] And now the object of the Queen's anger rode unsuspectingly into their presence.

They were met with an icy reception in Dublin. Stung into action by the Queen, the members of the Council made little attempt to hide their antipathy towards Garrett and their distrust of Essex. The latter was not permitted to accompany Garrett into the council chamber to plead in favour of his case. Outside Eleanor waited anxiously for the outcome and hoped that her headstrong husband would restrain his temper and not play into the hands of the government. But the councillors were not in a placatory mood and summarily demanded that he abide by the articles he had concluded with the Queen in England. Garrett contended that they had been signed under duress, but that he would agree to be bound by them as part of a more general settlement, otherwise the terms of the articles would render him the only undefended lord in the country and thus easy prey to his many enemies. Goaded by the overbearing attitude of his inquisitors, he refused to hold his estates at the Crown's pleasure or to forfeit those of his castles which it had held before his restoration. He would accept the Queen's pardon, but would not on any account 'repair into England to be a spectacle of poverty to all the world'[19] in order to receive it. Asked to submit pledges for his future conduct, he pointed out that both his son and his youngest brother James, still a minor, were in the keeping of the Crown. 'If neither my son, being my only son, nor my brother, whom I love, nor the possession of mine inheritance, as before granted can suffice,' he bitterly stated to his tormentors, 'then to the justice of God and the Queen I appeal upon you all.'[20] But his appeal fell on deaf ears. In the Council's opinion, the Earl of Desmond was not in any position to make demands, but should be prepared to accept whatever decision regarding his future they deemed appropriate. Temporarily in the Council's power but also under Essex's protection, Garrett reacted quickly when rumours of his impending imprisonment and removal to London reached his ears. Flight from Dublin was now imperative, and he called on Essex and Kildare to honour their pledges of protection. Essex was disgusted at the nature of the Council's proceedings against the Earl of Desmond. 'The manner of Desmond's answer might with honour have suffered a toleration,' he protested. 'The mischief is without remedy, for I am bound with the Earl of Kildare, by our words and honours, to safe-conduct Desmond to the confines of Munster.'[21] Essex was as good as his word, and, despite some resistance, he and the Earl of Kildare conducted Garrett and Eleanor safely away from Dublin and out of the clutches of the Council.

Throughout the long journey towards Munster Garrett's companions continued to exhort him to comply with the Queen's demands. At Kilkenny they were joined by the Earl of Ormond, who, carefully making sure that Essex was within earshot, loudly harangued Garrett, urging him to mend his ways and become as loyal a subject as he. Antagonised by the presence of his enemy, and as the safety of his lordship drew near, Garrett grew more reckless and sneered contemptuously at Ormond's advice. Let the loyal Earl of Ormond dispose of his private army, and he, Desmond, would do likewise, but not before. At the borders of Desmond Eleanor and Garrett parted with their unusual escort and, surrounded by their welcoming clansmen, returned to Askeaton. From Eleanor's point of view, the mission had been a failure. The Crown seemed intent on continuing to make impossible demands on her husband, demands which not only would leave him undefended but would be opposed by his dependent lords and clansmen in Munster. The Queen seemed likely to persist in displaying her personal dislike and distrust of him. There were elements in Desmond, Eleanor realised only too well, who would welcome Garrett's further alienation from the Crown as a means to accomplish their own designs. Eleanor had sought to attain the middle ground for her husband, but without apparent success.

With the Queen's threat to have him proclaimed a rebel still hanging over his head, Garrett summoned a meeting of kinsmen and tributary lords at Askeaton. It may have been as a result of this conference that the famous 'combination' or deed of association was compiled—though the date of this document was to be hotly disputed in later years. According to one version of events, the deed was signed on 18 July 1574, while another version places it exactly four years later, in 1578. Even if (as seems quite likely) the latter date is correct, the language of the document graphically reflects the unsettled conditions in Munster and the truculent mood of its principal leaders at the time of Garrett's return from Dublin. The signatories stated bluntly that they 'with one accorde doe counsell and advise the Earle not to consent nor yield to any more than in his answer [to the Council in Dublin]'. They further advised him 'to defend himself from the violens of the Lord Deputy' and forewarned the Crown that they intended 'aiding, helping and assisting the Earl to maintain and defend this our advice against the Lord Deputy or any other that will covet the Earl's inheritance'.[22] The document unequivocally states the reasons which compelled Garrett and his adherents to undertake such a course of action. They did not stem from any great desire to remove or replace the English presence in Ireland, nor from any intention to join in an international religious conspiracy against Elizabeth. They arose from a basic and distinct desire to preserve their hereditary lands, powers and privileges. The deed of association was signed by Sir John of Desmond and by nineteen of Garrett's liege lords and kinsmen. Noticeably absent was the name of James FitzMaurice FitzGerald; however, the problems of dating the document make it difficult to determine the reason for his non-participation: it may have resulted from a decision to distance himself from any movement which did not further his own designs in 1574, or it may simply have been due to his absence on the continent in 1578.

The intentions of Garrett and his adherents, whether set down on paper or conveyed by spies, were soon brought to the attention of the irate Queen. The aspirations of the Munster lords and chieftains, however legitimate to their own minds, were to the Queen a deliberate affront to her sovereignty and totally out of line with her political principles. She was furious to learn of Garrett's permitted departure from Dublin Castle and vented her anger again on the unfortunate Fitzwilliam. 'We gave you no such authority', she wrote, 'to give a protection to him to come and go but to come safe and receive his pardon.'[23] The Geraldine might be given safe conduct to the Castle but not out of it. The intolerable situation drove the angry sovereign even to bribe Sir John with a promise of some part of his brother's lands, and to the further extremity of extending her offer to James FitzMaurice 'or any other of the leaders of his confederates, alluring them from him by such offers as seem reasonable'.[24] Eleanor's distrust of Sir John and FitzMaurice and her suspicions concerning their designs on her husband's patrimony were further heightened by the Queen's offer. This distrust, together with the fear of her husband being proclaimed a rebel, may well have prompted them to take the unusual and later controversial step of enfeoffing Garrett's estates to Eleanor's brother, Lord Dunboyne, and to Lord Power and John FitzEdmund FitzGerald of Cloyne, in trust for them during their joint lives 'with provision for his daughters and final remainder to his son'.[25] They intended to make Garrett's property legally secure from the Crown and family rivals, so that it could eventually be passed on to his son, who, should his father die proclaimed a rebel, would automatically forfeit his right to inherit. The document was later to be no more than a paper defence, however, against the steeled intent of the Crown to possess the vast Desmond estates.

Meanwhile the Earl of Ormond had been seeking an explanation of the seizure by Desmond partisans of his castle of Derrinlaur on the Suir. Garrett refused to answer, and in August Black Tom, with the backing of Lord Deputy Fitzwilliam, took matters into his own hands. They surrounded the castle and ran a mine underneath the walls.

Before they could spring it the entire garrison attempted to escape. but they were intercepted and put to the sword and the castle was captured. The method employed in the seizure of Derrinlaur had an immediate effect on Garrett. Fearful that similar tactics would be used against his own castles, he decided to surrender the disputed Castlemaine to the Queen and to seek her pardon. Eleanor followed her husband's submission with a personal letter to Elizabeth. She assured the Queen that her 'husband's departure from Dublin procedid not (God I take to witness) through any evill intencion towards yor Matie or dignitie but rather incencid by ungodly disturbers of the comon tranquillitie to conceave otherwise of your worthy honor than he had cause'.[26] She excused her long delay in answering previous letters from the Queen on the grounds that 'I durst not untyll nowe, that he hath both hastely repentid and duetifully performid suche things as was required by yr Matie Deputie and Councell of him, ones oppen my lyppes nor put penn to paper to intreat for your highnes mercifull clemency for him.'[27] In view of his submission, Eleanor asked the Queen 'to restore him unto favour'.[28] Eleanor's appeal and Garrett's submission would appear to have had the desired effect. Weary of the entire episode, the Queen agreed that the Earl of Desmond 'was in theory to reign supreme as a feudal prince and be a loyal subject'.[29] But independent feudal princes were an anachronism to the Tudors and to their concept of royal absolutism. The Earl of Desmond, on the other hand, would not—and indeed could not—abandon immediately the role in Munster society which was his fateful inheritance. There could, however, be only one winner in the struggle, and from the beginning the odds appeared to be decidedly in favour of the Tudor queen. Garrett's fate and fortune depended on how quickly and astutely he could make the transition to his new status while retaining as much of his hereditary position as the changed political circumstances allowed.

Eleanor at last breathed a little easier. The threat of proclamation and attainder had receded. Elizabeth had not pushed Garrett to the brink and beyond the limits imposed on him by virtue of his position in the Gaelic world of Munster. Her relief was further heightened in March 1575 when James FitzMaurice, together with his family and some other members of the Munster Geraldines, sailed from Glin for Saint-Malo in France. FitzMaurice departed ostensibly 'for the recovery of his health and to make friendship to come to the Queen's favour'.[30] In fact it was common knowledge that he sought international assistance to continue his religious campaign in Ireland. Whether he had Garrett's consent and blessing for this undertaking is uncertain, but it does not seem likely. For Garrett, at Eleanor's insistence it would appear, had refused to give FitzMaurice additional land in Munster as a reward for his services. Thomas Russell, the Desmond historian and an ardent admirer of FitzMaurice, writing later in 1638, blamed Eleanor for FitzMaurice's exile.

> For Dame Elleynor Butler, Countess of Desmond, [he wrote] and then the mother of one only sonne, opposed herselfe against this James FitzMaurice and with reasons, persuasions, teares and imploreings, persuaded the Earle, her husband, not to dismember his patrimony, but rather for to leave it whole and entire to his only son James FitzGarrett, who was then a young child.[31]

Russell expounded the belief that Garrett was either, as he states, 'conjured by his wife or rather not well established in his witts'[32] to deny FitzMaurice an estate. But Eleanor saw little reason to deprive her son of any part of his inheritance, particularly not for FitzMaurice. Eleanor wanted her son returned to her care, and her husband's future conduct must not jeopardise that event. Consequently when Garrett's kinsman and ally, the Earl of Kildare, was suspected of intrigue against the Crown and imprisoned, and when it was expected that 'Desmond will make extraordinary broils to revenge him',[33] Garrett, with Eleanor's restraining hand on his sword and on his lips, did and said nothing. Their son James was now four years old, and her longing to be reunited with him must have been intense. But still more intense was Eleanor's determination to protect him and his inheritance from the grasping ambitions of her husband's family. With Garrett reinstated in his lordship and with James FitzMaurice in exile, Askeaton seemed a safer haven for the young heir of Desmond. They opened negotiations with the English government for the child's return. Initially it seemed that their request would be swiftly granted, as James was brought from London to Bristol, where he was placed in the care of a Thomas Chester. With some impatience and disappointment, Garrett asked the Earl of Leicester to intervene and to obtain for them a licence 'to have the child brought hither, where', he assured the earl, 'he will not put Her Majesty or me to any charge until he be able to go to school, at which time I will return him thither'.[34] But the English Privy Council still deliberated and waited, and pending further 'trial and proof of his [Garrrett's] obedience and good conformity'[35] ordered that the child be detained in Bristol.

But despite the temporary setback concerning her son's return, Eleanor's hopes for a more balanced treatment of her husband by the English administration in Ireland and at the English court were further heightened in the late summer of 1575 by the news of the imminent reappointment of Sir Henry Sidney as Lord Deputy of Ireland. Generally Sidney had tended to take Garrett's side at court and in the Council in Dublin in an attempt to balance the inordinate influence and power of the Earl of Ormond. In Sidney's opinion, Black Tom had become, particularly by virtue of the Queen's preference of him at Desmond's expense, too powerful a subject and a threat to the balance of power in Munster. Momentarily a chink of light had begun to shine on her life as Eleanor looked forward in hope to better prospects.

6

Diplomacy and Intrigue

I vow to God ... I know her to bee as wicked a woman as ever was bred in Ireland and one that hath ben the chief instrument of her husband's rebellion. And if she bee licensed to go out, your lordship shall doo as good an act as ever you did in your life to this realme to cause hir hed to be stroken of or else to be kept in perpetuall ymprisonment.

Sir Warham St Leger to Lord Burghley, 15 May 1581

A timorous peace descended on Munster. The acrimonious struggle for power there had temporarily exhausted both sides. Desmond had retreated to Askeaton to lick his wounds and to consolidate his position. The Dublin administration, under the leadership of Fitzwilliam, appeared as exhausted as the country it had attempted to subdue. Harassed by an unending series of disorders, wearied by a constant stream of abuse from an uncomprehending sovereign, and hampered by a continuous shortage of money and supplies, Fitzwilliam gladly resigned his thankless and unwieldly charge, and Sir Henry Sidney reluctantly resumed the reins of office in September 1575.

Although overtly the Crown had accomplished little in the lordships of either Desmond or Ormond since the incident at Affane, over the intervening decade English policy towards Ireland had undergone a radical change and adopted a more thrustful approach. Until Affane, Elizabeth had been content to tolerate the independent tendencies of her Irish earls. As late as 1565 her chief secretary, Sir William Cecil, had cautioned the then Lord Justice of Ireland 'to stir no sleeping dogs in Ireland untill a staff be provided to chastin them if they will byte. Many things in common weales are suffered that are not liked.'[1] But by 1565 the sleeping dogs had been aroused and strained at the reforming leash of the Crown. The Crown searched frantically for a suitable stick with which to control them. The stick could be the olive branch of submission and loyalty or the sharp prickly thorn of confrontation. Ormond had chosen the first option, and, while Desmond had initially inclined towards the latter, he had been given a chance to choose again.

The government had changed its earlier wait-and-see policy towards Ireland and had embarked on the difficult road of reconquest. The change of policy stemmed from various sources. Over the decade Ireland had become a major drain on Crown revenue. Official expenditure in Ireland had soared from £18,975 in the 1560s to £31,847 in the 1570s, which, even taking the inflation of the day into account, was more than the state coffers could afford or the parsimonious Queen would tolerate. Furthermore, recent developments in international politics also seemed to demand more positive action in Ireland. The threat of foreign intervention in Ireland by England's continental enemies and its menacing potential as a backdoor into England constantly haunted English minds. The recent revolt by James FitzMaurice and his flirtations with a wider international conspiracy which sought 'to use religion as a catalyst to make a common cause of local grievances'[2] had frightened the English government. FitzMaurice's continued contacts with the French, Spanish and papal courts did little to allay the fear that Ireland might well become a base for the Counter-Reformation, then rampant in Europe. There was further alarm at the likely prospect of the formation of a confederacy between the powerful independent Irish lords such as Desmond, O'Neill and the Earl of Kildare. If such a confederacy received foreign support, it could well extend throughout the country and attract the Catholic lords of the Pale, who were already embroiled in a bitter dispute with the Crown over the payment of cess. And there were other interests which would welcome the vigorous assertion of English rule in Ireland. While Elizabeth might chastise her officials for the disorderly state of the country and the enormous expense of reconquest, English financial investors in the various colonisation ventures felt positively defrauded. Loyal administrators, like Sidney, Fitzwilliam and Perrot, who had sacrificed their careers and their health as they trudged through bogs and over mountains in a thankless attempt to subdue, inch by inch, the rebellious land, felt understandably frustrated. The time for reassessment had come, and in the present short-lived lull the Crown also took stock.

Despite the continued detention of her son, the next few years were to be the one period of relative tranquillity and normality that Eleanor would experience in her brief and ill-fated marriage to Garrett. Imprisonment, exile, deprivation and loneliness had been her lot as Countess of Desmond. Her moments of happiness with Garrett had been fleeting. They were constantly torn apart by the unsympathetic political maelstrom that raged around them. Yet their union had become strengthened and revitalised. Throughout the years of her life with Garrett, Eleanor's primary concern and *raison d'être* for her every action was to protect her husband's political and physical well-being and to safeguard the Desmond inheritance for her son. With an iron will and fierce physical energy, she braved every threat to the attainment of those objectives. Time after time, both by virtue of her letters and personal mediation, she demonstrated her undoubted intelligence charm and political acumen as she interceded for her husband when he spoke treason too loudly or was suspected of some ill-planned and ill-advised conspiracy. Almost every letter from Garrett to the Queen or to the Privy Council was accompanied by a letter from Eleanor, moderating the more arrogant tones of her husband's demands or seeking to dissuade the Crown from forcing her husband into an impossible position. She was his adviser during negotiations with government officials, and her restraining hand held him in check while with the other hand she strove to keep the English administration at bay. She understood better than anyone and was witness to the tremendous pressures exerted on her husband from all directions—pressure from the Gaelic lords of Munster, who expected him to observe and protect the customs and privileges of their antique world; the self-inflicted pressure imposed by his inordinate sense of position and lineage; and pressure from the most potent threat that had ever emerged to undermine his prized inherited powers, assiduously guarded by his ancestors for generations. Garrett looked to his wife for support to share the burden that seemed at times likely to overwhelm him. In the whirlpool of intrigue and subterfuge that swirled around him , hers was the voice of calm and reason, the one voice he could trust. Imprisonment he held in fearful dread, a nightmare to which he would never again submit as long as he lived. Eleanor well realised that if the Crown, for any reason, attempted to deprive him of his liberty, the effect would be to make a rebel of her husband. This she sought desperately to avoid. Lords who rebelled against the Tudors never emerged victorious, and, as witnessed by Shane O'Neill's fate, upon their demise their inheritance was forfeited to the Crown. Eleanor would endeavour her utmost to prevent a similar occurrence in Desmond.

But the respite from the turmoil and trauma of the preceding decade also afforded her time to enjoy the more personal pleasures and privileges pertaining to her position as Countess of Desmond. In the shady tree-lined walks among the gardens and orchards which surrounded Askeaton she resumed as best she could some semblance of a normal lifestyle. During the preceding unquiet years her daughters had been fostered among close relatives and friends, but had been lately reunited with their parents, and their number was now increased by the birth of another daughter whom they called Ellen. Askeaton reverberated with the happy sounds of its own Geraldine family, reunited and in residence once again after many long years of absence, and to the pleasant sounds of the more peaceful side of the Gaelic lifestyle. In the splendid fifteenth-century hall, situated on the west side of the castle, lighted by the famous intricate traceried windows, with wide embrasures and narrow stone seats on either side, the Earl and Countess of Desmond presided over more joyful festivities than Askeaton had known for some time. The great hall vibrated to the warm noisy clangour of Gaelic hospitality. The earl welcomed his many followers to partake at his table, not merely out of hospitality, but also because in Gaelic Ireland, where 'every Irish overlord held sway over people rather than territory',[3] a lord's prestige and power were measured by the number of his dependants. While the English Crown might rant and rave over the existence and extent of the Earl of Desmond's personal army, the reality in Gaelic Munster decreed that without this the earl was unable to rule. Without his army, the earl in effect forfeited his ability to protect himself and his dependants, the primary function of his role as a Gaelic overlord. But the actual upkeep of his army was the duty of his overburdened and overtaxed peasantry, whose plight, both in the Gaelic and anglicised parts of the country, was deplorable. Overlords were demanding and harsh masters. They showed little mercy, and little was expected from them. The peasantry patiently bore the brunt of their master's excesses, both in war and in peace, with a blind obedience. If hatred towards Garrett and his house surfaced in their hearts, it was quickly subdued. As their earl and countess, dressed in silken finery rode past their cabins, they briefly left the plough or the reaping-hook to raise the loyal shout of 'Shanid abú!' with a mixture of the pride and fear that had been instilled into them for generations.

The long summer days were spent hunting, following the swift red deer over the plains of Limerick and Cork and into the dark forests of oak and ash. The evening silence was punctuated by the tolling of the prayer-bell from across the Deel as the monks from the Franciscan abbey intoned their Te Deums over the bones of dead

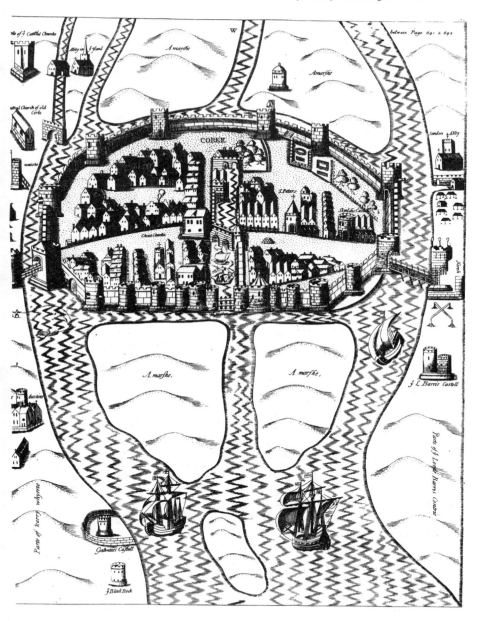

Cork city. A contemporary plan. (*Pacata Hibernia*).

generations of Geraldines. And in his travels, just as the sovereign Elizabeth in England was wont to quarter herself on her subject lords, so did the Earl of Desmond exercise similar but more ancient rights within his lordship in Munster. When he went to Tralee to collect his dues and rents, a fair was held there to honour his presence. It was attended by travelling merchants and traders who sold their wares and paid taxes to the earl for the privilege. The Mayors of Cork, Youghal and Limerick, over whom the Earls of Desmond claimed suzerainty, put on a brave show, opened their gates, displayed banners of welcome, entertained their lord lavishly, and breathed a sigh of relief and counted the cost when his official visit terminated. The earl presided over the palatine courts of Tralee and Any, appointed court officers, and was the ultimate arbiter in all judicial proceedings within the palatinate, dispensing justice by Gaelic law intermixed with elements of English law. Ships from Spain and France kept the earl in touch with developments abroad and also kept him provided with fine furnishings, wines for his table, and silk, tafetta and velvet for his and his countess's wardrobes. Whispers of more serious transactions reached Desmond from time to time as spies in the earl's pay brought reports of FitzMaurice's travels to the French, Spanish and papal courts in search of material assistance to fly the banner of crusade once again over Munster. But the threat which sought to shatter the tranquillity that like a soothing salve had almost healed the painful sores of the previous years was as yet far removed.

As if to augur a continuation of the peaceful respite, the Lord Deputy, Sir Henry Sidney, decided to undertake 'a mission of inquiry, conciliation, and administrative settlement'.[4] In response, the Earl and Countess of Desmond greeted him at Dungarvan and offered to conduct him on his journey through Munster. Despite their differences at their last meeting which had resulted in Garrett's long imprisonment in England, Eleanor knew that Sidney's antagonism towards the Earl of Ormond and his influence at court might be made to work in her husband's favour. She was also determined that Sidney should recognise that it was Garrett who was the premier lord in Munster, with as much authority and as capable to rule his palatinate as the supposedly 'loyal' Earl of Ormond. Sidney was suitably impressed, and in a spirit of friendship and cordiality the earl and countess escorted him into Cork city, where they were received by the citizens, as Sidney duly reported, 'with all joyfulness, tokens and shows, the best they could express'.[5] Eleanor's brother, Lord Dunboyne, joined their party at Cork, together with Garrett's brothers, Sir John and Sir James, who had lately returned from England.

Following the Geraldine's lead, the entire Munster nobility assembled together to attend the Lord Deputy. Thither came, as Sidney related, the chieftains of the three branches of the great MacCarthy clan: 'The Earl of Clancar, by the Irish styled MacCarthy More, was accompanied by his countess, the sister of the Earl of Desmond, and his infant children, the Baron of Valentia and the Lady Ellen. . . . The Lord of Muskerry, the wealthiest chieftain of the sept . . . and the Lord of the fertile lands of Carbery, Sir Donagh MacCarthy Reagh . . . accompanied by his two sons, Florence and Dermod Moyle.'[6] They were joined by the Earl of Thomond, the Archbishop of Cashel, the Bishop of Cork, the Viscounts Barry and Roche and the Baron of Lixnaw. To this glittering array of Munster aristocracy were added the lesser Gaelic chieftains like the O'Sullivan, O'Callaghan, O'Donoghue and O'Driscoll. As a further manifestation of Gaelic custom, Sidney received the five MacSheehy captains of the Desmond galloglass, bound in hereditary allegiance to their Geraldine overlords, though, as Sidney astutely observed, their status was hardly that of subordinates, 'the greatest being both in fear of them and glad of their friendship'.[7] And there too, as he gallantly reported to the English Privy Council, 'the better to furnish the beauty and filling of the city, all the principal lords had with them their wives during all the Christmas who truly kept very honourable, at least plentiful, houses'.[8] Sidney concluded his account by pointing out, perhaps as an incentive to the widowers and bachelors in England: 'To be brief many widow ladies were there also, who erst had been wives to earls and others of good note and account.'[9]

It was a great social event, and as such a rarity in the troubled times, a bright and joyful occasion, on the surface at least, as the interrelated Munster aristocracy mingled under the watchful but benign gaze of the English Lord Deputy. For Eleanor it was an opportunity to meet and exchange news with her sister, brother, half-brother, nieces and nephews and many other relations among the assembled nobility. It was Christmas time, and the festive season was lavishly celebrated. As principal lady of the province, Eleanor entertained Sidney, his entourage and the nobility and hosted banquets in their honour. The wine flowed freely, and the music was loud and merry as English and Gael celebrated the festive season of 1575. Alongside the gaiety and pageantry, however, lay the hard political realities. It was a suitable opportunity for Eleanor to capture the Lord Deputy's ear and to spell out the great pressures to which her husband was being subjected. She entreated Sidney to show patience and forbearance and promised to encourage her husband along the path of loyalty. But she also reminded him that Garrett's encounters with the Crown had so far done little to inspire his trust and obedience. Surrounded as he was by the trappings of the Gaelic world of which she spoke, Sidney could not fail to appreciate her dilemma, and accordingly spoke with friendliness and encouragement to her husband.

But Sidney did not allow the festivities to deter him from his duties as the Queen's representative. In the new year he set about the more serious business of his office. He presided over the court in Cork and heard civil cases there, tried by English law. He undertook an inspection tour of the city's defences and made provisions for their improvement and upkeep. On 1 February 1576, accompanied by Eleanor and Garrett, he departed for Limerick, where they received a reception as hospitable as Cork's from the mayor and citizens. The only ominous note struck by the Lord Deputy during his tour of Munster was to recommend a speedy appointment to the vacant post of President of Munster. He prophesied the return of James FitzMaurice and warned the Privy Council 'that all the loose people of this province will flock into him. Yea,' he continued, drawing on the knowledge he had perhaps gleaned from his talks with Eleanor, 'the lords, though they would do their best, shall not be able to keep them from him.'[10] After Limerick, Eleanor and Garrett parted company with the Lord Deputy, as he continued on his journey into Connaught, and returned home to Askeaton. There life continued in relative peace as before. Garrett saw to his vast estates, collected his rents, and exercised his customary privileges as overlord. To reiterate his palatine privilege and to stem any doubt in the minds of his tributary lords in the wake of Sidney's visit, he summarily ordered the Baron of Lixnaw and the freeholders of Clanmorris to attend at his palatine court at Tralee. In his own country Desmond's power was still absolute.

Despite Sidney's note of urgency, the presidency of Munster was not filled until the summer of 1576, when Sir William Drury was appointed as the second president of the province. Drury, a native of Suffolk, had been the governor of Berwick. He had a distinguished military career both by land and sea in England and on the continent. From nearby Askeaton the Earl of Desmond anxiously watched the build-up and concentration of English officialdom and military might as Drury established his headquarters at nearby Limerick and embarked on his presidency in a way that was bound to bring him into collision with the uneasy earl. Drury wrote enthusiastically to the Privy Council about the methods he had begun to employ. 'I began the assizes in Cork,' he reported, 'where I hanged to the number of 42. Of which some were notable malefactors, one pressed [i.e. pressed to death] and two gentlemen of the chief of the MacSweeneys hanged drawn quartered.'[11] Drury next turned his attention to the lordship of the Earl of Desmond. He was determined to curtail the influence and power of the earl in Munster, which he reckoned ran contrary to his own and would serve only to undermine his position as President. In order to compel the earl to reduce his army, which far outnumbered his own forces, he compiled a register of the earl's followers, for whose future conduct he held the earl personally responsible. He next attempted to extract cess, in money and in kind, from the earl's tenants in order to defray the expenses of his presidency. The earl bristled with anger at Drury's openly defiant attack on his position. Contemptuously he ignored Drury and complained directly to the Privy Council. The Council instructed Drury himself to investigate the matter, in the knowledge that their own earlier denial of sufficient means to maintain his administration in Munster had left the President with little option but to seek maintenance from the earl's tenants. As the earl's complaint was to be investigated by the perpetrator of the complaint, a fair and unbiased hearing was out of the question.

Drury next struck against the earl's most highly prized hereditary privilege, his palatine court of Kerry, which had been deemed void by the Irish Privy Council. Drury further contended that the palatinate had become the refuge of all the evil-doers of Munster and proposed 'to make a passage for law and justice to be there exercised', as he considered 'that it would not be safe among a great flocke to leave a scabbed sheepe nor good for a commonwealth to have nurseries for sinne'.[12] Drury started out for Kerry with the intention of establishing Crown courts there to prosecute offenders by English law. But the 'scabbed sheepe' of Drury's despatches, incensed at this blatant attack on his ancient privilege, called out his army and barred the Lord President's way to Tralee. Drury accused the earl of treachery and reported to the government that he was clearly intending to declare war on the Queen's army.

A direct confrontation, and one which would have far more serious implications for Garrett than Affane, seemed inevitable as the two forces formed battle-lines. If Garrett attacked or was drawn into battle by Drury, Eleanor realised that he would be proclaimed for treason forthwith, with dire consequences both for himself, his lordship and his family. Eleanor swiftly interceded with Drury. A contemporary observer rather graphically reported the meeting thus:

> Like a good Abigaell [she] went and met the lord
> president, fell upon hir knees, held up hir hands and with
> trilling teares praied his lordships patience and pardon,
> excusing as well she could hir husband's follie, saying
> that he had assembled all that companie onelie for a
> generall hunting.[13]

While the lady's excuse was somewhat thin, Drury, considering the
superiority of the earl's forces, accepted the countess's version of
events, but insisted nevertheless that he would procede to Tralee.
With great difficulty Eleanor restrained Garrett from attacking him. As
far as Garrett was concerned, Drury was merely one of the ever-
increasing band of 'unattractive outsiders, arrogant and ruthless men
whose system threatened a wide spectrum of the existing society,
from the learned class, the jurists, poets, and musicians to the men of
war'[14] and, more significantly, also threatened the power of lords like
Garrett. To the proud Earl of Desmond, the great gaelicised feudal
aristocrat of Munster, Drury was but a servant, a hireling, one of the
contemptible 'English churls' of inferior degree. But Eleanor realised
that Drury and his kind were but a symbol of the new English political
philosophy that had evolved towards Ireland. No matter how
disdainfully the Earl of Desmond might regard him, neither Drury nor
the policies being pursued by him in the name of the Crown would go
away. If Drury failed in his mission in Ireland, there would be a
hundred more like him to take up where he left off—and perhaps
with even more ruthlessness and less mercy.

Meanwhile in Connaught the Burkes strained against the severe
rule of the military governor there, Sir Nicholas Malby. Drury received
reports that Sir John of Desmond had incited the Burkes to rebel and
promptly apprehended him. Rumours reached Askeaton that Drury
intended to arrest the earl as well. Faced with the dreaded nightmare
of detention, Garrett fled for security with Eleanor and the children
into the furthermost part of Kerry and refused all offers, whether from
Drury or from Sidney, to negotiate. It was significant that rumours of
Garrett's impending arrest had emanated from London, where Black
Tom's influence within court circles was as strong as ever. Garrett's
flight and his point-blank refusal to obey the President of Munster
and the Lord Deputy could only serve to alienate him further from
the Crown and bring him a step nearer destruction. It was also to
Black Tom's advantage that Garrett's predictable reaction would serve
to keep Drury fully occupied in Desmond and leave him less time to
pry into the state of affairs in Ormond.

Professing his life to be in danger, the Earl of Desmond sounded the age-old call to arms as the year 1576 drew to a close, and soon over a thousand adherents flocked to his defence and to the defence of their ancient rights and customs. Safe within the confines of his palatinate and protected by his hereditary men-at-arms, Garrett boldly announced that no rent or cess would henceforth be forth-coming to the Crown from his lordship. The question of cess had become a vexed issue, particularly in the Pale, where Lords Baltinglass, Howth, Delvin and Trimleston had been committed to Dublin Castle when they attempted to voice their grievances on the matter to the Crown. While the Queen acknowledged that the system as then practised required some measure of adjustment, she was indignant that the normally loyal lords of the Pale should so boldly challenge her royal prerogative. Garrett by his pronouncement on the matter had, whether by design or accident, linked the grievances expressed by the lords of the Pale with his own resistance in Munster.

Eleanor spent the summer months of 1577 hidden deep within their Kerry fastness, secure, behind a natural shield of mountain, wood and marsh, from Drury, who scoured the countryside in vain. But as summer gave way to autumn she became uneasy that Garrett's continued absence from the rest of his lordship would weaken his control there and allow it to be usurped by others. She wrote to the Queen and to Sidney to explain that it was the fear of imprisonment, which was rumoured to have been imminent, that had caused them to flee to safety. But there was no immediate reply to her letters, and in the meantime the Queen continued her pointed policy of favouritism by entrusting the Lord Deputy to ensure 'that the Earl of Ormond's landes should be exempt from all cess'.[15] In vain Sidney urged her to reconsider. He warned her that her decision would not only result in a decrease in much-needed revenue, but, in the present circumstances, would be seen by the Earl of Desmond as further proof of the Crown's discriminatory policy against him. Mindful also of the situation in the Pale, Sidney further warned the Queen that her decision would 'be a precedent to others to sue for like immunities'.[16] To placate the earl and to allay Eleanor's fears, Sidney sent messages urging them to repair to either Drury or himself. The English Privy Council too wrote to assure them that the rumours of Garrett's imprisonment were totally false, and that it was believed that they had been instigated 'no doubt by some of your private enemies, that practise and would be glad to draw you into any undutiful action that might purchase unto you Her Majesty's indignation to the overthrow of your state'.[17] Eleanor concurred with the sentiments expressed, and she urged

Garrett not to play into the hands of his enemies but to make his peace with the Crown.

After much persuasion Garrett finally agreed to deal with Sidney, who forwarded the necessary letters of protection and arranged for the meeting to take place, significantly, at Kilkenny, the principal seat of the Ormond lordship. There at a ceremony in the cathedral in February 1578 the Earl of Desmond formally submitted to the Lord Deputy. Garrett was in great pain from the thigh wound he had suffered at Affane, and Sidney was taken aback at the apparent deterioration in the physical condition of the earl. 'I suppose there is least danger in hym,' he assured the Queen, 'beinge such an impotent and weake boddye, as neither can he gett up on horseback, but that he is helpen and lift up, neither when he is on horsebacke can he hym selfe alight downe without healpe.'[18] Sidney reconciled Eleanor and a reluctant Garrett with Drury and, as he reported, 'made them ffriendes in as good sorte as I could'.[19] He urged the earl to disband his army, as it was considered a threat to the Lord President's position and peace of mind in Munster. Drury was every bit as reluctant to make peace with Garrett. He privately considered that the Lord Deputy had dealt far too leniently with the troublesome earl, who, to Drury's mind, was the single greatest obstacle to peace and order in Munster. He was convinced that Sir John of Desmond, with the earl's prior consent, had conspired with the Burkes of Connaught to incite rebellion there. This belief was further strengthened when rumours circulated of a marriage between Lady Mary Burke, the daughter of the Earl of Clanrickard, and Sir John. He suspected that both the Earl of Desmond and Sir John had been and continued to be in contact and collusion with James FitzMaurice in his endeavours to elicit help from England's enemies abroad. Sidney, on the other hand, sought to portray Garrett 'as the least dangerous man of iv or v of these that are next hym in right and succession (if he were gonne) and easieth to be dealt withall'.[20] But perhaps both his critic and his erstwhile mentor both neglected to consider the passionate hereditary tradition of birthright, obligation and privilege that was invested in the feeble body of the Earl of Desmond and that would, when eventually unleashed, elevate the indecisive earl, almost against his will, into a noble and mighty warrior, a strong crusading lion. But in February 1578, as Sidney watched Desmond, grimacing in pain, being lifted off his horse and limping across the courtyard, he could not be blamed for dismissing such a possibility.

With another near confrontation narrowly avoided, Eleanor must have felt a great sense of relief at the outcome of their meeting with

Sidney. She ministered to Garrett's physical ailments which, despite his relatively young age, had incapacitated him greatly. For as well as the discomfort and pain he suffered from the aggravated thigh wound, the earl was showing the early signs of palsy, which was to develop further over the succeeding years. But with incursions by the Lord President into his preserve momentarily halted, he had some time to recuperate. All the signs augured well for a continuation of peace and time for the earl to make a slow but steady adjustment to the changed political situation. The Queen too would seem to have been affected by the air of reconciliation that had emerged. She wrote in friendly tones to Eleanor in appreciation of her

> good travail with your husband, to remove from him this vain fear of his apprehension and to leave off his number of followers. So have you [Elizabeth assured her, aware of Eleanor's personal motivations] declareth yourself no less wise and loving towards your husband for the preservation of his estate, which might easily have been utterly ruined if he had not by your good means been brought to the said submission.[21]

Sidney maintained a steady hand on the tiller of government in Ireland, and Garrett and Drury maintained an outward show of harmony in Munster. As further proof of his loyal intent, Garrett delivered into the Lord President's custody certain malefactors who had recently committed crimes within his lordship. Among them was the 'most notorious woman in all the coasts of Ireland',[22] the famous female sea-captain and pirate, Grace O'Malley (Granuaile) from Connaught. Garrett's soldiers had captured her as she led a raiding party from her ship in search of booty in Limerick. Drury communicated to Sidney the news of her capture and imprisonment by the earl:

> Grany O'Mayle, a woman that hath impudently passed the part of womanhood and been a great spoiler and chief commander and director of thieves and murderers at sea to spoille this province, having been apprehended by the Earle of Desmond ... his Lordship hath now sent her to Lymrick where she remains in safe keeping.[23]

Whatever part, if any, Eleanor played in yielding up the 'famous female sea-captain' to the Crown is not recorded, and her opinion and reaction to her husband's remarkable hostage is open to conjecture. She had doubtless heard tales of her exploits and extraordinary lifestyle as a sea-trader, pirate and mercenary. While pirates were numerous off the south and west coasts in sixteenth-century Ireland, a woman pirate of the calibre of Grace O'Malley was a phenomenon and a worthy hostage. Compassion for a woman's plight or a feeling of sisterhood did not concern Eleanor, so long as the capture and handing over of Grace O'Malley served as a means to pacify the Crown and protect her husband.

Despite the continued peaceful overtures, ominous storm-clouds had begun to gather on the horizon. In the summer of 1578 rumours came flying across the seas, propelled by emissaries from the papal and Spanish courts, that James FitzMaurice, suitably equipped, was homeward bound to raise the banner of crusade aloft over Munster. Messengers also brought despatches to Garrett and the Munster lords to advise them that FitzMaurice not only requested but expected their support and readiness to lead their followers behind the banner of Christ. James FitzMaurice was coming, with enough gold and arms from Christ's vicar on earth to persuade any doubting Catholic mind. Eleanor's nightmare was fast becoming a reality. The cursory truce between Garrett and Drury seemed destined to end with the recall in September of Lord Deputy Sidney, the sole buffer between Garrett and the more ruthless and grasping elements of the Crown. Drury himself was subsequently sworn in as Lord Justice in his place.

Eleanor and Garrett journeyed to Dublin to take their leave of Sir Henry Sidney. On 12 September 1578, as the tide lapped the city walls at Wood Quay, Eleanor with much trepidation and some sadness watched Sidney's departure from Ireland for the last time. Sidney perhaps better than most had come to understand their great dilemma and whenever possible had made allowances for their circumstances in his dealings with her husband. Sidney was undoubtedly a loyal, energetic and often ruthless Elizabethan official. But he also possessed rare qualities that were often lacking in his contemporaries in Ireland. Eleanor knew that many of her husband's treasonable outbursts and actions had never been reported by Sidney. He had shielded them from the arrogant petty Crown officials. His personal and political antipathy towards the Ormond clique at the royal court had, to a degree, worked to their advantage. There was a basic honesty and integrity about Sidney in all his dealings with them. While ever the devoted servant of the Crown, and in no way prepared to tolerate the Earl of Desmond's inclination to rule as an independent Gaelic chieftain, he was nevertheless willing to allow him the necessary time to adjust to the idea of becoming a reformed Anglo-Irish lord of the realm. As the ship slipped anchor and sailed down the wide estuary and into Dublin Bay, Eleanor perhaps realised that it took with it the last vestiges of peace and hope. She intended, however, to try to her utmost to preserve Garrett in some semblance of loyalty. If such a plan was to have any likelihood of success, it was essential to maintain a direct link with the royal court rather than risk deliberate misinterpretation by dealing through Crown intermediaries in Ireland. Sidney could yet be their ally at court and ensure that they received a fair hearing.

As the rumours about an impending invasion intensified, Eleanor wrote directly to the Queen to assure her of Garrett's continuing loyalty, stressing that he 'standeth as safe and sure a subject to her Matie and willbe as ready to spend himself and all he hath in her Maties quarrell as any within the Realme'.[24] She also asked the Queen to have her son released and returned to her, and Elizabeth promised to look into the matter. Eleanor sent the Queen 'as a token of my good will half duzen marten skins whereof I praye you some to take in good worth'.[25] To reciprocate the gesture, the Queen sent Eleanor a fashionable rich gown. Perhaps it was the self-same gown that Eleanor wore to the admiration and envy of all when she and Garrett presided at a banquet in Limerick held in honour of the newly appointed Lord Justice. The atmosphere was cordial, the earl and Drury appeared to be on friendly terms, and Drury reported significantly of their meeting: 'We won the Earl and Countess of Desmond to agree to and subscribe to a compositon for the alteration of their wonted manner of coyne and livery and the converting thereof into a yearly rent of £2,000.'[26] Eleanor's influence had helped to persuade her husband to relinquish the coyne and livery exactions in lieu of rent payments, a privilege which was the hallmark of the Gaelic world. She had brought him more than half way to meet the demands of the Crown and now looked for some reciprocal sign of generosity. She fully realised that her husband, in relinquishing his ancient Gaelic rights, must not be seen to lose face and risk losing his authority over his followers in Munster.

The Queen seemed eager to maintain and encourage the Earl of Desmond in his new-found loyalty. She wrote to both Garrett and Eleanor and again assured them that 'It was never our meaninge (as by some hathe been most unjustlie and maliciouslie given out) to dispossesse our subjects of our saide realme of their livinges.'[27] On the contrary, her intention was to see them live in peace and justice 'whiche', the Queen continued, 'if it hathe not been in our ministers

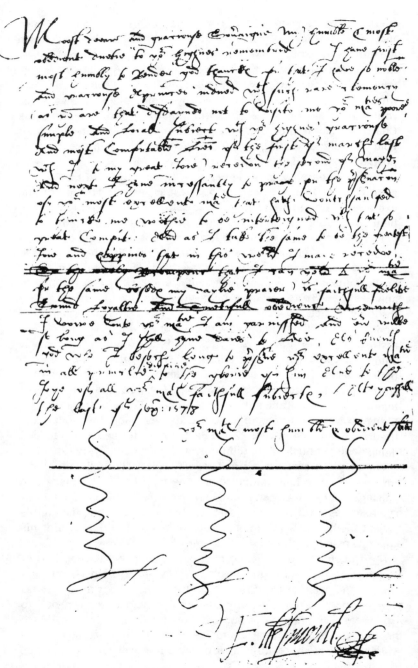

A signed letter to Queen Elizabeth I from Eleanor Countess of Desmond, 1578.

there, whom we wilbe as ready to punishe with all severity, if they may be justlie convicted of that faulte'.[28] In a personal message to Eleanor, Elizabeth again thanked her for her good advice to her husband and promised that the Countess of Desmond would 'find Us your good and gratyous lady when said occasion shall faule out wherein We may shewe you the proofe of our good meaning towards you'.[29] As a token of her appreciation the Queen despatched to Lord Chancellor Gerrard of the Irish Privy Council 'a gowne of clothe of gold'[30] to be passed on to Eleanor. The Chancellor, however, postponed the delivery of the gown until he could personally hand it over at a meeting with the Earl of Desmond, at which Eleanor was also present, when he placed it in her hands with, as he put it, the express purpose of making it possible 'by her help to have gotten the better end for the worth'.[31] There were no free gifts from the Crown.

Elizabeth kept one very important promise when early in 1579 Eleanor was reunited with her son. Almost six years had elapsed since she had seen him. James had been weak from birth, and the years in custodial care in England had not improved his health. His English apparel, accent and outlook made him seem strange and different in the eyes of his sisters who clustered around in wonderment at their timid new brother. The restoration of the Desmond heir caused quite a stir among the Desmond tributary lords and chieftains, not least among them the earl's brothers, who saw in the child the demise of their own ambitions and hopes towards the earldom. Like a tiny stormy petrel, the young boy appeared as the harbinger of the great tempest that was about to break over Munster. But for a brief time Eleanor's heart was full of tenderness and affection as she allowed the love she had stored over the years of his exile to flow over her delicate little son.

On 18 July 1579 the peace of Munster was shattered by a holy thunderclap that reverberated off the high mountain peaks of Kerry and sent shock-waves careering across the country to frighten the Council in Dublin and across the sea to stir Elizabeth and her government into action. James FitzMaurice FitzGerald, with a fleet of small ships, an army of 600 soldiers of Italian, Spanish, French, Portuguese, English and Irish origin, a quantity of arms and ammunition, a papal legate, a Spanish friar and a banner blessed by the Pope, landed at Smerwick harbour, where they dug themselves in at the old fort of Dún an Óir. The banner was a significant feature of the enterprise. It bore the arms of FitzMaurice and a crucifix and displayed the motto 'In omni tribulatione et angustia spes Jesu et Maria'.[32] The entire force was the net result of years of solicitation and exaggeration by FitzMaurice at the royal courts of Europe. The royal heads of Europe loudly applauded the crusading zeal of the Irish chieftain but were less than enthusiastic to back him materially. While in Rome FitzMaurice met the English Jesuit, Dr Nicholas Sanders, who helped him to elicit the meagre financial support for his cause from the Pope. Sanders had a reputation as 'a cold humourless unbending zealot'.[33] A former professor of theology at the Catholic university of Louvain, he was the author of an abrasively bitter but highly erudite and influential anti-Reformation tract. In the years before his appointment as papal legate to Ireland he had travelled widely and had access to and the respect of the Catholic princes of Europe. He was a tireless worker with a burning religious faith and an equally burning hatred for all that the Reformation represented. He saw in FitzMaurice and in his mission in Ireland the means to put his great energy and enthusiasm into effective action against the principles of the Reformation and to inspire the Catholic leaders in the country to resist the Protestant establishment. With a fierce determination and an absolute dedication to his principles, he turned his back on the serenity and security of Rome and willingly accepted the hardship and trauma of his Irish mission. Under his influence FitzMaurice declared his cause to be 'a war for the Catholic religion and against a tyrant who refuses to hear Christ speaking by his Vicar'.[34]

But FitzMaurice had tended to overemphasise the commitment or understanding of the Gaelic and gaelicised lords in Ireland to the aims of the Counter-Reformation, and had certainly overestimated the unifying force of religious zeal. The discontent of these lords sprang not from a sense of religious persecution by the English Crown, but from the Crown's endeavours to make Gaelic Ireland conform to English order. With such conformity went a dilution of the power of these aristocratic, despotic lords. Real religious persecution was yet a long way off in Ireland, and a revolt based on religious grounds alone was unlikely to succeed. To mould their crusade in Ireland into an effective branch of the Counter-Reformation movement, Sanders and FitzMaurice needed 'to make positive revolt out of negative discontent'[35] and to draw the lords and chieftains of Munster, especially the Earl of Desmond, into the religious net.

Under the influence of Dr Sanders, FitzMaurice despatched a letter to the earl. He urged his support for the banner of Christ and for the restoration of the Catholic faith in Ireland. His exhortation was couched in ominous terms:

God forbid that any Geraldine should stand in the field against the cross of Christ. I cannot tell what wordly thing would grieve me more than to hear not only that your honour would not assist Christ's banner but also that any other nobleman should prevent you in this glorious attempt. All that I write is spoken also to me good lady, your bedfellow, and to me good uncle, your brothers to all of whom I commend myself and also me bedfellow most heartily doth the like; trusting in Almighty God that as his holiness has made me Captain General of this holy war so your honour being head of my house will be the chief Protector and Patron of them, no less than me quarrel.[36]

The Pope, FitzMaurice further reminded Garrett and Eleanor, had promised that all who chose to fight under his banner should receive indulgences similar to those granted to all who had fought in the recent war against the Turks.

The arrival of FitzMaurice and his attempts to involve her husband in his crusade against the Queen had finally turned Eleanor's nightmare into a grim reality. All her years of haggling and bargaining with the Crown to win for her husband sufficient time to adapt to the changing political circumstances in Ireland seemed destined to be brought to nothing by the religious declamations of the returned exile. On a personal basis, there was little love lost between them, and, as in 1568–9, she suspected that the religious overtones of FitzMaurice's mission to Ireland hid a deeper and more devious plot against Garrett. She had heard the rumour that FitzMaurice had openly declared his aspirations towards the earldom of Desmond during his sojourn on the continent. His crusading banner displayed his personal coat of arms. Her husband was in poor health again and daily seemed to grow more incapacitated. Gaelic society, she well realised, had little tolerance for physical weakness in its leaders. Her son was a child of only eight years and a long way from his majority and inheritance. The sprawling Desmond lordship needed strong, steady guidance to safeguard it against the pressures being exerted on it by divergent outside interests. Eleanor might well have wondered whether, in the event of Garrett's death, FitzMaurice's real motives would be revealed in a sudden bid for the earldom. The question of religion seemed to her but a cloak to mask more basic motivations. It had never been a strong issue in the politics of the day in Ireland. Church property had always been the target of attack and seizure by warring Gaelic chiefs, just as it had in recent years by the Crown. Church laws had generally fallen into decline, particularly those which sought to regulate social conventions such as marriage, where the old Celtic ethos prevailed. FitzMaurice himself was divorced, and numerous other examples from among Eleanor's own family and peers bear out the assessment of a modern historian: 'In no field of life was Ireland's apartness from the mainstream of Christian European society so marked as in that of marriage. Throughout the medieval period, and down to the end of the old order in 1603, what could be called Celtic secular marriage remained the norm in Ireland and Christian matrimony was no more than the rare exception grafted on to this system.'[37] The clergy were as lax in the practice and observance of their faith as the laity. The sacraments were performed haphazardly. Many of the monasteries were in a ruinous and decayed condition. The real dilemma posed for Garrett and Eleanor by FitzMaurice's arrival was that Garrett would be, out of necessity more than by desire, prevailed upon to join the rebellion and thus be proclaimed a traitor and have his estates confiscated by the Crown. If, on the other hand, unlikely as it might then have seemed, the entire country were to rise in defence of the Catholic religion, and if the rising were to prove successful, then Garrett must not be left out in the cold. They had to play for time to determine which way the wind was likely to blow.

They despatched an innocuous letter to Lord Justice Drury to inform him of what he already knew, that James FitzMaurice had landed at Dingle. 'If need shall require,' Garrett assured Drury, 'I am ready with all mine to venture both my life and theirs in Her Majesty's quarrel.'[38] Drury was not impressed, and to test the earl's intent he ordered him to accompany an English detachment which was to set up camp some miles distant from the invasion force. Garrett agreed and with the English reconnoitred FitzMaurice's fortifications at Smerwick. Meanwhile his brothers, Sir John and Sir James, met secretly with FitzMaurice and Dr Sanders. The Geraldine historian Russell, writing in 1631, stated that Sir John actually agreed to join with FitzMaurice at this time, with the sole intention, as Eleanor had long since suspected, of deposing his brother as leader of the Geraldines and eventually becoming Earl of Desmond in his place. Russell further maintained that Sir John was motivated by 'a private grudge and hatred to ye Countesse of Desmond'.[39] Whether impelled by personal ambition or hatred of Eleanor, or inspired by the religious zeal of Dr Sanders, Sir John decided 'to performe some piece of service whereby hee might give them assurance of his faithfull meaning to doe them service and not to leave any after meanes to recant or shirke back'.[40] The 'piece of service' with which Sir John chose to demonstrate his commitment to the crusade astounded everyone and was destined to have inescapable repercussions for his brother.

Despite the apparent loyalty of the Earl of Desmond, Drury, still mistrustful, sent Henry Davells, a Devonshire man long resident in Ireland and on friendly terms with the Desmonds, to confirm the earls' allegiance. Davells was particularly friendly with Sir John, who, it was said, was his godson. Davells inspected the camp at Smerwick and concluded that with a few score soldiers it could easily be captured. He requested the Earl of Desmond to provide him with the necessary troops. Unwilling to commit himself to either side, Garrett lamely excused himself on the basis 'that his musketeers were more fitted to shoot at fowls than at a strong place and that his gallowglasses were good against gallowglasses but no match for old soldiers'.[41] Davells, together with his associate, Arthur Carter, the provost-marshal of Munster, set out to report back to Drury. They lodged overnight at an inn in Tralee. There, in the middle of the night, Sir John, accompanied by his brother Sir James and some supporters, burst into the room and killed both Davells and Carter in their beds. News of the murders was received with disbelief in most quarters. One opinion was that the crime was committed with the full knowledge and consent of James FitzMaurice, while others stated that he condemned the treachery of the act but not the act itself. Dr Sanders was said to have called the murder 'a sweet sacrifice before God'[42] and to have absolved Sir John and Sir James of the crime. For the Earl of Desmond the murder of Davells and Carter had even more far-reaching effects on his precarious position. He openly expressed his shock and revulsion and hurried back from Dingle to Askeaton. Drury would probably suspect him of being implicated in the murder, and both Eleanor and Garrett could well believe that the crime was intended to force his hand and alienate him further from the Crown. The Crown reacted predictably and Drury promised 'liberall rewarde to anie that should bring me the head of James FitzMaurice or of Sir John or his brother James of Desmond'.[43] Thus Garrett's brothers were formally proclaimed rebels by the Crown and placed in the same camp as James FitzMaurice.

But the murder of Davells and Carter had other implications for Garrett's position in Munster. When FitzMaurice landed in Dingle Bay, Garrett had an army of over a thousand men under his direct leadership. Scarcely one month later, as he hastened back to

Askeaton after the fateful crime at Tralee, less than sixty of his followers chose to follow him. The remainder, whether with or without his consent, formed part of the new army of the crusade under James FitzMaurice and Sir John of Desmond. It was rumoured in Dublin and London that the Earl of Desmond had in fact covertly allowed his army to aid FitzMaurice so that the earl himself could appear loyal until further aid from Spain arrived and until other lords such as Clanrickard, O'Neill and Kildare had decided to join the crusade. However, it seems clear that since 1576 Garrett, with Eleanor's encouragement, had been making a genuine attempt to adjust his status in Munster, to conform to the demands imposed on his position by the Crown, and to maintain some semblance of loyalty to Elizabeth. But the transition was undoubtedly a painful one for him. To add substance to the rumours, it could be argued that old habits die hard, especially in the case of the Geraldine earl whose pride would not allow him to accept any diminution of his traditional powers and thereby might lead him to conspire secretly with FitzMaurice. It could be further argued that Garrett had little choice in the matter, and that his obligation to the Gaelic world that sustained him, and to his tributary lords and clansmen over whom he claimed jurisdication, in turn demanded of him that in the present circumstances he should favour an act of rebellion. But it was clear, to Eleanor at least, that elements on both sides, for more devious reasons, sought to provoke her husband to throw off his loyalty to the Crown. He was in ill-health; and if he died, it must not be as an attainted rebel. There was no advantage to be gained either for Garrett or their son from rebellion unless it could be emphatically assured of success, and for this massive foreign assistance must be forthcoming. Despite the assurances of FitzMaurice and Sanders of further aid from the Pope and from Spain, none had materialised, nor had FitzMaurice been successful in his attempts to establish a widespread confederacy of lords and chieftains throughout the country. To Eleanor it appeared that Sir John had usurped her husband's control of his liegemen, who, exhorted by the preaching of Dr Sanders, had found a new cause on which to expend their martial skills and energies and be amply rewarded with plundered booty and papal gold. Life under Garrett in recent times had tended to provide little scope or reward for their fighting abilities. The earl was a feeble and sickly man; a leader who could not mount his horse unassisted could scarcely be thought fit to command their allegiance, especially when a more active leader, such as James FitzMaurice, seemed anxious to employ their skills.

While Garrett pondered his unenviable dilemma, Drury, who had fallen ill in Dublin, sent into Limerick the recently appointed President of Connaught, Sir Nicholas Malby, who with great severity had subdued all attempts to aid FitzMaurice in Connaught. Malby at once began to harass the rebel army. FitzMaurice and Sir John struck camp at Smerwick and moved out towards Limerick. They soon parted company, however, over differences regarding the leadership of the enterprise. FitzMaurice, with a small group of supporters, hurried through Tipperary and Limerick in an attempt to outflank Malby and enter Connaught. While passing through the country of the Burkes of Castleconnell his followers removed two horses from under a plough and took some booty. Theobald Burke, the chief's son, pursued them, and in the ensuing fracas FitzMaurice was shot dead on 18 August 1579. So abruptly ended the career of the man who, whatever his personal motivations, was the first to introduce religion as a political issue in Ireland, and the first to use it as a means to consolidate resistance to the Crown. Despite developments on the continent, however, the religious question in Ireland was yet an unsteady peg on which to hang the banner of revolution. The Gaelic annalists were fulsome in their praise of FitzMaurice. 'His death', they recorded, 'was the beginning of the decay of the honourable house of Desmond, out of which never issued so brave a man in all perfection.'[44] His former adversary, Sir John Perrot, acknowledged him as a 'man very valiant, politicke and learned as any Rebyll hath byn of that Nation for any yers'.[45] But to Eleanor, FitzMaurice had been the monster of her nightmares, the one who sought, deliberately or otherwise, by virtue of his very presence and intentions in Ireland, to dispossess her husband and his family and embroil them in a cataclysm that, once started, could be ended only by victory or defeat.

Sir John of Desmond assumed the vacant command of the insurgent force. Meanwhile Sir Nicholas Malby proceeded to snap at the Earl of Desmond's heels, bombarding Lord Justice Drury and the Council in Dublin with accusations of his disloyalty. Drury decided to investigate personally the allegations against the earl while at the same time dispersing the rebel detachments left behind by FitzMaurice in Kerry. Accompanied by the Earl of Kildare, Eleanor's brother the Baron of Dunboyne, and the Baron of Upper Ossory, Drury marched south and established camp near Kilmallock. He next prepared to dislodge the rebel garrison at Smerwick and thereby raise the old contentious issue with the Earl of Desmond—the invasion of his palatinate. The pressures on the Earl of Desmond were now immense. Eleanor's brother, on Drury's instruction, counselled him to repair to the Lord Justice; at the same time Dr Sanders, Sir John and his clansmen pressed him from the opposite side to prohibit Drury passage through the palatinate. His own pride cried out that he, the great Earl of Desmond, should not be so ordered hither and thither by subordinates and Crown servants. The cloud of melancholy and despondency returned as the earl shut himself up in his fortress at Askeaton and brooded over the hateful trap in which he was caught.

Drury sent a delegation led by the Baron of Upper Ossory to negotiate with him. At first Garrett refused to meet them, but Eleanor again prevailed on him to at least hear the baron out. The delegation was eventually ushered into the presence of the earl, who sat at a table with Eleanor by his side. The baron duly delivered Drury's instructions to the earl to attend his camp at Kilmallock. At this, Garrett's frail composure snapped, and with a sudden violent movement he upended the table and, as was duly reported by Drury,

> fell into an extreme rage protesting that he wolde never come to William Drury nor where Malby was a counsellor, and that he wolde presently be master of the fielde, that if the Justice came to Kerry he should have nothinge there and rather than Englishmen should come to Dingle he woulde rase the towne.[46]

All the pressures that beset him from all sides seemed to erupt in this outburst to the baron and his delegation. His pride recoiled from any dealings with petty officialdom, whose confiscation and abrogation of his powers had alienated him from his people and reduced his status in Munster. The palatine rights of his Kerry kingdom were the only vestige of prestige and self-respect which remained. If his sovereignty over Kerry was violated by Drury, he would be left with nothing. It was just too bad if FitzMaurice and his army had chosen it as the launching-pad for their crusade against Elizabeth. He alone, and not Lord Justice Drury and his lackeys, would see to the demolition of the fortifications and to the dispersal and expulsion of the remnants of the rebel army there. His fury was clearly beyond all control, and Eleanor shivered as she listened to her husband rage against the Queen—

> the red calioghe [hag] let hir doe what she like, affirminge that she and hir frendes had undone him and turning to a marchant of Lymericke there present he said he wold leave Lymericke and Corke as naked as his nayle.[47]

The English emissaries present were hurriedly told that the hag in question was the earl's wife, and this version of the remark was duly reported to the Privy Council in London. But the Irish lords present knew well that in Ireland the derisive nickname was applied to the red-haired Queen of England.

The Baron of Upper Ossory and his fellow-delegates departed to convey the earl's reply to Drury. Eleanor and her brother tried to reason with the overwrought earl. Finally she sent his secretary, Morris Sheehan, to explain Garrett's dilemma and excuse his conduct. Drury agreed to temporise with the earl and promised that he should have safe conduct to his camp near Kilmallock. Garrett agreed to meet the Lord Justice, who received him courteously and asked his opinion on how best the rebels might be resisted. Garrett suggested that pledges should be first given by his tributary lords, such as the Earl of Clancar and Lords Barry and Roche, and the other lords in Munster over whom he claimed jurisdiction. By this means, Garrett assured Drury, the lords would be less likely to join with the rebels and thereby undermine his position as an ally of the Crown. The lords, many of whom were present at the conference, resented this suggestion and protested vigorously to the Lord Justice that, in order to prohibit the earl from joining forces with his brother, he should also be required to 'put in his onely sonne pledge for maintayning the warre against his bretherne'.[48] Smarting at this further insult from his dependent lords, Garrett went 'into a newe passion and started from the boarde'[49] and angrily stalked off. Drury, however, agreed with the lords' proposal and refused the earl permission to depart until his son should be delivered as hostage.

Eleanor awaited Garrett's return at Askeaton. A party of his followers rode up to the castle and demanded that she deliver her son to be taken as a hostage to the Lord Justice. Eleanor refused. She could trust no one, least of all Garrett's supposedly loyal followers, most of whom had in any case defected to his brother, Sir John. She decided to put her case to the Lord Justice in person, and with a small guard set out for the English camp, having first hidden her son in the lake fortress of Lough Gur. Drury received her graciously and sympathised with her anxiety over the fate of her son. He agreed to her proposal that when conditions proved safe she would place the child in the custody of the Mayor of Limerick, and that, on the strength of her promise, her husband should be released immediately. Together Eleanor and Garrett rode quickly out of the camp to the remote safety of Lough Gur.

The crusade under the leadership of Sir John had meanwhile lost much of its original appeal and impetus. Sir John lacked the prestige and authority to extend the rebellion throughout the province and draw support from the lords and chieftains there. Dr Sanders realised there was only one person who could effectively revitalise interest in the crusade and to whom the uncommitted chieftains and disorderly clansmen would respond. But the Earl of Desmond still held aloof, reluctant to be drawn. He had little of FitzMaurice's crusading zeal. His own intransigence and the arrogant antics of the Crown officials in Munster were far more likely reasons to cause his complete alienation from the Crown. If the religious crusade could be used to stimulate 'the rankling sense of injustice dating from the Carew episode earlier ... and the consequent sense of insecurity of tenure on the part of the great landholders',[50] Garrett's present grievances against the Crown could be easily exploited for the cause of the Counter-Reformation in Ireland. As the English administration seemed determined to humiliate and strip him of the remaining vestiges of his traditional power, they intentionally or accidentally pushed the earl into the arms of Sanders. The Jesuit besieged Garrett with letters and messengers to convince him that his secular status could now be guaranteed only by his assuming leadership of a spiritual crusade. Messengers arrived from Ulster and Connaught where the Mayo clans, under the leadership of Richard-in-Iron Bourke, the husband of his former captive, Grace O'Malley, merely awaited his call to arms. Spies brought news that Drury, who had fallen ill again in Dublin, had been unable to secure much-needed supplies and forces from the Crown. Sanders renewed his promise of additional aid from the Pope and the King of Spain and tempted Garrett with promises of the glory and prestige that the Crown sought to deny him. Eventually Garrett made a secret rendezvous with Sanders and Sir John. He gradually became more withdrawn from Eleanor, who saw her influence over him being steadily eroded by the zealous exhortations of Dr Sanders. She tried in vain to reason with him, but his ego and pride had been aroused. Against the machinations of Dr Saunders she was no match, and, as was reported to the government, 'the corruption of the Erles disposition is such as manie tymes he nether regardeth frend nor wive'.[51] But for the present he maintained his show of loyalty and accompanied Drury on an expedition against the rebels, now led by his brothers, at Kylemore wood.

As events began to overtake her and as her influence over Garrett lessened, Eleanor's fears for the safety of her son increased. She had established a good relationship with Lord Justice Drury; like Sidney, he was one of the few English administrators who had come to understand and appreciate her dilemma. For different reasons they had both worked for the same objective, to maintain Garrett in some degree of loyalty to the Queen. Both had begun to falter under the pressure of their respective missions. Drury was in very poor health and had been consistently denied adequate provisions to perform his duties in Ireland. And now news of Drury's imminent departure for England reached Eleanor—her last contact with the more reasonable elements of the English administration was about to disappear. The safety of her son now weighed heavily on her mind. She feared that Sir John or Dr Sanders might well kidnap him to ensure and retain her husband's support. Garrett also feared for the safety of his son at the hands of his brothers, whom he later accused of attempting 'to imbrue their cruel hands with the blood if my wief and sonne, whom Sir John mortalie hated'.[52] Perhaps also with an instinctive sense of the turmoil that was about to engulf them, she decided that the child would be safer and might evade the taint of rebellion in the custody of the Crown. Drury was the only person she could trust to ensure the boy's safety out of Munster. Eleanor first journeyed with her son to Limerick city, where it was reported that

> The Countesse of Desmond (with the Erles consent as shee saith) brought hir only son the Lord Garrett [*sic*, for James] to Limerick and delivered him as hir assurance (for so shee termed it) to the Attorney and Recorder, from whome he was sent for to the campe within two daies after, because it was doubted that the Erles faction in Limericke should convey him awaie and that the Lord Justice has also vehement presumption that he should have been by the Erles followers (especiallie the gallowglas) sent as a pledge into Spaine for perfourmance of such promises that have been made by them to Doctor Saunders.[53]

Eleanor accompanied her son to Drury, who was about to set out on his final painful journey towards Waterford. It was a moving encounter between the dying old war-hardened soldier and the troubled countess torn in two by her desire to protect her son and having to place her trust in the very institution that sought to destroy his father. In their past dealings Drury had shown her a crusty courtesy and had come to respect her political and diplomatic abilities, and he now understood her fear for the child's safety. It was a heart-rending scene as the tall women bent down to embrace her small son and hold him close, aware that it could quite easily be for the last time. The pale, timid child, who since his birth in captivity had continued to be a captive of the tragic fates that buffetted his family, clung tightly to his mother, fearful from past experience that he was yet again about to be condemned to a dark, menacing life behind locked doors and among strange unfriendly faces. Drury reassured Eleanor, but as she looked into the haggard face, perhaps seeing death in his tired eyes, she felt a momentary icy stab of fear and begged him to do all he could to ensure that the child would be treated gently. With a breaking heart, she lifted her son onto the saddle beside one of Drury's officers and watched the cavalcade slowly disappear down the narrow rutted track.

Following the departure of the Lord Justice from Limerick, Sir Nicholas Malby was appointed temporary governor of Munster. He instituted the final campaign of attack and humiliation which was eventually to push the vacillating Earl of Desmond over the brink. A flurry of correspondence between the two sides preceded the action. Malby curtly summoned the earl to appear before him at Limerick. He further sent him a proclamation against the rebels which he ordered Garrett to have published throughout his lordship. Garrett haughtily replied to the effect that his service 'against the rebells would be more available than his presence ... in Limerick',[54] and he complained that Malby's army had plundered his tenants. Malby promised the earl 'much honour and favour ... if he will get that papistical arrogant traitor Sanders to be arrested'.[55] Garrett reciprocated by giving Malby some useless information on the actions of his brothers. Malby, without recourse to the Crown or to the Council in Dublin, set out on his own initiative, ostensibly to flush out the rebels but in effect to plunder the earl's lands. On 3 October 1579 he was confronted near Monasternenagh by the forces of Sir John of Desmond in battle array. A fiercely fought pitched battle ensued until eventually the English pikemen penetrated the rows of galloglass and kern and the rebel army slowly gave ground. Sir John and Dr Sanders escaped into the woods along the Maigue river. When news of the defeat reached Askeaton, the earl hurriedly forwarded his congratulations to Malby. Malby was unimpressed. He was convinced that the earl was involved with the rebels. 'He is the onlie man that did seeke to cutt my throate,' he informed the English Privy Council, 'the onelie arch traytor of Mounster, his two brethern are but ministers to serve his vile disposition.'[56] Malby's accusations were as yet based on conjecture; tangible proof of the earl's active implication in the rebellion was more difficult to establish. But conjecture and rumour seemed sufficient for Malby, whose Puritan outlook led him to despise all that Garrett represented and to work determinedly for his destruction.

Eleanor's abilities as a mediator were powerless against such intense and irrational behaviour. There was no one in the Council in Dublin with whom she could intercede in order to persuade the government to call off its mad dog in Munster. Her husband had temporised with the administration for months, but the Crown had also violated agreements made with him. Fired by puritanical religious zeal, Malby now prepared to exact a terrible penalty from the House of Desmond. He burned and pillaged his way through the earl's Limerick estates up to the barred gates of Askeaton castle. He pitched camp across the river from the castle, in and around the abbey. From a window of the castle Eleanor watched the final act of violation and degradation committed against her husband. The proud earl notified the English Privy Council of Malby's action at Askeaton:

> The saide Sir Nicholas encamped within the Abbie of Asketin and ther most malitiosslie defaced the oulde monuments of my ancestors, fired both the abbie, the whole tower and all the countrie therabouts and ceased not to shote at my men within Askyten castle.[57]

The thoughts that flashed through the earl's mind as he helplessly watched the very heart of the Desmond heritage being ravaged, and the bones of his ancestors and of his first wife being thus dishonoured, have not been recorded. He must have felt a dreadful sense of humiliation as he realised that the once mighty Earl of Desmond had been rendered so powerless that he could not prevent such an outrage, perpetrated by a lowly captain of the Crown within sight of his own fortress. In his despair he appealed to his rival, the Earl of Ormond:

> Your mother's grave hath beane most spitefully used by Sir Nicholas Malbye. It hath beene broken so that nowe there remaineth no monument thereof. I bescheche your consideraccion of my cause and howe I have ben persecuted by a Captain that hath no authoritie to do the like.[58]

But whatever vague sympathy or fear that Black Tom might have felt for his neighbour, the old wounds of their personal feud were still raw, and the vast Desmond estates were clearly more attractive if, as seemed ever more likely, their proprietor was destined to be proclaimed a traitor.

The final push came from Drury's successor, Sir William Pelham, who had been appointed Lord Justice of Ireland in October 1579. One of his first acts was to appoint the Earl of Ormond as military governor of Munster. He also issued a patent to Ormond, 'who having the keeping and custodie of the young Lord Girald [sic] sonne and heir to the erle of Desmond was by a warrant willed to deliver him to Captain Dachworth and he to bring or conveie him to the Castell of Dublin'.⁵⁹ During his journey in Drury's custody to Waterford the child had fallen ill. As Drury's own condition had worsened, it was decided to leave the Earl of Desmond's son in the care of Black Tom and to hurry to Waterford with the Lord Justice. Drury subsequently died there on 3 October without being able to discharge the undertaking he had given to Eleanor. Pelham was not only determined that Desmond's son would be put well beyond the grasp of all factions in Munster, but was also planning to use the boy as a valuable bargaining counter to obtain his father's submission. Rumours flew like sparrows from tree to tree across Munster, and their burden was that the Earl of Desmond had finally declared for the rebels. Pelham neglected to check the accuracy of the rumours, but summoned the earl to his presence. Still secure in his stronghold at Askeaton, the earl declined to put his head into the lion's mouth. Pelham threatened to execute their son. There was no time to appeal to the Queen. If Garrett went to Pelham, there was every likelihood that he would be promptly imprisoned. It was decided that Eleanor should once again attempt to intercede on his behalf. 'I have sent my wife to declare the causes of my present stay', he informed Pelham, 'and how my country has been burnt and spoiled, my castles taken and myself misused.'⁶⁰ But Pelham was not prepared to listen and received Eleanor coldly. He informed her that he would not be hoodwinked by her or by her husband like previous Crown officials. Her husband, he was convinced, had all along intended to rebel. Eleanor pleaded with him not to push her husband beyond the bounds of reason. She reminded him that they had voluntarily given their only son as proof of the earl's good intentions. She graphically described the outrages perpetrated by Malby on her husband's property and the provocative sacking of Askeaton abbey. She also reminded him that as a subject of the Crown her husband had the right to the Crown's protection. Pelham momentarily drew back and agreed to give the earl one final chance. With perhaps spiteful intent he chose the Earl of Ormond to act as mediator and, through him, presented a set of unacceptable demands: that Desmond must submit to the Lord Justice; that he must deliver Dr Sanders into Crown custody; that he must surrender Askeaton and Carraigafoyle castles to the Crown; and that he must join in the campaign against his brothers and serve under the command of the Earl of Ormond. Pelham must have known well that the Earl of Desmond had neither the power nor the will to comply with such demands.

Eleanor realised the futility of her mission and the calculated unacceptability of Pelham's remission demands and returned to Askeaton to be with her husband. Ominously, Pelham moved his forces ever closer to Rathkeale while he sent Ormond once again to negotiate with Desmond. But the latter's presence merely served to antagonise Garrett even further. 'I will remain as true-hearted a subject to Her Majesty as any one that seeketh to undo me,' he informed Pelham and demanded 'that my servant may go with my complaints to Her Majesty and the Council, whose judgement I am contented to abide'.[61] But Pelham and his war-dogs smelled blood and, knowing the Queen's penchant for pardons rather than costly wars, reacted quickly. Without the permission or the knowledge of the Queen or the Privy Council, Pelham had the Earl of Desmond 'with sound of Trumpett'[62] proclaimed a traitor and thereby forced the earl, as one commentator noted, 'for his owne safety to run that course against his will'[63] to the waiting Dr Sanders. Significantly, the proclamation was signed by Pelham, the Earl of Ormond, his brothers, and Eleanor's brother, the Baron of Dunboyne, while some of the Catholic barons of the Pale, such as Lords Gormanston, Baltinglass and Delvin, refused to be signatories. On 2 November 1579 the proclamation was simultaneously announced in Dublin, Waterford, Cork and Limerick and in the towns and settlements throughout the country.

As news of the proclamation reached Askeaton, the awful significance of the event and its relevance to their position momentarily numbed Garrett and Eleanor into inaction. Thoughts of Silken Thomas and his uncles, their entrails scattered before the jeering mob at Tyburn, of confiscation, exile and defeat flashed through their minds. But Eleanor bestirred herself once more into action in a desperate bid to avert the disaster that had for so long loomed before them but had now been turned overnight into harsh reality. She flew to her horse, and, as was reported, 'within one houre after this proclamation, the Countess of Desmond came to the campe but the campe was before dislodged'.[64] Before there could be any change of heart on the part of the earl, Pelham had let loose his dogs of war. Almost gleefully Pelham reported the event to the Queen. 'Desmond has been proclaimed a traitor,' he wrote. 'Ormond has already drawn blood and kindled the fire in the midst of Desmond's country'—and, Pelham added significantly, 'I have left the prosecution of the war to him.'[65]

The insurgents now descended on Askeaton to claim their hereditary leader, who had, in their opinion, meditated and procrastinated for too long, and who must no longer be allowed to shirk his responsibilities. Despite her efforts to avert it, Eleanor watched the nightmare unfold as Garrett was caught up in the flood and borne headlong into rebellion. The courtyard was thronged with armed clansmen, their numbers spilling out beyond the castle walls. Garrett bade farewell to his daughters, who, like their brother, would become innocent victims of the folly imposed on their father. Garrett well realised the dreadful plight his actions had brought upon his wife and young family, and despite his best efforts to protect their inheritance from confiscation, he knew in his heart that there would be no spoils for the vanquished. There were no farewells between Garrett and Eleanor. For the following four desperate years, wherever the Earl of Desmond hid or lay down to rest, his wife would not be far from his side. Slowly and painfully he limped out into the grey November evening, already chilled by the first stings of winter. Under the sombre dark sky the fifteenth Earl of Desmond, the reluctant champion, emerged before his hereditary supporters. A hundred hands lifted the crippled lord onto his horse. The papal banner was unfurled over his head. The centuries-old Desmond war-cry 'Shanid abú!' gave way to 'Pápa abú!' as the Geraldine rode out at the head of a crusade he neither understood nor with which he could sympathise.

Signature of James FitzMaurice FitzGerald.

7

Rebellion

> The wrathful skies
> Gallow the very wanderers of the dark,
> And make them keep their caves: since I was man
> Such sheets of fire, such bursts of horrid thunder,
> Such groans of roaring wind and rain, I never
> Remember to have heard: man's nature cannot carry
> The affliction nor the fear.
>
> SHAKESPEARE, *King Lear*, III, ii

As news of the rebellion spread across the country, initially it seemed likely to provoke a wider conspiracy among the Gaelic and gaelicised lords. In Connaught the Gaelic clans of Mayo and Galway rose in support. Scots mercenaries poured into Ulster. In Leinster James Eustace, Viscount Baltinglass, a determined Catholic, conspired with the rebel chieftain, Fiach MacHugh O'Byrne. There was great unrest in Limerick city, and the mayor was taken prisoner by the insurgents. Sir John of Desmond plundered Kerry and burnt Tralee. The rebels plundered the lands of a grantee there named John Rowly and left him nailed to his castle door as a warning to others. Dr Sanders exhorted the leaders and promised more assistance from the Pope and the Most Catholic King of Spain.

But solitary in the sombre Escorial palace near Madrid the black-garbed lay leader of the Counter-Reformation, God's lieutenant on earth, Philip II, gloomily contemplated a batch of recent despatches from his spies in England which littered the desk before him. They were proof of the distinct lack of progress made to date against his heretic sister-in-law and her godless kingdom. But the blame could be squarely laid at Philip's door. His own intrinsic predilection for deliberation and detail was mainly responsible. Every despatch was scrutinised, every emissary personally screened and interviewed, and every detail gleaned was methodically stored in the dispassionate mind of the anointed head of the greatest and most Catholic empire in the world. Now that the House of Guise in France had become part of his orbit, and now that his control over the Netherlands was being gradually restored, there was time to contemplate how best to resume the divinely ordained crusade against Elizabeth and to fulfil his 'gossamer vision of a Europe purged of heresy and united in the ample bosom of mother church'.[1] Elizabeth had blatantly aided and comforted his rebellious and heretical Dutch subjects. Now with news to hand of a crusade in Ireland against her, led by an earl who sought his help, the King pondered over the direction of his religious zeal and political revenge against his sister monarch.

While the banner of rebellion, emblazoned with the cross of the crusade, had been placed in the hands of her reluctant husband, Eleanor was yet hopeful that Garrett's slide into ruin could be reversed. She herself had not been included in the Lord Justice's proclamation and was therefore not personally deemed to be a traitor; this left her free to negotiate with the authorities and to put her undoubted skill as a diplomat to further good use on her husband's behalf. But she had no contact whom she could trust in the Dublin Council. Everywhere she looked were people who had pushed her husband into rebellion. Her only remaining recourse was to gain direct access to the Queen and her Council in England and to make them aware of the circumstances surrounding her husband's proclamation as a traitor and subsequent rebellion. Elizabeth must be informed of the conduct of her officers in Ireland who, for disloyal and selfish reasons, had purposely alienated her husband from the Crown. Eleanor knew well the many servants of the Crown in Ireland and in England whose greedy eyes were fastened on the fertile acres of Garrett's estates. A push towards rebellion rather than a pull towards loyalty had presented the prospect of rich reward for energetic and ambitious officials. She resolved to make Elizabeth aware of what had been done to her husband in the Queen's name. Her letters to England were liable to be intercepted by the self-same officials, who least wished them to reach their destination. But there was another way. On 4 November 1579, two days after her husband was publicly proclaimed a traitor, a despatch, signed by Pelham, Ormond and Malby to the Queen's secretary, Sir Francis Walsingham, made the startling announcement: 'To be a solicitor that in respect since the proclamation, the Countess of Desmond hath left her husband that she may enjoy her jointure.'[2]

Even as Garrett was hustled away by his followers and as the great wood of Clonlish had swallowed him, Eleanor had put her plan into action. She obtained a meeting with her kinsman, the Earl of Ormond, to whom she revealed her intention to divorce Garrett, ostensibly because of the shame and ruin his actions had brought on her and on his house. She asked that her marriage portion or dowry should be returned to her in order that she might sustain herself. Initially her request was taken at face value. It was on record that she had long endeavoured to keep the earl loyal to the Crown, and she had letters from a grateful Queen to prove it. Divorce was common among the Gaelic and gaelicised aristocracy at the time. Ormond himself had been recently divorced. He promised to investigate the matter, but, aware of Eleanor's long devotion to Garrett, became suspicious of her sudden desire to obtain her jointure. Her real reason, to obtain funding to enable her to bring her husband's case to London, soon became apparent. But Eleanor still tried to bluster her way to the Queen. 'Now that it hath pleased God to wrap my husband into these late troubles,' she wrote to Ormond, 'I wish to repair to Her Majesty's preserve and desire you to send me a passport. I mind to take shipping at Cork or Kinsale.'[3] As Ormond deliberated over her request, Eleanor, desperate to attain her goal before Garrett, by some precipitate action, could put himself totally beyond all help, had some cattle rounded up and asked Ormond 'to make sale of such kine as I sent to your country to bear my charges in England for that both my husband and I have incurred certain debts in England, it is needful that you send me a protection to pass with my stuff and goods until I shall come to Her Majesty without any molestation'.[4] But Ormond suspected that her sudden desire to see the Queen was to plead her husband's case and to seek the assistance of the court faction sympathetic to him. Ormond informed her that he had not the authority to issue her with a pass, but that he would nevertheless intercede on her behalf with Lord Justice Pelham. However, he took good care to forewarn Pelham, telling him: 'I have had a letter from my Lady of Desmond. It is thought, I dare say, by those that wrote it to be cunningly penned and devised but the intent is easy to understand.'[5] Pelham, in any event, had no intention of allowing the Countess of Desmond access to the Queen. Already Elizabeth had sounded the first notes of disquiet about the peremptory way he had proclaimed the Earl of Desmond. Desmond's wife pleading her husband's case before the Queen with the support of the Cecil faction might well mean dismissal or even imprisonment. Pelham wrote his reply accordingly to the Earl of Ormond: 'I have considered of my Lady of Desmond's letter. Pray you stay your hand from these her vain petitions till our meeting and answer her letter with silence.'[6]

But Eleanor refused to accept silence as an answer. She demanded and received an audience with the Lord Justice. She asked him to suspend the proclamation of her husband until she could further negotiate with him. Pelham refused her request, but granted her permission to go to her husband and promised her 'that grace would be showid to her husband if he would consent to ye delivery of his brother and Doctor Saunders'.[7] Pelham warned her that she must return 'within certaine daies to live in the Pale or with the barron of Dunboine her brother'.[8] But she realised that Pelham would never permit her access to the Queen or retract the proclamation, short of Garrett's unconditional surrender. Eleanor gathered her few belongings, fled to join her husband, and failed to return within the allotted time. To damage whatever credibility she might have with the Queen, Pelham informed Sir Francis Walsingham 'that there is not any emonge the conspiratours that more encouradgeth the disloyaltie of them than she. And therefore I believe that her messadge is but collorable . . . to gaine intellegence for purpose.'[9]

By now, however, the Queen's disquiet over the proclamation of the Earl of Desmond and the continuation of the war had changed to anger. She ordered her Lord Justice to explain his actions. Pelham protested that Desmond had been covertly involved in rebellious conspiracy since the time of James FitzMaurice. To sting her princely pride, Pelham further informed Elizabeth that 'in all his skirmishes and outrages since the proclamation, Desmond crieth *Papa aboo*, which is the Pope above even above you and your imperial crown'.[10] But Elizabeth was not satisfied. Rebellions cost money, while pardons, particularly on conditions favourable to the Crown, cost nothing. She had learned of the attempts by the Countess of Desmond to gain her royal ear and knew of Pelham's efforts to prevent her. Elizabeth demanded a further explanation from her Lord Justice. But before Pelham could compose an excuse, the Earl of Desmond, as Eleanor feared, put himself beyond redemption by an inexplicable attack on the town of Youghal. The town was in a state of total unpreparedness for the assault. In the middle of a thunderstorm the rebel army, with Garrett at its head, entered through a breach in the walls. Then, amid scenes of wanton carnage and cruelty, Youghal was sacked. Houses were set on fire, citizens put to the sword, women ravished, and the Desmond hordes, with wild exultant cries, ransacked buildings and stuffed their clothes with gold and silver from the town's coffers. It was reported that the Earl of Desmond, Sir John and the Seneschal of Imokilly tore down the emblem of the Queen's coat of arms from the courthouse and hacked it asunder with their daggers. For four days and nights the rebels looted the town. Laden with booty and prisoners, mainly women, the Earl of Desmond and his crusaders marched away, leaving the town of Youghal in flames.

Eleanor's reaction to the sack of Youghal must have been one of disbelief that her husband should allow his own town to be destroyed. But her husband had succumbed to the religious fanaticism of the rebellion. Dr Sanders ardently preached the message of the Counter-Reformation and assured the earl that his secular struggle against the Queen in Ireland was part of a wider glorious crusade against heresy. The Pope and King Philip would soon come to his assistance, Sanders assured him. The Jesuit preached his message and in the language of the Counter-Reformation movement exhorted those who listened to lay down their lives in pursuit of the glorious quest. The Earl of Desmond listened with the rest and felt uplifted, no longer hamstrung by his physical deformities or political deficiencies. Religion elevated him to his true status as the great rebel Geraldine fighting the just cause of faith and fatherland. His letters to the Gaelic chieftains and the Catholic lords of the Pale reflected Garrett's belated conversion to the crusading cause and Dr Sanders's teachings. Writing to Viscount Baltinglass, Garrett explained that

It is so that I and my brothers are entered into the Defence of the Catholick Faith, the overthrow of our Country by Englishmen which had overthrown the Holy Church and go about to over-run our country and make it their own and make us their Bond men.[11]

And his former pride returned as messengers and letters of support flowed into his base at Newcastle from Turlough Luineach O'Neill, Fiach MacHugh O'Byrne, Baltinglass, and lords and chieftains from every province. They made extravagant promises of large reinforcements of Scottish galloglass and Gaelic kern. But promises were easily made, and the Earl of Desmond had yet to prove how much support his cause commanded abroad before the effusive pledges of his erstwhile admirers in Ireland would be translated into practical assistance. As the mournful winter winds howled around Newcastle, Eleanor perhaps knew that she was powerless to stem the fast-flowing tide which bore her husband and his house steadily towards their doom. She looked across the dimly lit room to where Garrett was seated with Dr Sanders, who dictated to a secretary the now familiar interwoven words of religion and rebellion. She observed the almost skeletal features of her husband, his sickly pallor

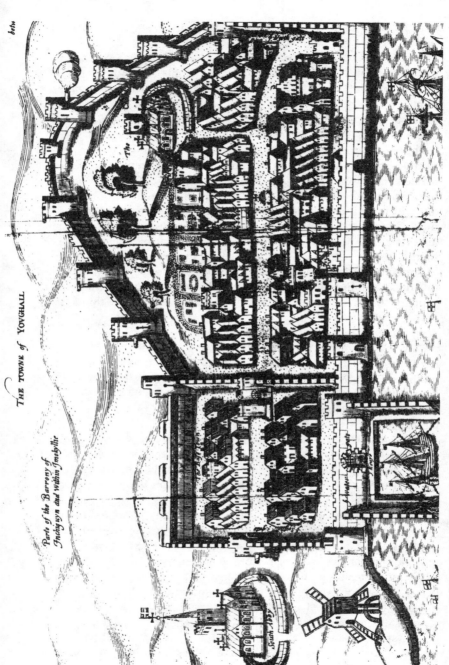

Youghal, Co. Cork in the 16th century. *(Pacata Hibernia).* Part of the Desmond lordship, sacked by its overlord, the 15th Earl.

and hunched shoulders. The winter campaign had taken further toll of his health. She thought of her son, alone in his dark cell in Dublin Castle. The servants she had sent to care for him had been dismissed, and Pelham had ordered 'that the constable of the Castle shall provide for his diett and wantes and that his nurse shall onely attend him there'.[12] Yet she was satisfied that even Dublin Castle was a safer haven for her child than his native Munster over which the storm was about to break.

For the hunt was on—surely the greatest manhunt in history, and for the most feeble prey that ever went to ground, though strangely revived for a time with the strength and power that sprang from a burning pride fuelled by a new-found religious zeal. While the Queen dithered to finance an all-out offensive against the Earl of Desmond, the Earl of Ormond took matters into his own hands. Passing between Askeaton and Newcastle, he burned and looted right up to the foothills of Slieve Logher. In a mission of vengeance he endeavoured to ensure that the lords of Desmond would never again pose a threat to Ormond. Hampered by appalling weather conditions and lack of supplies, Black Tom reluctantly returned to Ormond to wait for the new year and for Elizabeth to loosen the purse-strings to continue the campaign of extinction against his former step-father.

Towards the end of January 1580 two well-appointed ships arrived off Dingle. They carried letters for the Earl of Desmond and his brothers from the King of Spain. Garrett hurried to Castlemaine to confer with the King's messengers. Both the success of the rebellion and his own fate depended solely on help from the King. He told the messengers to urge their master to forward the long-awaited assistance without delay. He promised support from all the lords of the country and confidently declared that he would have a substantial army at his disposal. And indeed many hitherto undecided lords wavered to the cause during the early months of 1580. The Earl of Clancar was either compelled by Garrett or exhorted by Dr Sanders to join the rebellion. It was even rumoured that Edmund Butler, the Earl of Ormond's brother, who was married to Garrett's sister, had 'stood a little wavering and was to be doubted'[13] before being pulled back into line by his brother, Black Tom. But since the sack of Youghal, militarily Garrett had accomplished little. Ever fearful for his safety, like a shadow he flitted from Newcastle to Aherlow, to Adare, to Carraigafoyle on the Shannon, until he finally came to rest at the more secure fortress of Castlemaine. His landless adherents, while they awaited action against the enemy, looted and ravaged the countryside. The peasants, as ever, bore the brunt of their excesses

Walter Raleigh, one of the undertakers of the Munster Plantation.

King Phillip II of Spain. Brother-in-law to Queen Elizabeth I.

and sought the shelter of the woods and mountain foothills. Eleanor also had momentarily disappeared from view. There was no one with whom she could negotiate, and little reason for her to do so. She spent the winter months with her daughters between the fortresses of Castlemaine and Castleisland.

In the spring of 1580 the war recommenced with a vengeance. It was reported that King Philip of Spain had troops and ships massed at Spanish ports, ready to sail to Ireland in support of the rebel Earl of Desmond. Elizabeth's nightmare, that Spain could use Ireland as a backdoor into England, seemed likely to become a reality. The English court factions closed ranks and united to repel the foreign threat. The hitherto divided coteries led by Cecil and Walsingham were now of one voice. They urged the Queen to back Ormond and Pelham and to provide the means for an all-out offensive against the Earl of Desmond. Cecil, Ormond's one-time adversary, admitted:

> So must I merely say with others, *Butler aboo* against all that cry as I hear in a new language *Papa aboo*. God send you your heart's desire, which I know is agreeable to mine, to banish or vanquish those cankered Desmonds and to plant again the Queen's Majesty's honour and reputation.[14]

And finally, with the approval of the Privy Council and a reluctant nod from Elizabeth, the armed might of the Crown was unleashed on Munster. In March 1580 Ormond joined forces with Pelham at Rathkeale, and together they commenced a dreadful war of retribution. They divided their forces. Ormond moved to the Shannon side, Pelham kept inland, and they moved parallel to each other towards Newcastle. It was siad that they each kept track of the other's progress by the billowing clouds of smoke they left in their wake as they burned and pillaged their way west.

The country people fled for their lives before the new fury. But to Pelham every peasant or tenant who resided within the Desmond lordship was deemed a rebel, and the English scouting parties indiscriminately sought out and slew panic-stricken men, women and children. His despatches to the Privy Council unashamedly detailed remorseless acts of barbarity and deprivation committed against a largely defenceless peasantry. Exultantly describing a typical punitive raid, he wrote:

> The people and cattle flying before us in the mountains
> were followed by some horsemen and light footmen.
> There were slain that day by the fury of the soldiers above
> 400 people found in the woods; and wheresoever any
> house or corn was found, it was consumed by fire.[15]

The unfortunate people who were subjected to such treatment had
been shamelessly abandoned by their overlord and left to stand
defenceless before his enemies. The Desmonds, Dr Sanders and
their swordsmen were far removed, safe in their remote castle
outposts, out of range of the pitiful shrieks and cries of the
abandoned peasantry. In vain the people waited for the banner of
their hereditary protector to appear and save them from their doom.
But the great Geraldine lord did not come to their rescue, and
Pelham's soldiers and Ormond's galloglass found nothing to obstruct
them. Steel fell on unprotected bone and hacked its way over the
mutilated bodies of its unresisting victims. From the branches of the
Munster oaks the putrefying corpses hung in gruesome proof of
Pelham's progress. The once lush pasturelands were reduced to a
blackened heath as Ormond sated his revenge on his old enemy and
Pelham, one of the new breed of Puritan military commanders,
merely did his job.

But Munster was not ravaged only by the armies of the Crown. As
the Earl of Desmond and his army withdrew into the remoter areas,
they burned and looted everything in their path. Every fortress
between Castleisland and Tralee had been demolished to prevent
their use by the enemy. Cattle were seized and driven into secret
valleys and hidden recesses in the mountains to provide sustenance
for the fighting men. The peasantry were left to fend for themselves
as best they could, and any who remonstrated were summarily dealt
with.

Some of the stronger castles such as Askeaton, Newcastle, Adare,
Glin and Carraigafoyle, directly in Pelham's path, yet stood intact,
secure in the impregnability of their thick stone defences.
Carraigafoyle on the Shannon was considered one of the most
formidable. Its destruction was to open a new chapter in military
warfare in Ireland. Carraigafoyle commanded a strategic position and
guarded the entrance to the Shannon estuary. It was at this time
garrisoned for the Earl of Desmond by a mixture of papal and Irish
troops under the command of a Captain Julian. In view of the
expected aid from Spain, defence of the castle took on a new urgency.
Garrett undertook to overhaul the defences of the castle. Unable to

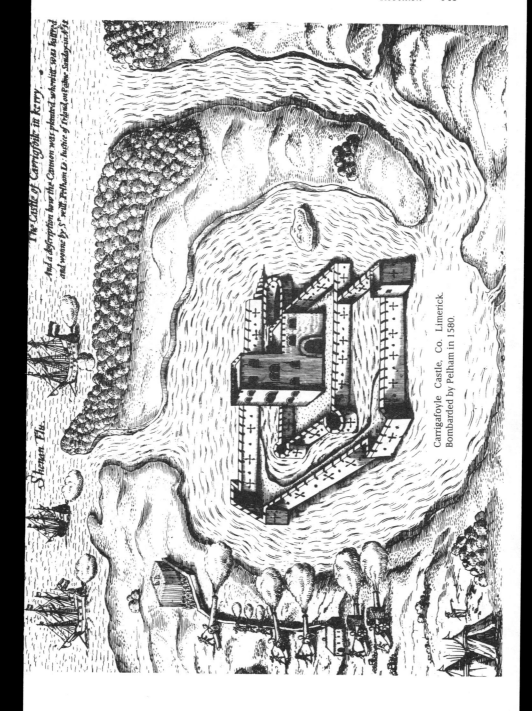

The Castle of Carrigfoile in Kerry.

And a description how the Cannon was planted, wherwitt was battryd and wonne by S.r will Pelham L: Iustice of Irland and Pettie Sonday, 1580.

Shenan Flu.

Carrigafoyle Castle, Co. Limerick.
Bombarded by Pelham in 1580.

risk a journey which would bring him into close contact with the enemy, he decided that Eleanor should convey the secret plans and instructions there. With a small escort she set out on the hazardous journey. Although she was not technically a wanted rebel like her husband, she yet could not afford to fall into the hands of the Crown forces, or even to attract their attention. She successfully eluded English scouting parties from the nearby armies of Pelham and Ormond and eventually safely delivered her husband's instructions to Captain Julian, who without delay put them into effect. Great earthworks were constructed on the estuary side of the castle to provide additional protection for the ships daily expected from Spain. On the landward side two separate ditches with a wall and a further earthwork were erected. Every chink and cranny in the outer walls of the castle was filled with masonry to prevent besiegers from obtaining a foothold. In Garrett's estimation, and indeed by the military conventions of the day, Carraigafoyle was rendered impregnable.

But the earl was not familiar with the more recent developments of modern warfare. English ships, under the command of Sir William Winter, anchored off the castle with a cargo of new siege guns. Garrett's defensive modifications, the earthworks, ditches and smooth masonry, could not withstand the subsequent barrage as for two days Pelham pounded the defences of Carraigafoyle. On 29 March a breach was finally made in the barbican and then in the inner walls. Pelham's troops poured into the castle and spared none of the defenders. As the cannon and culverins boomed their relentless message of victory across the Kerry countryside, Pelham prepared to move against the heart of the Desmond lordship. The siege cannon were pointed at Askeaton, but there was little need to fire even one shell. On learning about the destruction of Carraigafoyle and the fate of the defenders, Garrett's garrison at Askeaton fled for their lives and as they departed set fire to the magazine, which blew the greater part of the castle asunder. Pelham appointed a strong garrison under Sir Peter Carew and Sir Henry Wallop in the ruins of Askeaton, while Sir George Carew and Captain Hollingworth were established in the adjacent abbey.

Reports about the destruction of Carraigafoyle and the partial destruction of Askeaton were quickly brought to the earl, who, with Eleanor, was then at Tralee where they daily awaited the promised aid from Spain. The fall of Askeaton must have been a severe blow to them. Not only was the castle a place of great significance in the Desmond heritage and history, but to Eleanor and Garrett it was something more—the place dearest to their hearts, the home in which they had snatched a few brief years of happiness and contentment.

As Pelham's army drew nearer, Garrett's followers, who had so vociferously and eagerly prevailed upon him to lead them in the great crusade, deserted him in numbers. There was still no sign of the Spanish aid promised by Dr Sanders. With the exception of a brief, isolated uprising by Richard-in-Iron Bourke in Mayo, Connaught had failed to rise in support of the crusade. There was a shortage of food and supplies, and Garrett's swordsmen preyed far and wide over the impoverished land and cursed the earl as the cause of their misery. To stem the tide, Garrett was reported to have threatened his followers 'that yf aid from Spaine and the Pope cam not before Whitsontide he would leave them to make their composition with the Englishe as well as thei colde'.[16] Numbed by the ferocity of Pelham's tactics, few could envisage such action. The English forces pressed ever closer, and the list of garrisons established by them grew. Captain Bouchier occupied Kilmallock, and Captain Wilks held Adare. The hunt was on for the Earl and Countess of Desmond, Dr Sanders and the earl's brothers. Each day scouting parties from the various garrisons scoured the forests, mountain foothills and the secret recesses of Aherlow for the fugitives. Eleanor's brother, the Baron of Dunboyne, joined in the hunt for his sister and brother-in-law. Pelham would not permit even a relative to remain neutral.

As the net tightened, the Desmond fugitives flitted from place to place. Everything now depended on Spain. Garrett became suspicious that Dr Sanders intended to desert him, and he therefore kept a close watch on the cleric who, for better or worse, had become his one remaining hope of salvation. In his present position there seemed little possibility that he could be reconciled with the Crown and restored to his title and estates. Only from a position of strength could he hope to negotiate successfully with Elizabeth. Dr Sanders with his foreign contacts was the means to achieve that strength. In the large rambling fortress of Castleisland they waited and waited. The winter had been severe with frequent frost and snow. The earl could scarcely walk. His personal physician, Maurice Lee, had deserted him and had sought Pelham's protection. Aqua vitae was now the only medicine with which he could obtain relief from the pain that racked his feeble body, and with which he could deaden his mind to the reality of their dreadful predicament. Eleanor had sent their daughters to be cared for in the few remaining houses yet friendly to them. She entrusted her children to the protection of her half-brother, Donal MacCarthy of Carbery, and her brother-in-law, Owen

MacDonagh MacCarthy of Duhallow, both of whom were subsequently imprisoned by Pelham when they refused to divulge the whereabouts of their charges. Eleanor sent another daughter to the care of her sister, the Countess of Clancar. The strain, both physical and mental, of her situation must have taken its toll on her. She had been sucked into the morass as, against her better judgement, her husband had succumbed to the pressures exerted on him from both sides. She had her opportunity to desert him and chance her luck with the authorities. But the persistence and constancy that were the hallmarks of her character were difficult to shed, even if she had wished to do so. Her influential position in the Desmond household even yet attracted the attention of the English administration. Pelham, in an attempt to reduce English unease at the ruthlessness of his campaign in Munster, sought through her brother to involve her in a government plot 'for ye apprehencion of John of Desmond and Saunders'[17] in return for Garrett's pardon. While there was little love lost between Eleanor and Sir John and Saunders, she had even less trust in the Lord Justice. She too had come, albeit reluctantly, to the conclusion that in the present situation the only solution to the dreadful dilemma was a Spanish one.

But the strain of watching and waiting had begun to affect the relationship between the fugitives at Castleisland. Sir John bitterly accused the earl of cowardice and inaction. After heated exchanges the brothers separated. Sir John led his followers on a series of wild forages, while Garrett made a short sortie into Limerick, where he was surprised by the ward out of Adare castle. In the ensuing engagement his horse was shot under him, and it was only with considerable difficulty, owing to his infirmities, that his followers managed to hustle him back to the safety of Castleisland.

In June 1580 Pelham and Ormond combined once more for an offensive against the Earl of Desmond. They drove the MacCarthys and O'Callaghans, together with their cattle herds, before them and advanced along the Blackwater on the long, energy-sapping trek into the palatinate of Kerry. News of their progress reached Eleanor and Garrett belatedly. With Pelham at their heels, there was little time for an orderly withdrawal from Castleisland, and, as Pelham reported, 'The erle of Desmond being ther with his ladie was forced to forsake his horse and betwixt some of his gallowglass to take to the bogg.'[18] Eleanor was forced to abandon several items of clothing from her personal wardrobe, which, together with some vestments belonging to Dr Sanders, were derisively torn to shreds by Pelham's soldiers. Aided by the strong arms of the galloglass, she fled into the night. Splashing and stumbling through the bogs and marshes around Castleisland, the cries of their hunters in their ears, the Earl and Countess of Desmond ran for their lives. Garrett fell exhausted, unable to continue, and had to be carried on the shoulders of his galloglass into the safety of the mountains. Here the fugitives took a brief respite and separated.

Eleanor, with a small escort, set out for Newcastle to throw the pursuers off the trail of her husband. On her journey she encountered, whether intentionally or by accident is uncertain, the admiral of the English fleet, Sir William Winter. Winter's fleet, since the fall of Carraigafoyle, had remained anchored in the Shannon estuary. He had made a rendezvous with Pelham, who ordered him to take the fleet around to Dingle Bay. As he returned to his post he encountered the Countess of Desmond. Eleanor informed him of the sequence of developments and events that had forced her husband into rebellion. She begged him to take a letter to the English Privy Council so that she might negotiate directly for her husband's pardon and for a cessation of the war in Munster. The pitiful sight of the distraught and dishevelled countess perhaps touched Winter, who agreed to forward her letter to England.

Eleanor sat down to compose the most honest and poignant letter of the entire tragic saga. It is at once a powerful and compelling document. It demonstrates her knowledge and understanding of the minds of those she sought to convince and change. She gives an objective analysis of her husband's shortcomings, but also insinuates her conviction that he had been pushed by Pelham and Malby into a rebellion that he did not want. 'My husband and his countrie have bene bled by persons who are in authoritie here,' she wrote, and reminded the Council of her husband's loyal conduct until the death of Sir William Drury. Then, Eleanor contends, Sir Nicholas Malby was allowed free rein in Munster and 'the place of Justice was void. Malbie', she asserts, 'marched therewith into my husbands countrie, murdered certaine of his men, toke and spoyled certaine of his castles, burned within houses old men and children and within churches bourned certaine monuments of his ancestors and, a thinge which', as Eleanor diplomatically assures the Council, 'greeved him most, openlie called him a traytor within the cytye of Lymerick.' Eleanor grasps the opportunity to explain how both she and her husband had been denied access to the Privy Council by English officials in Ireland. Despite her husband's later promise to dissociate himself from those she describes as 'his unnaturall brethern and the traitor Saunders' and the delivery of their only son to the Crown, her husband, she claims, had been left with no option but to join in the rebellion or be overrun. For her own part, she declares that after her husband had been publicly proclaimed a traitor she had indicated to Pelham and Ormond that she wished to leave Munster and go to the Queen, but this was denied her. She puts on record her suspicions concerning the evil intent of her brother-in-law, Sir John of Desmond, who, she claims,

> since the tyme I was married and especiallie settens yt shall be please God to send my husband a sonne ... hathe allwaies enveyied the prosperitie of my husband and by all meanes sought both in Englande and here to throwe him into some action, wherebie he might incure her Maties indignaction hopinge thereby (as nowe he doth manifest havinge shott at the marke which longe he desired) to come by the Erledome as with hope he hathe ben alwaies prevented by my meanes and the actions of those that loved my husband.[19]

In her letter Eleanor fearlessly apportioned the blame for her husband's rebellion, as she adjudged it, on both sides: on the vindictive and deliberately provocative actions of Pelham and Malby on the one side, and on the greed and jealously of her husband's brothers on the other, while between lay the devious aspirations and plots of Ormond, Sanders and the rest.

Winter accepted her missive for the Privy Council and promised that when the opportunity arose he would have it delivered. With thanks, Eleanor later rejoined her husband, determined to keep him alive until either the hoped-for Spanish aid arrived or until her letter produced a pardon from Elizabeth.

Meanwhile the hunt continued. There was to be no respite for the rebel earl and his adherents. From the sod cabins of the lowliest kern to cold mountain caves and to the dens of wild animals the Earl and Countess of Desmond crept stealthily. With a handful of faithful attendants, like 'deere they laie upon their keepings and so fearfull they were, that they would not tarrie in anie one place anie long time but where they did dress their meat, then they would remove and eat it in another place to lie'.[20] They ranged over the more mountainous and marshy parts of Munster. At times her husband had to be carried on a pallet while, ever watchful, she rode at the head of the band ready to sound the alarm at the first sight of danger. She endured many narrow escapes from pursuing English scouting parties, who were ever on the watch for her in the hope that by following her they might discover the earl's whereabouts. 'We had the Countess of Desmond in chase two myles', Captain Bouchier of the Kilmallock garrison reported, 'and myssinge her selfe took a great prey of three hundred kyne from her.'[21] It became too risky to travel by day. There were too many eyes, both native and foreign, ready to watch the movements of the fugitives and eager, to secure the silver on their heads. Munster was pockmarked with garrisons from which scouting parties daily emerged to scour the countryside. The earl's followers cursed their overlord and blamed him for the ruination of the crops and livestock and for their hunger. But the main thrust of their anger was directed against Dr Sanders. Even in the earl's company he was reviled by the people for his hollow promises of Spanish arms and gold. The earl's authority alone protected him, and for reasons that now had little to do with the religious crusade.

During the summer many of the Earl of Desmond's erstwhile allies, including the Earl of Clancar, O'Sullivan Beare and O'Sullivan More, O'Callaghan and O'Donoghue, submitted to Pelham, who continued his ruthless campaign against those still in rebellion. Rumours about the likely appointment of a Lord Deputy began to circulate. Pelham, anxious to secure the most credit, redoubled his efforts in his attempts to capture the rebel earl and his family.

> I give the rebels no breath to relieve themselves [he boasted to the Queen] but by one of your garrisons or other they be continually hunted. I keep them from their harvest and have taken great preys of cattle from them by which it seemeth the poor people that lived only upon labour and fed by their milch cows are so distressed as they follow their goods and offer themselves with their wives and children rather to be slain by the army than to suffer the famine that now in extremity beginneth to pinch them.[22]

As Pelham reported, the first signs of a serious famine had begun to appear as the devastated land and terrified people succumbed to the awful consequences of the long war.

Suddenly the focus of political attention was diverted from Munster to the hitherto loyal English Pale where James Eustace, Viscount Baltinglass, aided by Fiach MacHugh O'Byrne, raised the papal banner high over Leinster. This latest revolt was part of the wider intensification of the Counter-Reformation movement abroad.

Jesuit agents of the Counter-Reformation, Parsons and Campion, had been smuggled into England and were actively exhorting English Catholics to prepare for an invasion for faith and freedom. The objectives of the Counter-Reformation were espoused by Baltinglass, who, unlike the Earl of Desmond, exemplified the reforming zeal of the movement. Urged on by Dr Sanders, with whom he had maintained constant contact, Baltinglass displaced the Earl of Desmond and moved to centre-stage in the revolutionary crusade. He beckoned to Sir John and Dr Sanders to join him and together to move the thrust of the crusade to Leinster. Sir John had little patience or respect for his sickly brother, while Sanders had detected a marked falling-off in the earl's crusading fervour. The earl might well be the chosen receptacle for the seeds of the most holy revolution, but his own motives seemed to derive from more worldly and material considerations. The true crusading spirit and will of the Counter-Reformation appeared to Dr Sanders to be embodied in the revolt of Viscount Baltinglass, and to him Sanders made his way.

Eleanor and Garrett were now on their own. Despite the events in Leinster, there was no respite from Pelham in Munster. He wreaked havoc with the harvest, without which they would hardly survive another winter. Deserted by their relatives and allies, Eleanor decided to intercede again with the Lord Justice. She traced Pelham to Askeaton, where he received her amid the ruins of her castle home. The harrowing circumstances of her life during the past year had taken their toll of the gaunt and haggard figure who knelt before the Lord Justice and yet once again tearfully pleaded her husband's cause. But this time her tears had little effect. The resolute and pitiless faces of Pelham and his assistant, Geoffrey Fenton, were mirrored in Fenton's report of the meeting: 'The Countess came in . . . but with the same impudencie wherewith she hath covered her face since her last breaking out with her husband; yet taketh she uppon her to worke hym to submission.'[23] But Pelham would not relent, and once again refused Eleanor permission to present her husband's case at court. There was no option but to keep the field and survive the winter and hope that the rumours that had begun to circulate about Pelham's impending recall proved true. But Pelham's harassment continued unabated as he sought to isolate them further from their remaining supporters and to contrive their betrayal. It was rumoured that Sir John had secretly conspired with Sir Warham St Leger, the recently appointed provost-marshal in Munster, to betray his brother and secure a pardon for himself, while Rory MacSheehy, a captain of the Desmond galloglass, was urged by Pelham to capture Dr Sanders. Pelham warned Lord FitzMorris not to succour the fugitives. 'You have had in your country', he wrote to him, 'the traitor earl, his wife, his brother and Sanders, whom you might have apprehended if you had listed.' To ensure FitzMorris's future actions, Pelham informed him that his two sons would be detained 'until I may see some service done by you in delivering up some of the principal conspirators above named, dead or alive'.[24]

While the whispers and rumours flew, Garrett's half-brother, Sir James 'Sussex', was wounded on a plundering raid in Muskerry and captured by the Sheriff of Cork. He was delivered in chains to St Leger and imprisoned in Cork. After two months of physical and mental torture Sir James was executed in October 1580, as St Leger reported to the Privy Council: 'Sir James of Desmond who (by direction of the Lord Deputie) I caused to be hanged drawen and quartered at the gates of this town ... who yeelded to godward a better end than otherwise would have don if he had not dyed to death.'[25] James had pleaded in vain for summary decapitation, but the twenty-two-year-old rebel had to suffer the ignoble and gruesome form of execution reserved for traitors. He had faced his ordeal bravely. The English administration in Dublin noted his death and merely observed that 'the pestilent hydra hath lost another of his heads'.[26]

In September 1580 Arthur, Baron Grey de Wilton took office as the new Lord Deputy in Ireland. Pelham reluctantly surrendered the sword of office in the knowledge that he had failed to complete his mission against the Earl of Desmond and that the methods he had employed in Munster had found little favour with the Crown. Moreover, Admiral Winter had kept his word to Eleanor, and her letter had reached the Queen and aroused her anger. Elizabeth had little time for the Puritan fanaticism of Pelham and his kind, particularly where such zeal cost her money. Where loyalty could be purchased, even for a time, Elizabeth was willing to overlook the political and religious shortcomings of the individual. She had scant regard for the Earl of Desmond; she cursed him roundly for being a drain on her resources, and wished him dead or in exile. Yet the Countess of Desmond's letter made the Queen question the appropriateness of Pelham's precipitate actions against the earl and his subsequent policy of annihilation which had accomplished little but to devastate one-quarter of her Irish realm. Pelham felt bitter about the criticism, and his companion and aide, Sir Nicholas Malby, protested to the Queen's secretary on his behalf. It was unjustifiable, Malby stated, that the wordes of an infamous woman, the wyfe of a proclaymed traytor herselfe a nowtorious traytores, the great worcker of these wicked rebellions in the popes behalf should cary their credyt to deface the faythfull service of a dutyfull and honest servant.[27]

But Pelham's day had come and gone, and Elizabeth dismissed the protests as more urgent and disturbing events unfolded.

The untried but impatient Lord Deputy rashly carried the fight to Baltinglass and Fiach MacHugh O'Byrne, deep in the treacherous recesses and ravines of the Wicklow mountains, and paid the penalty. At Glenmalure the O'Byrne kern and galloglass decimated Grey's raw English recruits. The effects of the victory were instantaneous. In the north O'Rourke and O'Donnell rose in revolt, while Turlough Luineach O'Neill prepared to attack the Pale with an army of 5,000 clansmen. His rival, the English-educated Hugh O'Neill, the Baron of Dungannon, hid himself in the woods and loudly protested his loyalty to Elizabeth 'even if all the Irishry in Ireland should rebel'.[28] Sir John of Desmond besieged Maryborough, and Ormond was attacked by the rebels. To add to the explosive situation, Spanish aid arrived, undetected, at the ill-fated harbour of Smerwick.

The news of the uprisings and the arrival of the long-awaited aid from Philip spurred Eleanor and Garrett into action. The years of intrigue and subterfuge, of tears and humiliation, of deprivaton, hunger and loss seemed likely to be vindicated. The long lonely vigil was over. The King had kept his word; the army of salvation had arrived. As they urged their horses over the steep mountain passes towards Dingle, the depression and misery of their situation perhaps momentarily lifted and excitedly Garrett swore to avenge the wrongs they had suffered. As they topped the last hill before the descent to Dún an Óir, the promentary fort standing stark and windswept against the sea, their elation turned to disbelief. Instead of the army of well-appointed troops promised by Dr Sanders, they saw a force of 700 'poor simple bisognos, very ragged and a great part of them boys'.[29] Philip had sent aid to the crusaders in Ireland, but his interests in the Low Countries took precedence. It was significant that the majority of the troops were Italians. With the soldiers was Friar Mateo de Oviedo, the apostolic commissary, and Friar Cornelius O'Mulrian, the papal Bishop of Killaloe, and some Jesuit preachers. Ill-clothed and totally inexperienced in warfare, the soldiers quickly succumbed to the cold and damp of the Irish climate. Their leader was Sebastino di San Joseppi from Bologna, who must have been equally incredulous to learn that the pale sickly man who had to be lifted off his horse was the great Irish crusader who was to lead them to victory over the army of the English heretic queen. Philip had sent sufficient arms for the 4,000-strong army promised him in their despatches by the Earl of Desmond and Dr Sanders. Where was this great army? the Italians wanted to know. They were assured that over the hills the army waited. But San Joseppi would never know that beyond the high peaks of Slieve Mish lay a people decimated by war and famine, too hungry and unwilling to bear arms in a cause they did not even understand. A massive confidence trick had been practised by both sides, for which they would pay a costly penalty. Sir John and Dr Sanders hurried to Smerwick. The leaders sent urgent messages back to Philip to the effect that nothing less than 8,000 well-equipped and experienced troops could ensure the success of the crusade. Rashly Garrett outlined to the King the miserable circumstances of his situation, the seizure of his estates, his poverty, and how both he and his countess were daily driven from pillar to post in their own estates by the army of Philip's heretic sister-in-law. The effect of this plaintive tale on the cold, reserved Spanish King would be no more than an indifferent shrug of the black-caped shoulders and a detached resolve to pursue Christ's crusade elsewhere under the leadership of a less distressed captain.

Reports of the 'invasion' reached Dublin, where Lord Deputy Grey, who was impatient to blot out the embarrassment of Glenmalure, joined forces with the Earl of Ormond and made for Dingle. The Golden Fort (Dún an Óir) might provide him with the chance to restore his tarnished image. In Grey's army were Captains Raleigh, Zouche and Mackworth, while the poet Edmund Spenser acted as the Lord Deputy's secretary. At the beginning of November Grey pitched camp at Dingle. As the English army approached, the Desmond leaders and their supporters hurried away with empty promises of aid to the Italians. Admiral Winter sailed into Smerwick and cut off the chance of escape by sea. The siege of Dún an Óir commenced. Initially the Italians flew the papal insignia from the fort, but as the siege intensified it was replaced by a black and white banner. This was the signal to the Geraldine army to attack the English in the rear. But no army materialised, and the Geraldine leaders remained hidden. The Italians sued for terms, but Grey would consider only an unconditional surrender, to which, it was controversially reported, San Joseppi agreed. But the hero of Spenser's *Faerie Queene*, the brave knight Artegal, in his this-worldly identity of Lord Deputy Grey, ordered Captains Raleigh and Mackworth to implement to the letter of the law the prevailing rules of sixteenth-century warfare. The unarmed survivors of the siege, with the exception of a handful of officers, were mercilessly slaughtered. Six hundred died at Smerwick, a dreadful indictment of the sub-human cruelty of warfare and the tragedy of broken promises and incomprehensible and ineffectual alliances. San Joseppi and his inexperienced youths were the sacrificial victims of the deviousness of international politics fuelled by the raging flames of religious fanaticism. The shame of Dún an Óir must rest on the Puritan shoulders of Lord Deputy Grey, but also on Dr Sanders, the Earl of Desmond and the Geraldines, whose rash and empty promises had first lured and then abandoned the Italians to their doom. While Grey's action at Smerwick was sharply criticised by some factions at the English court, the Queen viewed it as a removal of a threat from her most bitter enemy to the security of her realm; accordingly she thanked and commended Grey for his endeavours. It is significant to note that there was no official remonstration by the Catholic powers, who, if the positions were reversed, would undoubtedly have done likewise.

Smerwick was for Garrett the final fateful step which placed him beyond all hope of return. His action had made reconciliation with the Queen now viritually impossible. He had aroused the deepest anger in Elizabeth as he had turned her greatest fear into stark reality by bringing England's most dreaded enemy into Ireland; for that the Queen would never forgive him. Garrett's great gamble had failed, and the fortunes of war were once again in England's favour. The risk of Spanish intervention in Ireland had receded; the honour of the Crown had been bloodily restored; Turlough O'Neill no longer threatened the Pale; the Burkes of Connaught had been subdued; and early in 1581 Viscount Baltinglass, his cause clearly lost, was attempting to flee to the continent. Hope abounded that the tiresome Earl of Desmond might do the same. For Eleanor the débâcle of Smerwick proved her long-held misgivings that Dr Sanders and his religious crusade was an inappropriate vehicle for restoring her husband to his lordship and powers. Garrett had been pushed onto the wrong horse. His physical and political limitations made him no match for the enormity of the situation which confronted him after Smerwick as he foundered in the wilderness. But Eleanor noticed a strange change in her husband. The religious motivation of the rebellion which he had briefly espoused was totally uncharacteristic of the earl. After Smerwick he had parted company with Dr Sanders, each embittered by his brief association with the other. Released from the pretence of espousing a cause in which he had no real interest, Garrett reverted to the cause which was life itself to him, the proud defence of the power and privilege of his title. The Queen, who after Smerwick considered the earl to be of little consequence, was amazed when it was reported that 'The Earle of Desmond who was thought to be either dead or fled beginneth to appear and to show himselfe, having assembled a great companie.'[30] The foreign 'Pápa abú!' exhortation of the crusade was replaced by the native war-cry of 'Shanid abú!' as the Earl of Desmond prepared to lead his followers in the only crusade he understood, the defence of his land, privileges and power.

For Dr Sanders the long, dismal, aimless campaign in Ireland had finally exacted its price. He had become totally disillusioned with the Gaelic leaders and their Gaelic ways, so different from the glorious crusade envisaged by FitzMaurice. The sodden woods and oozing bogs of Kerry had sapped the fiery zeal and burning energy of the scholarly agitator. While English steel had diligently sought his head for three long years, ironically it was the Irish ague and famine that eventually killed 'the supporting pillar of the Catholic faith'[31] somewhere among the briary thickets of Clonlish wood in the damp spring of 1581.

While Eleanor might well have been amazed at the change in her husband and his determination to continue the rebellion, her amazement was compounded by the policy of peace and reconciliation suddenly being preached by his bitter rival, the Earl of Ormond. For years he had opposed and plotted against Garrett and aided various officers of the Crown in the spoliation of his estates. Yet the extent, the fearsome results and future implications of the latest expeditions by the new breed of English officials and soldiers in Ireland frightened him. Enough, he deemed, was enough. Munster had already suffered more than enough. But Grey and the avaricious freebooting landless captains and officials in his retinue, eager for the spoils of war, would not be stopped. While the Earl of Desmond's estates and property were now easy pickings, Ormond could not help but wonder whether the greed and lust for land of the new breed of English military conquistadores would stop short at the lands of his enemy. Would equally greedy and suspicious eyes be eventually cast on his own domain and questions raised regarding his extensive powers? Black Tom had to tread warily lest his hesitancy be interpreted as disloyalty and his estates subjected to the same fate as Desmond's.

During the winter months of 1580–81 Eleanor lay low. Garrett seemed determined to continue the fight, and his rekindled resolution had also tended to make him stronger physically. Consequently when, in April 1581, the Countess of Desmond presented herself at Cork city to Ormond, the reasons for her sudden appearance were open to speculation. Eleanor was accompanied by her sister, and Ormond authorised protections for both women. Eleanor was examined before the Munster Commissioners, among whom was her former jailer in London, Sir Warham St Leger. They asked her if she came on her husband's behalf, to which she replied 'that she was not authorised by him to sue for him but did it of her owne head'.[32] She was then escorted back to her lodgings for the night with instructions to commit her petition to paper. Ormond permitted her sister to depart to live under the custody of their brother, the Baron of Dunboyne. It is difficult to ascertain the real reasons for Eleanor's unexpected appearance at Cork. Her husband was determined to continue a campaign in which she had suffered immeasurably. Perhaps she could take no more of the physical fatigue and mental anguish wrought on her by the rebellion. But her petition reflects a more likely reason for her visit to Ormond at Cork. One of Eleanor's principal characteristics was her constancy, and she probably realised that she might find in Ormond, who for personal considerations now also wished for a cessation of hostilities, a likely means to achieve the access to the Queen which she had sought so persistently. Desmond, she knew, despite his new-found pride and determination, could not hold out much longer, and Eleanor volunteered once more to be the first in line to test the Crown's mind.

Eleanor asked again for permission to take her case before the Queen so 'that my travell maye be a meanes to brede a generall quiet into this province and precure mercie to my husbande nowe driven to distresse'.[33] She did not directly request a pardon for her husband; Garrett had forfeited that right by aligning himself with a foreign power. She merely requested that she be permitted to seek the Queen's mercy for herself and her husband. Her dilemma, she stated, was such that 'as nature tyeth me to the companie of my Lord my husbande (who so unhapely is fallen into her Maties heavie displeasure) yet', she assured them, 'my dutie remembered to her Matie'.[34] She pleaded for the welfare and safety of her daughters who had suffered considerable distress and want during the course of their young lives. 'I doe also beseche your wisdom', she asked, 'that I may take my daughters with me into England or els to leave them with my ffrendes untyll my retorne out of England ... to remaine free and not as prisoners.'[35]

Ormond forwarded her petition to the Lord Deputy and Council in Dublin, where it was received and endorsed by Grey's secretary, the poet Edmund Spenser. Spenser, author of *The Faerie Queene*,[36] was

The Tudor manor built by Black Tom, 10th Earl of Ormond, at Carrick-on-Suir, Co Tipperary.

influenced in his writing of the epic by his term of service with Lord Deputy Grey in Ireland; it is believed that he based the character of the evil temptress Radigund on Eleanor. Grey and his Council were unmoved by Eleanor's petition and recoiled in assumed horror at what they termed 'so arrogant a petition made without submission or confession of her husband's horrible treason and her owne'.[37] They accused her of

> the treason of bringing in of strangers into this realme by the practize of her husband, and by all conjecture much furdered by her, hath in all reasonable opinion so aggravated her former offences as we see lesse cause nowe than before to graunt a matter so offensive to her highness.[38]

Grey sought to continue the policy of his predecessor Pelham and ensure that the Earl of Desmond would have little option but to continue in his rebellion, and that there would be no last-minute pardon as a result of any intercession of his wife with the Queen. Half a million acres of land was the prize for the victor. They were too near their goal to have it snatched away by the tears of the rebel's wife. Grey ordered that Eleanor was to be sent back to her husband so that her presence might slow him down; otherwise, Grey argued, 'he maie go with as few companie as pleaseth him from wood to wood and from bogg to bogg or to Spaine or Scotland when to warrant further help ... but', Grey reasoned, 'having hir in his train he cannot chuse whether he leaveth or goe'.[39] It was Grey's opinion that the Earl of Desmond 'hath more care for the said Countesse and her traine to leave them than he hath of himself'.[40]

Eleanor's case was not helped by the actions and interests of the provost-marshal, Sir Warham St Leger. He already had a foothold in Desmond which he hoped to extend. Furthermore, his differences with the Earl of Ormond at this time were common knowledge. Such was his animosity to Ormond that any sign that Black Tom favoured the cause of the rebel's wife would be seized upon by St Leger as proof of his disloyalty. He wrote to Lord Burghley, the Queen's chief secretary, to add a further impediment to Eleanor's passage to the Queen:

> In my simple opinion, ther can no good growe of her going thither. I vow to God ... I know her to bee as wicked a woman as ever was bred in Ireland and one that

hath ben the chief instrument of her husband's rebellion.
And if she bee licensed to go out, your lordship shall doo
as good an act as ever you did in your life to this realme to
cause hir hed to be stroken of or else to be kept in
perpetuall ymprisonment.[41]

The cries of the avaricious were sounding more strident against any
possibility, no matter how tenuous, which might deprive them of the
great prize so near their grasp. With the weight of official opinion
firmly set against her, and with Ormond's loyalty under question,
Eleanor knew that she was fighting a losing battle in her attempts to
gain access to the Queen. Ormond was powerless, even if he wished,
to help her. Suspicious of Black Tom's influence with the Queen, who
now talked of a general pardon, Grey accused him of dangerous and
suspicious tendencies and relieved him of his position as military
governor of Munster. Grey managed to persuade the Queen to
exclude the Earl and Countess of Desmond and Sir John of Desmond
from the amnesty. Thus with Ormond sidelined and Eleanor barred
from England, Grey ensured that the devastation in Munster would
continue until the Earl of Desmond was taken dead or alive in
rebellion. The scent of riches and privilege wafted stronger than the
acrid stench of decaying corpses and scorched earth as the eager
English bloodhounds leapt from the slips and tore after the prey.

Eleanor rejoined her husband in the wilderness for the final
agonising phase of the war. She had done everything within her
power to salvage something from the ruins. Stalked like wild beasts,
she and Garrett went to ground. The long winter months of 1581–2
were, according to the annals, notable for 'great wind, constant rain,
lightning and much tempestuous weather'.[42] Like demented
spectres they flitted across the decayed Munster landscape. They
were pursued without respite by Captain Zouche, an eager,
uncompromising officer in the Munster service. He reported that he
had almost caught the countess on several occasions, but Eleanor
had merely lured his posse away from where her husband lay, too
exhausted to flee any further. To the English soldiers the Countess of
Desmond became an obsessive figure, dominating their gossip and
nightmares. Stories of her evil, devious ways were peddled from
camp-fire to camp-fire. She became the object of their fear, hatred
and lust; the she-devil, the mythical harpy, the wanton. Was it true
that under the pretence of seeking pardon from the Lord Deputy she
had spied for the rebels? Was it not whispered that she was a witch?
What self-respecting woman—and a countess to boot—would

willingly live like a wild animal in the woods and bogs of this god-forsaken country? The soldiers savagely cursed her as the incessant rain soaked them to the skin and quenched the camp-fires. They swore at her as they spat the spoiled biscuit and chewed the tainted uncooked meat of their rations. They cursed her and the country that gave her birth as they vomited their guts out and shivered uncontrollaby with Irish ague and dysentery amid the oozing marshes and frozen mountain passes of Munster. Was it true that she traded her favours easily? The red-rimmed hungry eyes of the war-weary soldiers gloated at the prospect of her capture.

In the middle of a cold misty November night the soldiers' desire was almost fulfilled. A scouting party from the nearby garrison of Kilmallock came upon an isolated wattle cabin hidden deep in a wood. Eleanor, her nerves as taut as the strings of a crossbow, heard the sound of movement outside. She roused her exhausted husband. There was no time to awake the galloglass, who, shrouded in their great woollen cloaks, were asleep under the surrounding trees. Supporting her husband, she stumbled out of the cabin and into the darkness as the clansmen sprang to arms and engaged the English soldiers in a fierce battle. Desperately Eleanor looked for an escape. Before her was the dark outline of a river, swollen by the winter deluges. Behind her she could hear the victorious shouts of the English as they put the galloglass to flight. There was no escape. Quickly she helped Garrett to the river bank and into the ice-cold water. The river rose almost to their chins, which with difficulty they kept above the fast-flowing current. Hidden from sight by the overhanging bank, they waited. The soldiers surrounded the cabin, and Captain Zouche entered to effect the capture of the wretched fugitives. A makeshift bed stood in the corner, the coverings still warm to the touch. Zouche ordered a search for the occupants, convinced that they were still in the vicinity of the cabin. The soldiers spread out. They came to the river and searched the undergrowth above the bank. Underneath, Eleanor held the sagging body of her husband afloat, her body almost numb. She could scarcely breathe. Finally Zouche called off the search, and in silent agony she had to wait until the last sounds of the English posse faded and until the strong arms of the surviving galloglass came to her rescue and lifted them bodily from the river. Returning to the cabin, they found that Eleanor's clothing had been ripped to pieces and trampled into the mud by the frustrated soldiers. There was no time to recover. A voluminous Irish woollen mantle was wrapped about each of them, and they were carried into the night by the faithful Desmond retainers in search of another temporary shelter before sunrise.

While Zouche was to be yet again denied the capture of the elusive earl and countess, it was he who was destined to draw first blood in the renewed campaign at the beginning of 1582. Since the massacre at Smerwick and the subsequent death of Dr Sanders and flight to the continent of Lord Baltinglass, Sir John of Desmond had remained in Munster. Early in January he set out to rendezvous with the Seneschall of Imokilly near Castlelyons, Co. Cork. On information received from a spy, Zouche lay in wait for the rebel lord, and in the ensuing struggle Sir John was killed by a spear thrown by a former servant named Fleming. Thus the life of a turbulent, unscrupulous and bold Geraldine was brought to a bloody end. Sir John was the most active leader of the Geraldines and while he could be accused of many dark deeds and even darker thoughts, there was a certain decisiveness about his actions, in marked contrast to the vacillations of his elder brother. His antagonism to Eleanor and the deep mutual dislike that existed between them stemmed from many causes. Her Butler origins perhaps aroused his Geraldine prejudice; he resented her influence over Garrett which had replaced his own; furthermore, she had borne his sickly brother an heir, thereby eliminating his own chances to succeed to the coveted title. The decapitated body of Sir John of Desmond was hung in chains over the main gate of Cork city. There it remained for almost three years, a grisly spectacle, until the skeletal remains were blown by a storm into the river. Zouche despatched the head as a new year's gift to Grey in Dublin, while the Queen was presented with Sir John's 'fair torquoise [ring] set in gold'.[43] His estates in Co. Cork were later granted to Captain Thomas Norris and Sir Walter Raleigh, while the poet Edmund Spenser received the castle and lands of Kilcolman. The war-mongers and war correspondents of the long campaign were well rewarded.

The Earl of Desmond alone remained to carry on the resistance. It was reasonable to expect that he would capitulate, but the earl very rarely did what was expected of him. There was to be no surrender on his part. Moreover, the Geraldine supporters clung to him as their only means of salvation. If the earl received a pardon, it would be conditional, and preserve his life only. The estates of his dependent lords and clansmen were likely to be expropriated and parcelled out to the land-hungry English freebooters as payment for their services. The earl had no option but to continue the rebellion or at least stay alive until aid came from abroad or until Elizabeth relented. Garrett had become a prisoner of his heritage, and during 1582 his liegemen and followers once more flocked to his banner. The Crown became disturbed at the continued policy of spoliation being pursued in Munster. Even former perpetrators of the destruction, hardened campaigners like Raleigh and St Leger, echoed the Earl of Ormond's reservations for which they had previously condemned him. They expressed concern over the scorched-earth policy of Grey now that it seemed likely that the Desmond estates would be forfeited and divided out among them. Elizabeth swore at her Lord Deputy who, despite the resources she had given him, had accomplished little. Desmond the 'arch-rebel' still roamed free, and Munster was desolate.

The earl still held out, and, as one observer noted, 'he continued still in his old accustomed spoiling and wasting the countries and trusting to no house nor castell did shrowd himselfe in woods and bogs'.[44] From his hiding-place, deep in the wild Glen of Aherlow, the earl had reverted to attacks on his hereditary enemy and raided the nearby lands of Black Tom. He skirmished occasionally with the English patrols sent to track him down. Eleanor continued to accompany him, and as late as June 1582 Zouche reported yet another running encounter with the Countess of Desmond, whom he claimed he had 'distressed'. Although she had not been named with Garrett as a traitor in the original proclamation of 1579, Eleanor had loyally shared his hunted existence and had now been on the run with him for over two years, during which time she had endured the greatest hardship imaginable. Her physical and mental health was near breaking-point. Her devotion and loyalty had been tried and tested amid the icy waters of Munster's marshes and rivers, on the cold floors of huts and caves, in hunger and in the countless sleepless nights when every rustle and stir in the dark outside might herald the end. She had increasingly faced the wrath and vengeance of the Crown as she strove to intercede and negotiate on her husband's behalf. Whether physically unable to bear the terrible strain any longer, or, as is more likely, in yet another effort to intercede and seek terms by which Garrett could surrender, Eleanor suddenly appeared before Lord Deputy Grey at the English camp near Maryborough on 15 June 1582. Grey was moved by the emaciated lady who, in dirty ragged clothing, courageously stood before him to plead her husband's case. But with his usual self-righteousness and sense of duty, 'yet weighing the nature and quallitie of her actions and howe farre she might participate in the trayterous councelles and conspiracies of her husband', he had her conducted 'to the house of an honest merchant of Dublin there to remeine in estate of a prysoner untill . . . we might be directed how to dispose of her further'.[45]

In semi-captivity in Dublin, Eleanor awaited her chance to

intervene on her husband's behalf. But by now Elizabeth and her Privy Council wanted an end to the war, and an end to the troublesome Earl of Desmond who refused to surrender unconditionally. There were to be no futher negotiations or time-wasting interventions. Walsingham instructed Grey to withdraw the protection he had given to Eleanor and ordered that she was 'to retourne back agayne to her said husband within a certain tyme', after which 'if shee happen to bee taken she must then bee subject to such punishment as the laws will laye uppon her for her conduct'.[46] The Crown demanded the unconditional surrender of the Earl of Desmond so that his estates and property, thereby attainted, could be used to pay the vast expenses incurred by the war against him. His death, however, would also bring the same result. In the somewhat naïve belief that Grey shared his desire for rapprochement, Walsingham advised him:

> You should appoint some such person to delyver unto the countesse by waye of friendly advice that if she could persuade the said Earle her husband to come in and submitt him selfe simplie to her Maties mercie, the only waye hee can nowe take for his safetie, [the Queen might then consider] not only to leave him his liefe but also to use some further clemencie towardes him.[47]

But Grey neglected to put the Queen's offer to Eleanor, who was not aware that it had been made until some time later. Neither Grey, who was about to be relieved of his post, nor his administration wished for any last-minute chance of reconciliation. Fortunes and reputations were at stake.

During the summer months of 1582, while Eleanor awaited her fate in Dublin, she was allowed to visit her son, still incarcerated in the Castle. James was now eleven years of age, and Eleanor was greatly distressed at the conditions under which he was detained. She wrote to Lord Burghley and reminded him that she had voluntarily placed her son in the Crown's care, but that the 'boy now remaineth in the Castell of Dublin, without any kynd of learninge or brenginge upp or any to attend uppon him. . . . In consideracion of his innocency and tender yeares',[48] she urged that he should be transferred from the unsuitable environment of Dublin Castle and sent to England, where she hoped someone in power might take a friendly interest in his welfare and his future as the only son and heir of the Desmond earldom. As her husband would appear to have forfeited his last chance of retaining his title and estates, it was an appropriate time to remind the Crown of the existence of his son. If her husband's estates were attainted, the Queen might yet agree to restore at least part of them, together with the hereditary title, to his son when he came of age, as she had seen fit to do in the case of his kinsman, the Earl of Kildare. An English education and upbringing, as with the young Hugh O'Neill, Eleanor realised might be the most effective way to ensure her son's eventual succession to his inheritance. Her request for the child's removal to England was subsequently granted.

Eleanor, forced to rejoin her husband on the run, protested to the authorities against a decision which she maintained 'above all things in this world she abhoreth and ever hath and the greatest thing against her nature and bringing upp'.[49] She again asked to be allowed to plead her case before the Queen, but the stern, immovable faces of Grey and the Council gave her her answer. The unconditional surrender of her husband was the only eventuality they were prepared to accept. Wearily Eleanor returned to Garrett with the unchanged 'offer' of the Lord Deputy and Council. Infuriated, Garrett stepped up the tempo of his campaign against the Crown. He had nothing to lose. A demonstration of power and intent might yet induce the Crown to offer better terms to bring an end to the conflict. Moreover, the old Geraldine pride had been ignited as, for the last time, the Earl of Desmond mounted his horse unaided to instil the fire of battle into his war-weary liege lords and famine-stricken followers. All Geraldines who dared defy his call to arms were summarily dealt with. He was informed that four of them had accepted Crown pardons. He ordered their arrest. They were brought before him, and 'calling them traitors, he had them stripped naked and slashed to death by his kinsmen, every sword in the band taking part in their death'.[50] 'So shall every Geraldine be served who shall not follow me,'[51] the earl decreed. The rebellion shed the last vestiges of the pseudo-ideologies that had earlier motivated it. The inherent Geraldine aspriations for supremacy and independence resurfaced as the Earl of Desmond mustered his hereditary men-at-arms into line in the final attempt to halt the march of time. 'Misery had given the man courage. . . . English ruthlessness threw him back into the life mould of the Gaelic captain.'[52] Significantly, as he began Garrett took the fight to the territory of his rival, Black Tom of Ormond, and plundered Tipperary along the Suir valley to the borders of Waterford. At Knockgraffon, near Cahir, he soundly defeated Ormond's brothers to put a winning touch to the age-old feud. He was supreme in the palatinate of Kerry, where the English garrisons cowered for cover from the renewed wave of Geraldine fury. Garrett's old ally, the

Seneschal of Imokilly, plundered east Cork and west Waterford and looted the Earl of Ormond's grand new house at Carrick-on-Suir. The starving kern and weary galloglass flocked to the Earl of Desmond's standard in a final furious drive in defence of the archaic world that had bred and sustained them. Their overlord for the first and final time assumed the dignity and stature of a hero, and as such was destined to become a legend in the annals of tradition and folk memory.

By now Eleanor's term of protection from Grey was drawing to an end. She had not succeeded—perhaps had not wanted to succeed—in persuading Garrett to seek a conference with the Lord Deputy and Council, who were agreeable 'to meet therle 20 myles from Dublin if shee by any persuasion may drawe her husband thither'.[53] Eleanor requested an extension of the protection, and this was granted. She also asked for a ten-day truce for Garrett and his followers, but this was denied. Eleanor brought three of her daughters, Margaret, Joan and Katherine, into Cork city and obtained Crown protection for them. There the web of intrigue and double-dealing enveloped her. She obtained an interview with Sir Warham St Leger, who bluntly informed her that Garrett's life might be spared under restraint in England but that his restoration was not negotiable. St Leger better than anyone knew that such terms were repugnant to the earl, and in any event he had no desire to see the earl reconciled with the Crown and to risk losing his own chances to a slice of the Desmond estates. At the same time as his offer to Eleanor, St Leger warned the Privy Council in England: 'Desmond if received to mercy, will ever be a hollow-hearted subject.'[54] He informed the Queen that Desmond had embarked on a new conspiracy with Spain and was planning another invasion. But Elizabeth was weary of the long campaign and still was susceptible 'to have the rebellion ended without blood'[55] and urged that Desmond be induced to surrender. But too much blood had already been shed, and the Queen's hopes were frustrated by her own officers' greed as well as by the earl's new-found enthusiasm for his cause.

It is ironic that the saga of the capitulation of the House of Desmond should be terminated by the self-same feud with which it had started—by one last conflict between the original combatants. Elizabeth had run out of money, ideas, and patience regarding the Desmond rebellion. The age-old rivalry between two Irish lords could achieve what a series of her best administrators and military men had failed to do. She left it to her old friend Black Tom to bring the bitter war to an end. Despite the misgivings of her officials in Ireland, she appointed him Lord General with a force of a thousand soldiers and power to grant pardons to all rebels in the Earl of Desmond's camp. By this time the plight of everyone in Munster had become desperate. The famine raging there for many months had spread across the country to the walls of Dublin city. In Munster, particularly towards the west, the situation was beyond belief. 'The lowing of a cow or the voice of a ploughman was not heard from Dingle to the Rock of Cashel,'[56] the annalists recorded.

Ormond's plan was to confine the Earl of Desmond to one locality, preferably within Kerry, which had suffered particularly severely from famine and devastation. From Clonmel, Ormond drove Garrett, Eleanor and their followers before him towards Kerry, while the garrisons of Limerick and Kilmallock attacked his seneschal, Garrett and Eleanor fled into Kerry before Ormond's determined onslaught. One by one the earl's allies deserted him and accepted the pardons readily offered them by Black Tom. The Baron of Lixnaw submitted, as did Lords Roche and Barry. The greatest blow to the Desmond cause came when Garrett's long-time friend, the Seneschal of Imokilly, fearful for the welfare of his only son, then in the custody of St Leger, made his submission to the Earl of Ormond. Deserted but for a few galloglass and retainers, Garrett and Eleanor made the exhausting journey over the mountains towards Kerry. They were hunted day and night without respite. Eleanor's female attendants were captured by the soldiers while, aided by a heavy fog, Eleanor and Garrett barely effected their own escape. Garrett's health had further deteriorated, and the galloglass took turns to carry their lord on their shoulders as they sought to evade the relentless hunters who sniffed the scent of the kill. Eleanor sought to negotiate with Ormond for suitable terms, but Ormond would not agree to anything less than Desmond's unconditional surrender. Ormond had also joined the ever-increasing pack who clamoured for the anticipated spoils. He claimed all the Desmond estate on the grounds that his mother was the sole heir of the eleventh Earl of Desmond. His claim had been noted by his enemies who sought to discredit him at court. 'The Lord Generall', it was said, '. . . sometime useth speech of a title he hath to all Desmond's lands and seemeth to think he hath well deserved the same, though he had no title thereunto.'[57]

The extent of the despair and the hopeless sense of isolation experienced by the Earl of Desmond was revealed in an unprecedented appeal for help to his enemy Ormond. Abandoned in the wilderness by his friends, he now turned to his enemy as the last resort.

As I may not condemn myself of disloyalty to her Majesty, [he wrote to Ormond] so cannot I excuse my faults, but must confess that I have incurred her Majestie's indignation; yet when the cause and means which were found and devised to make me commit folly shall be known to her Highness, I rest in an assured hope that her most gracious Majestie will both think of me as my heart deserveth and also of those that wrung me into undutifulness, as their cunning devise deserveth.[58]

As Black Tom could quite easily qualify for the latter category mentioned by the earl, he refused his offer to parley without first receiving Desmond's total surrender. In vain Eleanor pleaded Garrett's position with Black Tom and his abhorrence to be 'destrainte of libertie, a thing' which she well knew 'he can not indure for he acounteth it more greyvous than death'.[59] But Ormond's reply was to pursue the campaign with increased ferocity. The tally of 'traitors put to the sword'[60] mounted. Captains, galloglass, constables and kern fell at the hands of Black Tom's army. There was to be no clemency for Desmond. Rumours reached Ormond that Garrett intended to escape by sea to Spain. He penetrated deep inside the hitherto inviolate palatinate of Kerry. Through Castleisland, Castlemaine and into Dingle, Ormond's forces encountered little resistance from a people beaten by war, want and hunger and whose lord, like a wild animal, had been reduced to live in the wastelands of his lordship.

Finally, towards the middle of June 1583, Eleanor came before the Earl of Ormond and unconditionally submitted. Ormond reported to the Queen that the countess 'put her self holye to your majesties mercye', and added: 'This poer lady lamenteth greatlye the follye and lewdness of her husband whome reason could never rule.'[61] While Eleanor might well have lamented, it was perhaps not for the reason which Ormond felt obliged to report to Elizabeth, but because she had said her final farewell to Garrett, for whom she had never ceased lovingly to work and intercede. In the wild wastes of Slieve Logher, where they had taken a final refuge together, they had decided to part. He had become hampered by her presence and needed total freedom of movement if he was to continue to evade his pursuers. At least that perhaps was the excuse he chose so that she might be spared the fate that hourly awaited him. She was the mother of his heir, whose fortune and fate would require all her great reserve of energy and intelligence if something was to be salvaged from the

Desmond ruins. And she could still continue to intercede with the authorities on his behalf. Her health was beginning to feel the effects of the long years of hardship she had been forced to endure. Her durability and resilience could only be marvelled at and admired. She had withstood without protest hunger and deprivation. She had shared her husband's brief glory and long humiliation. More politically able than he, she had never openly criticised his oftentimes inexplicable behaviour and actions; instead she had worked to expose the devious plots of his relations and the shortcomings of Crown officials; and in her dealings with the Crown she had shown no little skill as a diplomat. As Garrett watched her disappear from view with the vain hope of further conciliation with the enemy or flight to the continent, the fighting spirit must have finally evaporated from his emaciated body. Without her, it would be as much as he could do to hide from the bloodhounds that were fast following behind him.

The long hunt finally came to an ignoble end within the recesses of Garrett's treasured palatinate. At the beginning of November 1583 he had run to ground with about twenty followers in the wood of Glanageenty about five miles east of Tralee in the parish of Ballymacelligot. Ironically, in view of what was about to occur, this was the country of the O'Moriartys, among whom Garrett had been fostered. His remaining galloglass captain, Goram MacSweeney, had been captured and executed by Ormond. The Earl of Desmond lay exhausted, 'concealed in a hut, in the cavern of a rock'.[62] His followers had gone to scour the barren countryside for sustenance. On the southern shore of Tralee Bay they seized a number of cattle, the property of Maurice O'Moriarty, pillaged his house and assaulted his wife. The O'Moriartys were incensed and sought the assistance of the English garrison at Castlemaine to track down the plunderers. Accompanied by six soldiers, the O'Moriartys tracked the cattle to Glanageenty. They fanned out, and one of them, Owen O'Moriarty, climbed a hill which overlooked the steep glen below. A fire flickered in the distance. As the first light of dawn on 11 November gleamed fitfully through the swirling morning mists, they attacked the camp in the glen. The guards ran for their lives. The attackers entered the cavern, where an old man was asleep on the ground beside the fire, attended by two frightened young boys and a woman. The old man roused himself. A soldier of the garrison, Daniel Kelly, lunged with his sword at the slowly rising figure and almost cut off his arm, while another hit him a glancing blow to the head. 'I am the Earl of Desmond,'[63] the old man cried out. The attackers were astounded.

They had stumbled across the most wanted and hunted fugitive in memory. Visions of the bounty offered for his capture dead or alive spurred them into action before the earl's followers could regroup and return. Kelly bound the earl and they tried to drag him through the woods. But Garrett could not walk and the wound in his arm was bleeding profusely. After a hurried conference, Kelly raised his sword a second time and decapitated the earl. With the grisly trophy clutched in his hand, Kelly and the rest hurried back to Castlemaine to claim their reward. The head was sent to Kilkenny, and Ormond forwarded the prize to the Queen.

> God of his goodness who be praised for ever hath answered your L. expectations [he wrote to the Privy Council] by cutting of that wicked member whose head I have thought good to send by this bearer to her Matie as a profe of the happie ende of his rebellion.[64]

Elizabeth eyed the head of the Earl of Desmond in death as coldly as when alive and ordered it to be impaled on London Bridge. Ormond ordered a search for the earl's body, but loyal Desmond retainers concealed the remains and later interred them in a small chapel at Kilnamanagh near Castleisland. The 'old' fifteenth Earl of Desmond was in fact aged about fifty-one at the time of his death.

Eleanor received the news of Garrett's death at Kilkenny or Cashel, where she was residing with her daughters under the protection of the Earl of Ormond. Whether she was shown the ghastly trophy as it was prepared for despatch to England is unknown. Perhaps, despite the cruel and often barbaric customs of the time, she was spared the ultimate anguish. The sense of inevitability about the outcome of the long struggle against time and the Crown, and the future daunting role yet to be played if she was to salvage something for herself and her family from the wreck, perhaps helped to ease the pain and sense of loss at Garrett's cruel end. She had done everything within her power to avert the catastrophe. Her wayward husband had become a prisoner of his pride, of his heritage and of the past, with dreadful consequences for himself and his house. As yet Eleanor had only begun to reap the bitter harvest he had sown.

'And thus', a contemporary chronicler recorded, 'a noble race and ancient familie descended from out of the loines of princes is now for treasons and rebellions utterlie extinguished and overthrowne.'[65] The dead earl had bequeathed a terrible legacy to Munster, to his wife and children, and to his dependent followers. 'And as for the great companies of souldiers, gallowglasses, kerne and the common people who followed the rebellion,' the chronicle continues,

> the numbers of them are infinite, whose blouds the earth dranke up and whose carcases the foules of the aire and the ravening beasts of the feeld did consume and devoure. After this followed an extreme famine, and such as whom the sword did not destroie, the same did consumé and eat out.[66]

The death of the Earl of Desmond closed the final chapter of the history of medieval Munster. In death Garrett inadvertently attained the greatness and prestige that eluded him during his life. For tradition and literature chose to depict him as one of the great symbolic patriotic figures of history. In a perceptive comment on the process, Seán O'Faolain has written:

> Natural tradition, reaching above individual human weakness, translated him into one whose equal was not in nobility, honour and power. It is fantastically untrue, and yet in its truth is the power and poetry of Ireland, and in its untruth her indifference to all her children whom she sacrifices ruthlessly to her needs.[67]

But the facts reveal the personal ambitions and the defects that motivated Desmond in his campaign against the Crown. The absence of any ideological nationalistic stimuli does not detract from his actions, but on the contrary helps us to sympathise and identify with the basic human urge to survive and rule that compelled him to strive against the tide of time and gave meaning to the tribalistic war-cry of his house, 'Shanid abú!'

Signature of James FitzGerald, the Súgan Earl of Desmond. (He first signed this petition 'James Desmond' but it was returned by George Carew, President of Munster, for signature as James FitzGerald).

8

The Pauper Countess

> I and my childrin have tasted of so moche
> myserie thattt I protest unto your honnor I
> knowe no waye howe to preserve me and them
> from perishing by famyne except her Matie
> do nott relieve us.
>
> Eleanor, Countess of Desmond, to
> Lord Burghley, 4 September 1585

The death of the earl and the end of the Desmond rebellion were causes for public celebration in Cork, Waterford, Limerick, Galway and Dublin. Garrett's death was hailed as a joyful deliverance from long years of turmoil and devastation. If a sense of loss and sadness was felt by the adherents of the House of Desmond, it was expressed in secret. The earl's allies one by one submitted and gladly accepted the pardons offered them by the Earl of Ormond. The galloglass and kern hid their weapons and lay low until a new leader might emerge from the ruin and require their services in a new conflict. The terrified tenantry and peasantry crept out of the woods and mountain refuges and returned to the plough to till the despoiled land and to await the arrival of new masters. 'Munster had suffered a violent upheaval, and time was needed to organise the new departure which, from the viewpoint of the state as beneficiary of the FitzGerald collapse, the occasion demanded.'[1] The Earl of Desmond, possessor of a great estate, had been slain *in flagrante bello*, and this 'was deemed and constitued an immediate attainder, in which instance the heir was irrevocably bound'.[2] Desmond's rebellion and subsequent death 'threw into the hands of the Crown the vast tracts forfeited by Desmond and his adherents and which were now to be parcelled out to new possessors'.[3] But before the spoils of victory could be distributed among the waiting freebooters and adventurers, a commission of survey was first established to determine the precise title and extent of lands claimed by the successive Earls of Desmond. The potential prize, over half a million acres of Munster, was worth the brief delay.

While the legal wrangles regarding the appropriation of her late husband's property got under way, Eleanor attempted to pick up the broken and empty pieces of her life. She was thirty-eight years old, still in the prime of life, yet with the vicissitudes and deprivations of a lifetime behind her. But her agony was not over. Her circumstances were difficult and her future uncertain. As the wife of a rebel, she could expect little sympathy for her plight. As an active participant in the rebellion, she knew that her life was in jeopardy should the full force of the law be brought to bear. She rested for a time with her daughters, under the protection of the Earl of Ormond at Clonmel, and waited for the dust to settle. She was accompanied by a few female attendants, some Desmond retainers and her confidant and friend, Morris Sheehan. Her son was still a prisoner in Dublin Castle, but arrangements to have him transferred to the Tower of London were in train—for other reasons than for the furtherance of his education, as Eleanor had initially requested. The heir to the Desmond estates might be more easily forgotten if he were concealed among the tombs of the Tower, where his sequestered existence would be less likely to trouble the consciences of those about to perpetrate a great fraud against the defenceless child. The prospect of salvaging something for her son from the ruins of his inheritance seemed remote, but Eleanor never dismissed a chance, no matter how slim, in the cause for which she had fought and schemed so desperately. Despite the antagonism of the Butlers towards her husband, Black Tom was content to allow her and her daughters to remain in sanctuary in Ormond. He urged the Crown to adopt a policy of reconciliation and to honour the pardons he had granted the rebels. 'Deal earnestlye with her highness', he asked Burghley, 'that no new devices be wrought to thrust those into a new rebellion, whiche have beehaved them selfes dutifullye and done service sins their submissions.'[4] Ormond's concern, however, arose not merely from a desire for reconciliation but from a deep-rooted sense of self-preservation.

Eleanor hoped that the reconciliatory policy preached by Ormond would enable her to recover something from the wreck of her husband's estate. With this in view, in December 1583 she solicited Ormond's assistance to secure a formal pardon for herself and her family and to lodge a claim to part of the forfeited estates. Ormond was willing to secure her a pardon and wrote to the Lords Justices in Dublin on her behalf: 'My very good LLs. the Countess of Desmond, hath beene an ernest sutor unto me to writt to your LLs for pardon.'[5] However, regarding her intention to secure part of her husband's estate, Ormond was less enthusiastic. 'She clameth', he wrote, 'to have a great porcion of therle of Desmond's lands for her joyntor.'[6] In an attempt to prohibit her from making a claim to her husband's estate, the Irish Privy Council curtly signified to Ormond 'their disapproval of any pardon to the Countess of Desmond'.[7] But Eleanor refused to be deterred and persuaded the earl to plead her case for a pardon directly to the Queen. In January 1584 she met with qualified success when the Queen notified the Dublin administration:

> We are also content that the lady of Desmond shall have
> her pardon with some such conditions annexed thereto as
> shall be thought convenient for her quiet behaviour.[8]

Elizabeth could well afford to be magnanimous in victory. A pardon was an insignificant exchange for one of the greatest prizes that had ever fallen into her lap.

By now the clamour of claims to the escheated estates had reached a crescendo, and Eleanor's own tentative approaches were pushed aside in the rush. The hordes of undertakers, adventurers, Crown administrators and soldiers who queued up for the great pay-off were joined by the remnants of the House of Desmond who sought their share. Garrett's elder half-brother, Thomas Roe FitzGerald, whose claim to the earldom had beeen disallowed in 1558 in favour of Garrett, now came forward, together with his son James, and personally petitioned the Queen to restore to them the Desmond estates, which they claimed were rightfully theirs. They further argued that since neither had supported the Earl of Desmond in the late rebellion, there was no impediment to their case. Their pleas, however, fell on deaf ears. Eleanor again entered the fray with a claim to lands in Limerick. Ormond notified the Crown of her intent. 'She claymeth', he wrote, 'to have had a conveyance from her husband afore his entering into rebellion for the most part of his land in the County of Limerick.'[9] Whether the conveyance was actually produced or not is uncertain, but her claim was taken so seriously by the Irish Privy Council that they withheld her pardon until the matter could be satisfactorily resolved.

Eleanor and her daughters were still living on charity, and their future position and welfare in Ormond had become precarious. They could not remain there indefinitely. Already Eleanor's persistent claims to the forfeited estate of her husband had embarrassed her current protector by countering his own claim to the lands. Consequently during the early months of 1584 the Council in Dublin brought pressure to bear on her to forfeit whatever claims she was reported to have to her late husband's estate. 'Before I could receive my pardon', she later testified, 'I was fayne to enter into recognizences of £10,000 that neither my self nor eny other to my use shall make tytle, challenge or entrye, to any dower, jointor or thirds of eny parte of my husband's lands.'[10] She was further obliged to agree that neither she 'nor eny of my five comfortles children shall nott departe this realme, neither can I obtayne licens to go in to England to be a petitioner to her Matie'.[11] The Council's policy of alienation, implemented against her husband with dire consequences, was to be continued against his widow and children lest the Crown should relent and deprive the waiting hordes of avaricious entrepreneurs of even a small part of the great prize. She was to be denied even the restitution of her dowry and was condemned to live on the charity of others. Ormond was ordered to provide 'a diet of 10d per diem for her self her daughters and weeman',[12] and on this meagre subsistence the Countess of Desmond and her household were expected to exist.

She was abandoned by the Gaelic world whose cause her husband had sought to champion. Few of his Gaelic and gaelicised allies wished to associate with or be seen to assist the traitor's wife. Her brother, the Baron of Dunboyne, had also deserted her in her need. The English-educated James Butler had matured in the mould of his overlord Black Tom. He had little of the sympathy or tolerance for the Gaelic world that had absorbed his brother-in-law and brought about his downfall. He had become a prominent member of the 'Old English' aristocracy, loyal to the Crown and more concerned with matters of land, title, cess and the recusancy laws than with any attempt to hold back the tide of time in defence of an outmoded way of life. For Dunboyne the enemy was not the Crown but the new breed of English adventurers whose appetite for land and wealth might not be appeased by the acquisition of merely the attainted lands of a rebel. To succour a rebel's wife and children, even one's own sister, might well be used by the enemy to discredit him with the Crown. Moreover, Eleanor had quarrelled with her brother over his refusal to yield up lands bequeathed to her by her father as part of her dowry and which she had entrusted to her brother before the rebellion. As ever, Eleanor was left with little option but to rely on her own efforts and wits in the continuing battle to survive.

For almost a year Ireland had been administered by two Lords Justices until in June 1584 Sir John Perrot eventually assumed his appointment as Lord Deputy. On his departure from England, the Queen imparted to him her usual impossible requirements for 'good' government in Ireland, which, put briefly, were 'to increase the revenue without oppressing the subject, to reduce the army without impairing its efficiency, to punish rebels without driving them to desperation, and to reward loyal people without cost to the Crown'.[13] The most pressing issue that faced Perrot was the settlement of the Desmond estates; and the knowledge of Munster that he had acquired during his term as Lord President there made him a suitable candidate for the job. In June the proposed commission to survey the escheated lands was established under the direction of Vice-Treasurer Sir Henry Wallop, Sir Valentine Browne, Surveyor-General Ashford, and two auditors. Wallop was an able property administrator, and the work of the commission progressed steadily. It is significant that, like many of his fellow-administrators in the Irish service at the time of the Desmond collapse, Wallop was richly rewarded from the escheated estates, being granted the ancient Geraldine seats of Askeaton, Adare and Croom.

Perrot's attention was initially diverted to Ulster, where he took the field against a large force of Scots mercenaries whom he suspected of being part of a plot concocted by the Scottish King against Elizabeth. After a brief but ineffective campaign, which elicited a sharp rebuke from Elizabeth against 'such rash unadvised journeys',[14] Perrot returned to Dublin and prepared to summon the first parliament since 1569.

Eleanor had alerted the Lord Deputy to her plight, and initially Perrot seemed well intentioned towards her. He ordered that she and her family should be removed to his custody and that provision should be made for them in Dublin, but appeared to be in some doubt as to what to do about her long-term future. 'We think her estate to be verie bare,' he informed the Queen, 'and much she lamenthed and desyreth to be sent over to your Matie. We have no warrant to proceide against hir by lawe, to send her over, to bayle her or relieve her.'[15] He requested the Queen 'to geve some direction concerninge her'.[16] While he awaited instructions he had Eleanor and her entourage brought from Clonmel and housed within the precincts of Dublin Castle. Eleanor's plight was indeed pressing. Without money or means, abandoned by friends and relations, she had been reduced to the status of a beggar.

> So as I and my children have lived in such calamitie [she recorded] thatt if my lo: Deputie had nott taken pittie of me and them in relevinge us owtte of his Lops: kitchin we might have starved with honger: for in my necessitie all

my kinsmen and frends have utterly forsaken me.[17]

In Dublin Castle Eleanor visited her son, then awaiting his imminent transfer to London. James was thirteen, old enough to comprehend the enormity of the tragedy that had befallen his house with such disastrous consequences for his future. For a fleeting moment Eleanor was reunited with her pitiful son, to whom she could give no tidings of freedom or hope and whose future she could only expect be be as miserable as his short past, a life sentence of captivity, darkness and exploitation. As the day of his departure loomed nearer, Eleanor pleaded with Perrot that the child should be accompanied to London by his nurse and one of his elder sisters. Little attention had been given by either side to the fate of the heir to the Desmond title. At that time, it has been pointed out, 'in Ireland men were too busy in a fierce struggle for life and lands to concern themselves about the fortunes of a child whose patrimony was gone, whose legitimate place was taken by another, and who would have been—even had the Queen left him to his fortunes—equally set aside as from his youth unfit to command in troubled times so powerful a sept'.[18] The dark vaults of the Tower closed over the child who was fated to spend sixteen long years in captivity, totally forgotten and ignored by the powers to whose care he had been entrusted. Eleanor and her remaining daughters continued their life of humiliation and despair in the Castle, defenceless and destitute and fed only by the morsels which fell their way from the Lord Deputy's table; and there they awaited the outcome of the new parliament.

Perrot convened parliament in April 1585. Twenty-seven counties were represented, mainly by the 'Old English' group. While some Gaelic chieftains were present in both houses and others were invited to attend as observers, many Gaelic-held areas were not yet represented. The city was *en fête* for the occasion, and the narrow cobbled streets were thronged with lords and chieftains and their retinues from the country. Eleanor looked on with the rest at the endless parade of Gaelic chieftains and anglicised lords dressed in their obligatory English apparel. She saw her husband's old fellow-conspirator, Turlough O'Neill, choking in the doublet and hose of his new-found allegiance, yet prepared to put on the loyal show to preserve his interests. Beside him rode the greatest single threat to his position in Ulster, his second cousin, the handsome English-educated Earl of Tyrone, the young Hugh O'Neill, who had been well rewarded for his contrived loyalty, his help in suppressing the rebel Earl of Desmond, and his share in the savagery that had subdued and despoiled Munster. Thither came Eleanor's brother, her brother-in-law the Earl of Clancar, and the former friends, allies and liege lords of her husband. They perhaps avoided the accusing eyes of his destitute widow and children as they trooped into Perrot's parliament to vote for the formal attainder of their former overlord. But Eleanor could not blame them for their sudden conversion to the Crown. As she had all along counselled her husband, survival was the key, and adaptation was the means to survive. Loyalty to an antique and doomed world was a luxury which could no longer be afforded or tolerated.

The parliament was an acrimonious one. Perrot was thwarted in every move by officials in the administration who were antagonistic towards him and by the lords of the Pale, who continued to oppose the Crown's wish to replace the old system of cess by a land tax. Perrot was opposed and failed in his attempt to enact a measure suspending Poynings' Law which, if successful, would have enabled legislation to be passed by the Irish parliament without recourse to England. Religion for the first time began to emerge as a divisive political measure. Until then the Crown had been prepared to tolerate dissent from the religious settlement in Ireland because it feared that any attempt to impose the reformed religion would lead to even greater civil unrest. 'It was more important that the Queen should rule Ireland than that Ireland should abandon the Pope.'[19] But now, with the ideological struggle between Catholicism and Protestantism encroaching on the political issues of the day, and with the power of Spain threatening her throne, Elizabeth was forced to change her ambivalent attitude to religion. Catholic Ireland was a danger to England's security. By their intervention in the Desmond rebellions Philip II and the Pope had already attempted to capitalise on this fact. While the more radical Puritan elements of both the Irish and English administrations sought the implementation of laws against recusants in Ireland, Perrot well realised that for the moment the strength of numbers ensured 'the impossibility of coercing the majority into conformity',[20] and therefore plans for the introduction of penal legislation were, for the moment, postponed. But Perrot's temporising attitude and generally pacific policy towards the Gaelic lords and chieftains, combined with his public antagonism to the more radical elements within his administration, provoked the latter's jealousy and hatred and were eventually to lead to his downfall.

In the second session of the new parliament the long-awaited bill of attainder against the late Earl of Desmond and his adherents was introduced. Whether Eleanor was involved in the subsequent attempt to prevent the attainder of her husband and have the Desmond estates returned to her in trust for her son is uncertain. However, given her astute political knowledge and her ability to negotiate and intrigue as well as the next, it is likely that she plotted and was party to this final attempt to secure that for which she had endured and sacrificed so much. To thwart potential claims to the estates, a measure was first pushed through parliament by the government which stipulated 'that all conveyances made, or pretended to be made, by any person attainted within thirteen years before the Act, shall be entered on record in the Exchequer within a year, or be void'.[21] Before the bill of attainder could be introduced, however, Sir John FitzEdmund FitzGerald rose in the chamber and submitted the original feoffment 'by which the late Earl of Desmond had placed all his estates in trust for his wife and son, at a time when he was wholly free from all taint of rebellion'.[22] There was uproar in the house. Panic-stricken potential grantees of the estates clamoured for an explanation. Sir Henry Wallop was speedily despatched to determine whether the late earl's deed of association with his adherents, signifying his intention to rebel, had been signed by him *before* the execution of the enfeoffment of his lands. If it had, then by the terms of the new act the earl was deemed to have forfeited his estate. If, however, the date of the feoffment preceded that of the document containing the deed of association, then the Crown's claim to the Desmond estate was invalid. 'In the entire collection of the State Papers of England, no document exists that was of equal importance as to its absolute correctness of date, as this one, for on none other ever depended the transfer of estates so vast and so valuable.'[23] The feoffment, as preserved among the Carew Papers in Lambeth Palace, bears the date of 10 September 1574, while the deed of association is dated 18 July 1578, four years later. Wallop claimed that the deed of association bore the incorrect date and should have read 18 July 1574, thus putting it 'seven weeks earlier than the execution of the feoffment'.[24] He based his conclusion on the contents of the first sentence of the deed of association, which reads: 'Whereas the earl had assembled his kinsmen and others after his coming out of Dublin . . .'[25] This, he contended, referred to the earl's escape from detention in Dublin in November 1573.

Given the extent of the fortune that depended on the issue, as well as the anxiety of the Crown and the avaricious expectations of the waiting undertakers and speculators, it is not beyond the bounds of reason to suspect the authenticity of Wallop's evidence. It certainly seems strange that the matter was only raised in the first place because Sir John FitzEdmund FitzGerald, who had been a signatory to the deed of feoffment, was convinced that a miscarriage of justice was about to be perpetrated against the Countess of Desmond and her son. Throughout the duration of the Desmond rebellion FitzEdmund had been a model of loyalty to the Crown and had dissociated himself completely from the rebellion of his kinsman. He explained his actions regarding the feoffment to Sir Francis Walsingham as having no ulterior motive other than a sense of justice and fair play: 'I thought it my parte to tell, onely in discharge of my conscience and honestie before God and the worlde, not as a thinge I wished allowed.'[26]

FitzEdmund's efforts were doomed to failure. Parliament accepted Wallop's theory, and the final attempt to prevent the forfeiture of her husband's estates and title came to nought, leaving Eleanor and her children abandoned and, in view of her undoubted support of FitzEdmund, ostracised by those in power. Had she succeeded, then 'the vast estates of the earl must have slipped through the fingers— matchless for their tenacity—of Her Majesty, and a multitude of enterprising English gentlemen must have returned home'[27] empty-handed. The act of attainder of the Earl of Desmond and his chief supporters 'and the vesting of their lands, without inquisition, in the Crown'[28] was passed without a whisper of protest from the Gaelic and gaelicised chieftains and lords present, much to the delight and relief of the potential colonists who now lined up for the division of the spoils.

After the attainder of her husband and the confiscation of his estates, the fortunes of the countess and her family rapidly deteriorated. Perhaps to punish her for her attempts to prevent the forfeiture, Sir John Perrot withdrew his assistance, and Eleanor and her young daughters were thrown into the streets of Dublin and onto the charity of anyone touched by their plight. Most of her acquaintances resolutely turned their backs on her. However, Eleanor still retained her insight into the political arena and her ability to exploit the many factions and coteries that it contained. She turned for help to Perrot's implacable enemy, Adam Loftus, the Archbishop of Dublin, who agreed to alert the Crown to the extremity of her circumstances in Dublin.

> I assure you [he wrote to Burghley] hir case (being chargid with childrin) is so miserable that seldom the lyke hath bene sene in a woman of hir calling. All hir frends ... have quite forsaken hir: so as if yor L, with the rest of that

> honorable board, be not a mean to hir Matie, to grant unto
> hir some portion to releive hir and hir childrin, there is no
> doubt but that shortly they all will goo a beginge.[29]

But the government was slow to come to the aid of one who had
almost successfully denied it the ultimate victory and spoils in
Munster. The cold unfriendly streets of Dublin held more terror for
Eleanor as the winter drew near than the wastelands of Munster. She
was heavily in debt to the merchants and traders of the city. Her
credit was fast running out. The desperation of her plight as she
scrounged food and clothing for her needy and hungry children she
conveyed in her own letter to Burghley:

> I and my childrin have tasted of so moche myserie thatt I
> protest unto your honnor I knowe no waye howe to
> preserve me and them from perishing by famyne except
> her Matie do nott relieve us.[30]

But winter came and went without any assistance from the Crown.
With her ragged, frightened children clutched around her, she
tramped the streets of Dublin in search of sustenance. In a city that
had recently felt the effects of a famine for which her husband was
blamed, few doors were opened to her, and the faces of the citizens
were as cold as the icy winds that blew through the narrow streets.
Once again she wrote to remind Burghley of her wretchedness and
poverty:

> At the present time my miserie is such that my children
> and myself liveth in all wante of meat drinke and clothes,
> having no house or dwellinge wherin I with them may
> rest, neither the aid of Brother or kinsman to relieve oure
> necessitie which is so myserable that I see my poore
> children in manner starve before me.[31]

Eleanor's desperate appeals for charity were ignored in London. The
memory of her husband's rebellion and of her personal involvement
in it were still vivid at court, where antagonism to anyone connected
with the Desmond cause still ran deep. Walsingham had never
favoured the Earl of Desmond or his house, and his dislike of Garrett,
greatly magnified as a result of his rebellion and association with
England's enemies, was transferred to his widow. Memories of the
effects of the rebellion were constantly recalled, as in December 1585

when the Crown rewarded the Earl of Desmond's executioner, Daniel Kelly, 'in consideration of his having slain the traitor Desmond'.[32] The Queen incessantly bemoaned the vast amounts expended in the suppression of the rebellion. And as the extent of the damage and devastation of the forfeited Desmond estate became apparent, there were growing doubts as to whether forfeiture of the land would ever recompense the Crown for the outlay it had expended in securing it.

But Elizabeth was also confronted with more urgent and important issues in England which diverted her attention from Ireland and from the pleas of an impoverished rebel countess. Around her the tempo of national and international intrigue had reached a crescendo. Plots against the security of her realm and conspiracies against her life daily ebbed and flowed with the political tide of events. A plot among English Catholic gentry, aided and abetted by the Spanish ambassador to England, to assassinate her had earlier been uncovered. The plot hinted at the involvement of the Queen's cousin, Mary Stuart, who despite being kept under close confinement in Sheffield, continued to scheme against her cousin with unrelenting enthusiasm, conspiring with the King of Spain, the Pope, the Duke of Guise, and her son James VI of Scotland. Mary attracted the attention of the international conspiracy which sought Elizabeth's overthrow and death. Every scheme had hitherto been unsuccessful; nevertheless, Mary, who 'seemed to thrive on adversity and derived renewed hope from every defeat',[33] persevered. As the prospect of war with Spain grew ever more likely, and the plots against Elizabeth grew more desperate, Protestant feeling in England, both among the people and in the parliament, against Mary Stuart and her foreign Catholic fellow-conspirators grew more angry. Puritan opinion demanded her head, and Elizabeth's counsellors advised her that she was sheltering within her kingdom 'the daughter of sedition, the mother of rebellion, the handmaid of iniquity and the sister of unshamefastness'.[34] But Elizabeth had constantly refused to permit the execution 'of a divinely ordained sovereign ... it set a dangerous precedent'.[35] During 1586, however, Mary exceeded her previous indiscretions in a reckless new plot against the Queen. This time the wily Walsingham had baited the trap and gathered the necessary evidence. Elizabeth was left with little option but to sanction the trial and execution of her cousin. But before that momentous event Philip of Spain finally made up his mind 'that the retribution of heaven upon the heretic and monstrous Queen of England had been too long deferred'.[36] He considered Elizabeth's imminent downfall to be God's expressed will, and himself to be the chosen instrument to put that will into effect. Elizabeth and her subjects, on the other hand, believed that England was the final bastion of hope for the world against the insidious incursions of the Catholic confederacy led by the Pope, the King of Spain and the Catholic faction in France, driven by the lust for power of the Medici and their Valois dynasty. 'The odds had been taken, the sides drawn, and Europe waited and speculated on which of them, Elizabeth of England or Philip of Spain, was the shining messenger of the Lord.'[37] It was not surprising that the welfare of a countess of the realm, no matter how destitute and deprived, received little attention in the midst of such critical affairs.

For Eleanor the crisis facing herself and her children was as important as Philip's designs on England. Rebuffed at every level, in May 1586 she again solicited the help of Archbishop Loftus, who agreed to write to the government on her behalf. The archbishop's appeal was blunt. He could himself vouch for the countess's extreme necessity, he told Burghley, and

> could not resonably denye, being an eye witness of her extreme mysery ... to make knowne ... how in truthe she standeth at this Prsnt: being not hable to sustaine her selfe or her poore children with necessary foode, but are ... lyke to famishe if her Matie do not grant bestowe some portion upon her for her relayfe.[38]

But, as before, the archbishop's request failed to get a response.

Eleanor was now at her wits' end. She faced the prospect of prison as her bills mounted and the merchants and money-lenders clamoured for payment. Secretly she prepared to embark for England in a last-ditch attempt to plead her case at court. But she was prohibited by law from leaving Ireland without special licence from the Lord Deputy. She had, moreover, signed bonds, which had been guaranteed by members of the Munster aristocracy, to that effect. Undeterred, however, during the latter months of 1586 she begged and borrowed from every available source to fund her mission. But some of the lords who had guaranteed her bonds, like Viscount Roche of Fermoy, who was bound for the sum of £100, grew uneasy about her intentions. They urged her to reconsider her proposed flight to England. She refused. Finally Lord Roche alerted Lord Deputy Perrot to Eleanor's plans. He begged Perrot that, in view of his dutifulness, his own bond of £100 should not be forfeited. Perrot's cryptic reply did little to relieve his anxiety. 'Touching the countesse of Desmonds going into England,' wrote the Lord Deputy, 'yt is more than I knowe, neither can she goe without licence from me so to doe, which she is not like to have.'[39] But before Eleanor could attempt her escape to England in early 1587, her plight was finally brought to the attention of the Queen, who decided that 'the Countess of Desmond should have a pension of one hundred pounds Irish'[40] and ordered Sir John Perrot to pay her. On the strength of the promised pension, Eleanor obtained additional credit from the Dublin merchants to feed and clothe herself and her children, though, as she later divulged, 'I owe duble for everything I hadde.'[41] Her indebtedness to the merchants increased as Perrot declined to pay her the pension out of his administrative costs. Her situation was indeed desperate. 'Her creditors (being not paid of their former debt) would no further lett her have meate, drinke nor any other necessaries.'[42] Eleanor could take no more. Towards the end of 1587 she managed to obtain a passage to England; she departed, leaving her daughters in care in Ireland.

She made her way to London, and for the following twelve months she followed the court in the same state of abject poverty and debt as she had endured in Ireland. Even if she had the means to influence or bribe those in power to gain access to the Queen, political developments made an audience virtually impossible. Throughout the early months of 1588 rumours of an imminent invasion by Spain preoccupied Elizabeth and her Privy Council. After months of speculation the great Spanish Armada lumbered into the English Channel 'to visit the censure of God upon a middle-aged female'.[43] Despite ample warning, England was ill-prepared to meet the challenge. All through the summer, as Elizabeth moved her court from place to place, Eleanor followed patiently in her wake with her petition. She had to maintain a low profile. Passions and prejudices had been aroused in England against the Catholic Spanish threat to which her name in the past had been linked. The court bustled with frantic activity as messengers hourly brought despatches with the latest reports on the sea battles in the Channel, and the Queen and her counsellors held lengthy meetings on matters of state and security. But Eleanor persistently and patiently waited her chance. She had become used to isolation, hostility, humiliation and poverty and the quiet resignation that such conditions induce. She had been somewhat encouraged by Burghley, who had looked on her presence kindly enough, though he could as yet spare little time to examine her case in detail.

She meanwhile contrived to visit her son in his lonely cell in the Tower. What memories must have come flooding back as she traversed the self-same passages to be reunited with her son as she had done to be reunited with his father some twenty years previously. She found James in great distress from an ear ailment which was being treated by the prison physician without much success. His general health had, not surprisingly, remained fragile. The damp and stale air of the Tower did little to relieve the general malaise that had afflicted him since birth. He had become both institutionalised and anglicised, a passive prisoner of his unnatural life, nervous and apprehensive lest he incur the displeasure of those in charge of him. His later correspondence is proof that Eleanor's concern regarding his lack of a formal education had been rectified by the authorities. A schoolmaster, with a salary of £13 13s per annum, had been appointed to educate the young prisoner. He was taught to express himself well and to write in a bold clear hand. His literary style, taking into account his youth and lack of experience of the world, was frequently 'very superior to that of the statesmen to whom his letters were mostly addressed'.[44] There was little else Eleanor could do for her son who seemed lost to her and to the world.

When the Spanish Armada had finally disappeared towards the North Sea, eventually to be battered and broken on the jagged, unfriendly rocks of the Irish coast, Elizabeth resumed her more mundane duties. She agreed to receive the Countess of Desmond and hear her petition. Eleanor had her audience with the Queen at St James's Palace in early October 1588. Elizabeth wore her fifty-five years well. After the glorious repulse of the Spanish threat she appeared every bit the

> Goddesse Heavenly Bright,
> Mirror of grace and Majestie divine,
> Great lady of the greatest Isle, whose light
> Like Phoebus lampe throughout the world doth shine [45]

of Spenser's *Faerie Queene*. Elizabeth could still dazzle her subjects into love and loyalty by the very radiance of her attire. It was irrelevant to her adoring subjects that the famous red hair was now a red wig; her ruddy complexion was liberally aided by the application of rouge and rice powder; and the regal presence that emanated from her slight frame owed much to the sheer opulence and weight of her wardrobe. Good Queen Bess had saved her subjects from a fate worse than the fires of the Inquisition, and now more than ever 'she could still marshal words and command emotions'.[46] And there was little competition or threat to her looks, wardrobe or majesty from the

A signed petition from Eleanor to William Cecil, Lord Burghley, Secretary of State (above). 1597.

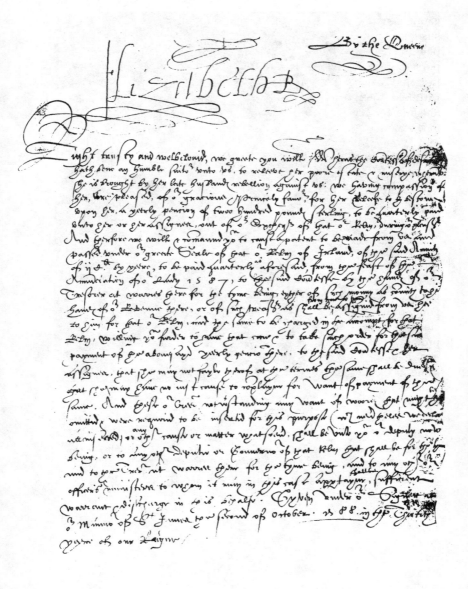

A letter signed by Queen Elizabeth I, to Sir William FitzWilliam, Lord Deputy of Ireland, with instructions for the payment of a pension to Eleanor, Countess of Desmond, 1588.

gaunt, tattered, dispirited countess who knelt before her to beg for sustenance to provide herself and her family with the bare necessities of life. Sheer pity alone would have moved Elizabeth to loosen her purse-strings. And as Eleanor explained the extremity of her situation in Ireland and how the Queen's previous pension of £100 had been withheld from her, Elizabeth's sympathies were undoubtedly aroused. She immediately forwarded new instructions to her Lord Deputy:

> Wee having compasson of hir unhappᶦe and miserable estate whereunto she is fallen, rather by hir said husband's disloyaltie, than by anie hir owne offence, are pleased for hir owne reliefe to bestowe on hir a yearely pension of two hundreth pounds sterling to be paid to hir quarterly out of our excheqr of that realme.[47]

But past experience had made Eleanor suspicious of the Crown's servants and the way in which they dealt with the instructions they received. She reminded the Queen that her previous order to the Lord Deputy and Council in Ireland for the payment of her pension had gone unheeded. Elizabeth consequently despatched a personally signed and sealed letter to her officials in Dublin, commanding the prompt payment to Eleanor of her pension so that, as she stated, 'she may have no just cause to complayne for want of payment of the same'.[48] But bureaucracy seemed destined to thwart even the Queen's orders. For an addendum to the Queen's letter subsequently noted that payment of the pension was to be for some months 'stay'd upon a doubt moved by Mr Soliciter'.[49] Meanwhile, her mission apparently accomplished, Eleanor unsuspectingly returned to Ireland in high expectations of some measure of respite from the misery and misfortune to which she seemed destined to be forever subjected.

On her return she found that Sir John Perrot had been recalled and that Sir William Fitzwilliam had succeeded him as Lord Deputy. But the change in personnel brought little relief to Eleanor, for she found Fitzwilliam's administration as reluctant as its predecessor to comply with the Queen's instruction concerning her. By December 1588 she had received only part of her pension from the Council in Dublin, and she therefore decided on a different course of action. She requested the English Privy Council that she might be paid her pension out of the English rather than the Irish exchequer. The Queen was agreeable, and accordingly in early 1589 Eleanor, accompanied by her daughters, Morris Sheehan and a small retinue, departed for England and settled near Westminster. But there were other reasons besides the receipt of her pension that lay behind her decision to move to England.

The dismemberment of her late husband's estates had begun. The lands to be planted were among the richest in the south. It was originally the intention of the Crown that seignories or chief grants not exceeding 12,000 acres were to be created for the principal grantees, or undertakers as they became known. But wily lawyers contrived to extend the grants for their clients beyond the proposed limits, and many grantees, notably Sir Walter Raleigh, ultimately became owners of estates of over 40,000 acres, much more than had been intended by the Crown. The principal grantees were required to plant their estates with English tradesmen. The grants were made in socage, with a head or quit rent payable to the Crown. The plantation was widely advertised in England as a great opportunity to acquire an estate and fortune at little cost. The native Irish were prohibited from becoming tenants or undertenants of the new proprietors. However, the initial aims of the Munster plantation were gradually distorted and undermined. The majority of the undertakers became absentees. Their estates were managed by agents who readily employed Irish tenants. Ireland's reputation for political unrest and racial turmoil deterred the more suitable English farmers, who refused to be lured by promises of wealth to such a wild and unstable country. But the hardened veterans of Grey's expeditionary force showed little such hesitancy and eagerly grasped the spoils of war. In Counties Waterford and Cork Sir Walter Raleigh and Sir Christopher Hatton received large estates. Sir Edward Denny, Sir Warham St Leger, Sir Thomas Morris, Hugh Cuffe and the poet Edmund Spenser all received attainted Desmond land and property in Co. Cork. In Co. Limerick the main beneficiaries were Francis Berkeley, Sir William Courtney, Richard and Alex Fitton and Sir George Bourchier, while Edmund Fitton received over 11,000 acres in Counties Waterford and Tipperary. The long bloody hunt to extinction of the former proprietors had been vindicated and the pursuers had reaped the rewards. But no provision was made for the widow and heir of the attainted earl. A burning ambition, however faint the hope, to yet salvage some part of the forfeited lands was responsible for Eleanor's latest move to England. Residence in London would enable her to petition her case directly rather than try to negotiate through the unfriendly and antagonistic administration in Dublin.

She also sought more regular access to her son James, still a prisoner within the Tower. The conditions of his confinement there, as with many of his fellow-prisoners, allowed him 'the libertie of the

Tower ... and accesse of all his friends'.[50] By a special warrant dated 28 July 1590 Eleanor was granted access to her son, whose health was again giving cause for concern. As well as a physician, he now required the services of a surgeon, while the list of medicines supplied by the Tower apothecary grew at an enormous rate:

ii Bottels of serope of iii pints apeace
ii pourgatives
iiii ownces of perfumed lossengis for his nostrells
iiii ownces of serope for his nostrells
iiii ownces of Unguente for his eare
iiii ownces of Implaster for his eare
iiii ownces of pilles of Masticgini
ii drames of pillemics
i drame of Trossecs deterra sigillata.[51]

These were just part of the list of pills and potions prescribed for the various maladies that wracked his unhealthy physique.

It was while she was in London that Eleanor first made the acquaintance of the man who was to occupy the central place in her future life. This was Donogh O'Connor Sligo, then at court to petition the Queen for the restoration of his title and estate as the heir of his uncle, Sir Donal O'Connor Sligo, who had died in January 1588 and whose estates had been seized by the Lord President of Connaught, Sir Richard Bingham. In their past misfortunes and present straitened circumstances, Eleanor and Donogh had much in common.

The family of O'Connor Sligo were a branch of the royal house of the O'Connors of Connaught and were genealogically connected with Rory O'Connor, the last high king of Ireland in the twelfth century. The earliest historical references to the O'Connor sept of Sligo occur at about the time of the Norman invasion. In the succeeding centuries, following a series of dynastic feuds, the O'Connor clan split into three permanent divisions: O'Connor Roe, O'Connor Don and O'Connor Sligo. The O'Connor Sligo sept eventually settled in the area roughly equivalent to present-day Co. Sligo. A member of the sept bore the title King of Connaught between 1318 and 1324. By the sixteenth century the O'Connor Sligo was the acknowledged overlord of the area. But O'Connor dominance in Sligo was dependent on the O'Donnell chiefs of Tyrconnell (Donegal), who claimed a suzerainty over Sligo. Owing to internal difficulties in Tyrconnell, the O'Donnells were from time to time unable to put their claim over Sligo into effect, but the threat always remained for the O'Connors, who constantly sought, through alliances with the O'Donnells' enemies, to cast off the shackles of O'Donnell dominance. To the south-west of Sligo lay the lordship of the Norman de Burgos or, as they had become, the MacWilliams, the Lower MacWilliam of Mayo and the Upper MacWilliam of Galway, the latter of whom had been created Earl of Clanrickard by Henry VIII.

Sligo occupied a strategic position between Ulster and Connaught— a circumstance whose significance, as the sixteenth century drew to a close, was not lost on either side. Donogh's lordship technically incorporated the barony of Carbury, with Sligo town as its central point. He claimed the castles of Sligo, Ballymote and Collooney. Sligo castle had a chequered ownership, and it was to feature prominently in the subsequent war between the Ulster chiefs and the Crown. It was consequently to protect themselves from the heavy exaction of the O'Donnells that the O'Connor Sligo turned for help to the English administration which was beginning to extend its influence into Connaught. Donogh's uncle, Sir Donal, had in 1568 made an indenture with the Queen which he interpreted as a reaffirmaiton of his overlordship of Sligo but which the Crown later claimed related to the overlordship of the barony of Carbury only. However, the grant from the Crown allowed him to maintain his rights of overlordship of the county, and the Crown tended to support him in his struggle against the O'Donnells. The agreement between O'Connor Sligo and the Crown worked well until it was suddenly jeopardised by a dramatic but not unexpected change in the political climate. This new dispensation was emphatically marked by the arrival in Connaught of Sir Richard Bingham as Lord President of the province in 1584.

succeed Sir Nicholas Malby as President of Connaught. While Perrot adopted a mainly conciliatory policy towards the chieftains and lords of the province, Bingham's policy was that of the sword. Bingham was a stern military campaigner who carried out his orders to the letter. He perceived his duty to be the extension of English law into all parts of Connaught in the shortest time possible, allowing little scope for the Gaelic chieftains to adapt. The divergent policies pursued by Perrot and Bingham were bound to bring them into conflict. One of the first incidents to spark off their latent mutual animosity involved Donogh O'Connor Sligo. Bingham began his campaign in Connaught by seizing the O'Connor Sligo castle of Ballymote, ostensibly as a precaution against an invasion by Scottish supporters of Mary Queen of Scots. But Bingham also recognised the advantage of securing a strong foothold in Sligo and thereby controlling the pass from Ulster into Mayo and the rest of Connaught. Sir Donal appealed to London

and went personally to see Perrot in Dublin in 1584, where the Lord
Deputy issued him with letters patent officially confirming the
original agreement signed with the Queen, though excluding
Ballymote and twelve quarters of land. In the following year Perrot
concluded the famous Composition of Connaught, whereby in lieu of
cess a rent of ten English shillings or one Irish mark was introduced
on every quarter of arable land containing 120 acres in the province.
Certain lands were allowed rent-free to principal lords, but their
positions as elected heads of their traditional dependent clans were
abolished, and each chieftain was made responsible for his own sept
and agreed to hold his estate under the English law of primogeniture
instead of in accordance with the Gaelic custom of election. In
relation to Sligo, the Composition 'merely put into formal feudal
language the terms of the earlier agreement'[52] between Sir Donal and
the Lord Deputy. Sir Donal continued to hold his estates of the manor
of Ballymote and was granted all his lands free of the Composition
rent. On his death in 1588, despite the seizure of Ballymote and Sligo
by the Crown, his heir Donogh seemed likely to inherit a substantial
lordship.

Sir Richard Bingham, however, refused to recognise Donogh as his
uncle's legal heir. 'The heir is base born and illegitimate,' he wrote to
the Earl of Leicester, 'and the land, especially Sligo itself, by descent
and lawful inheritance is now thrown into the lap of Her Majesty.'[53]
Although a commission of inquiry subsequently found Donogh to be
the legitimate heir, Bingham persisted in his opposition and moved
his brother, George Bingham, into Sligo castle. While the dispute
raged on, ships of the Spanish Armada came crashing in upon the
Sligo coastline, and rumours reached the English court that the
Spaniards who had survived were planning to invade Connaught in
support of the Ulster chieftains. Possession of Sligo castle took on an
added significance, and the question of Donogh's right to inherit was
again investigated. In an attempt to persuade the Crown to reinstate
him and to repudiate the accuations of the Binghams, Donogh took
his case to the English court. It was there that he became acquainted
with the widow of the famous rebel Earl of Desmond, who had come
to court on a similar mission to plead her case for a pension and
some portion of the attainted estates of her husband.

The similiarity of their status at the English court, coupled with the
fact that the success of both their petitions depended greatly on
whatever patronage and influence was extended to them by Lord
Burghley, was perhaps instrumental in establishing a bond of
friendship between them. Both were exiles, political outcasts, in poor

circumstances and without friends. Of the two, Eleanor's position was the more extreme, especially in terms of her future financial and political expectations. Donogh, while presently regarded as politically dispensable by the English interest in Connaught, might soon become a vital factor to the Crown—and this possibility increased as the months passed by and the situation in Ulster deteriorated. But meanwhile both had to endure the tedious and slow court procedures regarding their petitions. With little money to speed or influence the process, they had little option but to assume the patience and humility of the penniless and the powerless. And the weeks stretched into long futile months of waiting and hoping for redress as they hesitated awkwardly on the outer fringe of the court circle, unwelcomed and ignored. There is no evidence to suggest that their relationship at this stage was anything more than that of fellow-sufferers and friends.

Both initially made little progress with their petitions. Eleanor's pension was not readily forthcoming from the tight-fisted admini-stration, while Bingham continued to press the Crown against the reinstatement of Donogh in Sligo. Eleanor mainly resided in London near Westminster and, being unable financially any longer to follow the court to plead her case, settled under the care of a widow, Alice Pynnock, who, it was recorded, was paid the sum of £85 'for the diet of the Countess of Desmond'.[54] Together with her pension and inheritance, Eleanor also sought further concessions from the Queen. By her entry without licence into England she had in effect transgressed the conditions of her pardon and had 'therby forfeited certain bonds wherein she is entered for the performance of the clause'.[55] The Queen eventually agreed to overlook the transgression and ordered the Lord Deputy to ensure that any future bonds made for her continuing good behaviour 'should not be hurtful or prejudicial unto her for that which is past'.[56] Slowly, over the years, Eleanor was beginning to experience some semblance of toleration if not favour in court circles. Her old enemy Walsingham was dead, and Sir Robert Cecil had joined his father, Lord Burghley, at the forefront of Elizabeth's administration. The younger Cecil was willing to extend a little sympathy and understanding to the long-suffering countess from Ireland. The brilliant, delicate, hunchbacked statesman became her main refuge and hope.

While Eleanor's fortunes at court seemed likely to improve as the years passed, the expectations of her friend, Donogh O'Connor Sligo, also seemed likely to bear fruit. In 1596, as the political situation worsened in Ireland, the Crown considered it expedient that Donogh should return to Ireland and be restored to part of his inheritance. For the 'civilising' hand of English education had begun to wear thin on England's supposedly loyal earl, Hugh O'Neill of Tyrone. From the fastness of his Ulster kingdom he noted Bingham's savage chastisement of Connaught, where the Mayo Bourkes, after three unsuccessful attempts to restore their ancient rights, had been ground into submission and their hired Scottish mercenaries butchered and drowned on the banks of the Moy. He watched Bingham's advance into Sligo and his unrelenting campaign against O'Rourke of Breffny, who had sheltered some Spanish castaways from the ill-fated Armada.

Alarm-bells sounded in the cunning, pragmatic mind of O'Neill as Bingham attacked Maguire's lordship of Fermanagh, the last remaining bastion of O'Neill's hitherto impregnable kingdom of Tyrone. The shadow of the dead Earl of Desmond might well have returned to haunt O'Neill and remind him that the bitter fate he had helped to bring down on Desmond faced him now in Ulster. But it was still too soon to show one's hand. There were too many intangible obstacles yet to be overcome before his great plan could be put into operation. Despite the suspicions of the English administration in Dublin, he must continue to appear Elizabeth's loyal and loving earl. He consequently bawled like a child before the Council in Dublin and tearfully protested his loyalty on old Fitzwilliam's shoulder to stifle the charges that he was involved in a conspiracy with Spain and Scotland against the English Crown and to absolve himself of the murder of his kinsman, Hugh Gaveloch O'Neill, a contender by right of Gaelic law for his position as chief of the O'Neills. But in December 1591 he helped to effect the dramatic escape of his relation and future ally, the young Red Hugh O'Donnell, whom Perrot had imprisoned in Dublin Castle as a hostage for his father's loyalty in Ulster. O'Neill sought to mould the red-hot lust for revenge of the young Tyrconnell chieftain and the seething general discontent of the Gaelic chieftains of Ulster into a watchful, calculating patience until the time was ripe for confederacy and rebellion.

While O'Neill played a waiting game, Red Hugh attempted to reassert O'Donnell supremacy over Sligo, extend his power and influence further into Connaught, and seek or extract support there for the forthcoming war with the Crown. Sligo was the key to success in the conflict, and both sides realised its strategic importance. The methods employed by Bingham in the province were called into question as officials in the administration in Dublin, jealous of his success in Connaught, attempted to have him removed from office.

O'Donnell was eager to take advantage of Bingham's misfortune and raided unhindered through Sligo and Roscommon. In 1595 he seized Sligo castle, which was garrisoned by the Lord President's brother, and thereby achieved unhindered access into Connaught. It was against this background of events that the English government, in a bid to stop O'Donnell's growing power in Connaught, decided that Donogh O'Connor Sligo should be reinstated in his lordship forthwith 'in the hope that he could be used as a buffer against the commonwealth which O'Donnell appeared to be creating in Connaught'.[57]

Donogh returned to Ireland in 1596, while Eleanor remained on at her lodgings in Westminster. While Cecil had managed to have her pension restored to her, with directions that it should be paid at quarterly intervals, in the long term it seemed unlikely that her financial position would improve significantly. A pension of £200 per annum would hardly restore her to a lifestyle that befitted her rank and status. Furthermore, despite Cecil's intervention on her behalf, it continued to be paid sporadically at the whim of petty officials in Ireland and England. Her petitions to Cecil continued in the same vein as before. 'My great wants and extremities, the daily dearness of victuals ... urges me to be more troublesome,'[58] she wrote to him in May 1597 in an attempt to secure a more permanent cure for her financial straits. If Cecil could not secure her part of either her jointure or the estate of her late husband, Eleanor requested that he act on her behalf as matchmaker. She explained that she was willing to extend her offer 'to any in England or Ireland that would be pleased to marry either myself or my daughters'.[59]

Her request was not as extraordinary as it might appear. She was now over fifty years old and had endured widowhood for fourteen years. The political stigma attached to her name was gradually receding, although her distinct lack of a fortune or dowry did not enhance her matrimonial prospects. But fortune took a hand to find her a mate. Cecil was at this very time seeking, by the establishment of a network of marriage alliances in Connaught, to create an opposition among the local aristocracy to stem the growing support for the confederacy of Ulster chieftains. He had already successfully concluded a marriage alliance between O'Connor Sligo's sister, Maeve, and the prominent chieftain of the Mayo Bourkes, Tibbott-ne-Long, the youngest son of the redoubtable sea-captain and pirate, Grace O'Malley. The marriage had produced satisfactory political results, and the former rebel chieftain looked likely to adhere to the Crown in the coming conflict with O'Donnell. It would appear that

Cecil considered that a marriage between Eleanor and Donogh would serve a similar useful purpose, while having the additional advantage of removing from the court a persistent petitioner whose humbled estate was a constant reminder of the Munster tragedy.

It was arranged that Eleanor would return to Ireland. Cecil had already secured the restoration of her estate in Munster which her brother had withheld from her. The Queen also wrote on her behalf to the Lord Deputy

> to signify unto you our good liking of the retourne into the realme of the Countess of Desmond, for the opinion we have conceived of her good and lawful behaviour, towards us and our state, so we have now bin pleased to confirme the same unto you by those our own letters. . . . We require you to yealde unto her your favourable assistance in all her lawfull good causes as she may from time to time stand in need thereof and agreeable to the degree she holdeth.[60]

Cecil also obtained freedom of movement for her between Ireland and England. Cecil's diplomatic wizardry and Eleanor's persistence had finally achieved a small but, from Eleanor's point of view, significant victory.

In September 1597 Eleanor and her daughters prepared to leave for Ireland. On her departure she acknowledged Cecil's kindness towards her and showed her appreciation as best her circumstances would allow. She presented him with a gift of an Irish harp 'humbly praying you to accept the same, the rather that the sending comes from a thankful mind'.[61] Then, with a lightened burden and the hope of better fortune, Eleanor set sail for Ireland and a new beginning.

King James I whose court Eleanor visited as a petitioner.

Hugh O'Neil, Earl of Tyrone meets the 2nd Earl of Essex, 1591.

9

The Chatelaine

Hecuba: Fortune veers: be brave,
   Sail with the stream,
   Sail with the wind of fate.
   Do not run your ship of life
   Headlong into the billows of disaster.

   EURIPIDES, *The Trojan Woman*

Casting aside the mask of loyalty and co-operation, Hugh O'Neill, Earl of Tyrone, had revealed his real designs by 1595. Throughout his career his actions had been ever stimulated by his driving ambition for greatness and power—objectives which had once appeared attainable by loyalty to the Crown, but which now seemed more likely to be achieved by espousing the cause of Gaelic Ireland, which he had initially sought to destroy. In February 1595 he sent his brother Art to capture the Blackwater fort, which he had formerly helped the Crown to establish. He was proclaimed a traitor in June, and on the death of the old chieftain, Turlough Luineach, he assumed the Gaelic title of 'The O'Neill'. With his young ally, Red Hugh O'Donnell, he set about establishing an effective unified opposition to England's expansionist designs in Ireland. To this end the Ulster lords re-established communications with the Spanish court, not merely for gold and ammunition, but for that which Desmond had earlier sought, an effective Spanish force to support the proposed rebellion in Ireland. And Spain seemed eager to assist in a new campaign in Ireland against England. But even as the ships and supplies assembled at Cadiz in June 1596 England's sea-dogs, Essex and Howard, destroyed them in a daring attack on the port. A further attempt later in October fell foul of the weather. O'Neill had to buy time, and he and O'Donnell therefore renewed negotiations with the Crown. The Queen, ever anxious to pardon rather than become involved in expensive warfare, accepted the excuses. Secretly they continued to conspire with Spain. In an attempt to extend the association, they called on 'the gentlemen of Munster' to join the Ulster confederacy and to 'make war with us'[1] in a final desperate attempt to preserve the remnants of the Gaelic world. The Munster patrimony of her late husband and the Sligo lordship of her new husband were destined to become part of the concluding chapter of the long saga of Gaelic resistance of which Eleanor had such bitter experience.

On her return to Ireland from the English court, Eleanor married Donogh O'Connor Sligo. She was then about fifty-two years of age, while her new husband would appear to have been a few years her junior. Donogh was a sober, solid chieftain, not given to the wild excesses of his contemporaries, but more concerned to seek to consolidate his position and his estates than to engage in active rebellion against the Crown. While socially it could be said that she had married beneath her status, her marriage to O'Connor Sligo was a welcome respite from the years of misery, loneliness and ignominy she had endured since Garrett's rebellion and death. Moreover, from a personal point of view, the marriage seems to have been a happy one. She continued to be referred to as the Countess of Desmond and adhered to the active and independent role she had adopted throughout her life. She obtained possession of the small estate in Tipperary which her brother had earlier sought to withhold from her, and together with her new husband she journeyed to Munster to inspect her domain.

Her new home was to be her husband's lordship of Sligo, which the Queen had restored to him with the exception of the castle and lands of Ballymote. But on their arrival there they found the lordship had been overrun in their absence by Hugh O'Donnell, who still retained possession of Sligo castle. Eleanor and her husband initially settled at Collooney castle, from where Donogh made vain attempts to stem the ravages perpetrated on his estates and on the estates of his tributary lords, such as the O'Harts and the various O'Connor septs, who expected his protection against the exactions and rapine of O'Donnell. Donogh in turn depended on the Crown to protect him from O'Donnell, and in particular looked for help from the English administration in Connaught. But after Bingham's suspension in 1596 the Connaught administration had almost collapsed and was unable to meet its obligations to the Gaelic lords who sought its protection. Consequently many of the lords who had sided with the Crown and were willing to administer their estates by English law were forced to align with O'Donnell.

In December 1596, however, Sir Conyers Clifford was appointed Chief Commissioner of Connaught (he was subsequently promoted to the vacant post of President of the province in September 1597). Donogh had become acquainted with Clifford at court and was at hand to welcome him at Galway and accompany him on a tour of the province. His friendship was rewarded when Clifford recaptured Sligo castle and installed Donogh there with a garrison. Donogh reciprocated by inducing his brother-in-law, Tibbot-ne-Long, the most powerful chieftain in Mayo, to make terms with the Crown. Tibbott had become disenchanted with O'Donnell's bid for supremacy in Mayo, and he had become further alienated from the Ulster confederacy when O'Donnell had imposed his own candidate for the highly prized MacWilliam title against the wishes of the Mayo Bourkes. Tibbott controlled a fleet of galleys, previously operated by his mother, the indomitable Grace O'Malley. Clifford and O'Connor Sligo combined with their new ally to expel O'Donnell's MacWilliam from Mayo and left Tibbott in sole command there.

The new Lord Deputy, Thomas Lord Burgh, carried the fight against the confederacy into Ulster. He recaptured the Blackwater fort and established a garrison there. Clifford meanwhile, with the assistance of O'Connor Sligo, simultaneously attacked Ballyshannon castle, but was forced to retreat to Sligo. Clifford could do little but establish Donogh at Sligo castle and hope that he could hold out against O'Donnell until further assistance could be had from England.

While her husband strove to hold his position in Sligo, Eleanor was embroiled in a legal battle with her brother, the Baron of Dunboyne, over possession of the disputed estate in Tipperary. Despite the Crown's grant of the lands to her, the baron sought to have his sister's right contested by law. During the course of 1598 she journeyed to Dublin and to Tipperary to prepare her case against her brother. In the intervals she resided at Sligo and became acquainted with her husband's political friends, foes, family and relations. Once more she found herself surrounded by intrigue and conspiracies of the type that she had experienced in Munster. The political situation was moving to a climax. Messengers from O'Donnell and from Clifford each urged her husband to a different side in the coming conflict, while spies from both sides reported their every move. No one could be trusted. Allegiances changed as quickly as the tide, and today's friend could be tomorrow's foe. Eleanor became acquainted with her husband's sister Maeve and her enterprising husband, Tibbott-ne-Long, the son of her late husband's former prisoner, Grace O'Malley. The famous female sea-captain and pirate still lived on in Mayo and like Eleanor had successfully petitioned the Queen for sustenance and protection. At the present time both she and her son favoured the Crown as a less evil option than to endure the exactions of O'Donnell. But, as Eleanor well realised from bitter experience, the loyalty of the minor lords and chieftains to either side was transitory and depended on the ebb and flow of the political tide. Just as Garrett had expediently, for his political survival, sacrificed Grace O'Malley to the Crown, so had he a few months later eagerly sought and obtained the support of her husband and her sept in his rebellion against the Crown. But such was the political reality of sixteenth-century Ireland, where even the latest confederacy against the Crown was motivated by a desire for personal and political gain rather than any real sense of patriotic duty.

With the position in Sligo at apparent stalemate, Donogh received letters of recommendation from Clifford to Sir Robert Cecil, the Queen's secretary of state, for the restoration of the castle and lands of Ballymote. Eleanor and Donogh went to Dublin, where he embarked for London. Eleanor remained in Dublin to prepare for the impending lawsuit with her brother. The baron demanded that her right to the disputed estate should be tried by common law, but, as she explained in a petition to Sir Robert Cecil, 'to be tried by a jury of the citizens of Dublin where her brother is more favoured than she'[2] could hardly be deemed justice. She requested instead that her case should be determined by the Irish Privy Council or in the Court of Chancery, where she felt there would be less bias against her. Cecil agreed to have the matter further investigated, but political events once more intervened as Ireland was plunged into a rebellion that threatened to engulf the entire country.

In August 1598 Sir Henry Bagenal, with an army of over 4,000 men, was sent north to relieve the fort on the Blackwater. O'Neill, O'Donnell and Maguire combined to defeat him decisively at the battle of the Yellow Ford. The result of the battle transformed the campaign of the Ulster chieftains. 'A wave of feeling that was like one vast geyser of long-suppressed discontent', as Seán O'Faolain described it, 'gushed up and smothered the colonists until within a few months Tyrone was virtual master of Ireland and could see the outline of a rapidly forming confederate army.'[3] But if the exultant feeling was to persist and have effective results, it would take time for the yet unfamiliar notion of nationhood to penetrate the fiercely independent minds of the multitude of chieftains and lords who feared and saw in the aims and ambitions of O'Neill and O'Donnell merely an attempt to subject them and rule over them. Already in

Sligo and Mayo the peremptory actions of O'Donnell had alienated the principal lords there. It was difficult for O'Connor Sligo or Tibbott Bourke to see any exalted nationalist motivation in the plundering raids of O'Donnell on their territories.

In Munster, however, the effects of the victory were instantaneous and opened a new chapter in the death-struggle of the House of Desmond. And Eleanor as wife and co-conspirator of the last earl could not fail to become involved as the survivors of her late husband's family grasped the life-line thrown to them by O'Neill. Garrett's nephew, James, the son of his disinherited half-brother Thomas, rose up out of the ashes of despair and defeat to lay claim to the estates and title of his uncle. Eleanor's reaction to the claim was bound to have been antagonistic. Quite apart from the position taken by her husband in the present conflict, she retained her hope that her son would be restored to at least some part of his father's estate. The adherents of her late husband shared her view and referred contemptuously to James FitzThomas as the Súgán (straw-rope) Earl. But with the support of O'Neill, the cowed and dispossessed liege lords of Desmond rose up, if not in support of the claims of FitzThomas, then in support of the only apparent means to wreak their vengeance on the usurpers of their former lands and to regain their hereditary patrimony. With the assistance of O'Neill's captains, they ravaged and plundered the terrified colonists. The confederacy spread. O'Neill's son-in-law, Viscount Mountgarrett, together with the Earl of Thomond's brother, the Baron of Cahir, and the Kavanaghs of Leinster, swiftly joined with O'Neill. The former Geraldine fortresses of Newcastle, Shanid, Adare, Pallas and Tarbert were hastily abandoned by the new owners, who fled bag and baggage back to England, never to return. Edmund Spenser, burned out of his estate at Kilcolman, conveyed the sense of horror and misery of the colonists:

> Out of the ashes of desolation and wasteness of this your wretched Realm of Ireland, vouchsafe to receive the voices of a few most unhappy ghosts of whom is nothing but the ghost now left buried in the bottom of oblivion.[4]

But there was no immediate relief forthcoming from the Crown. And the Desmond adherents, after sixteen years of repression and confiscation, took a bitter and bloody revenge and showed the planters little mercy. Black Tom, the Earl of Ormond, was once again given the task of suppressing the new Desmond revolt. Sternly he warned FitzThomas:

We need not put you in mind of the late overthrow of the
earl your uncle, who was plagued with his partakers by
fire, sword and famine; and be assured, if you proceed in
any traitorous actions, you will have like end.[5]

But the new Geraldine leader had grown tired of waiting for the
Crown to reward him for his long loyalty and for his opposition to his
late uncle. Lack of reward and a renewed ambition now made him a
willing ally of O'Neill. But in the terminology of the rebellion he
replied to Ormond that 'Englishmen were not contented to have our
lands and livings but unmercifully to seek our lives by false and
sinister means under colour of law.'[6]

Events in Desmond could not fail to attract Eleanor's attention and
involve her in the claims and disputes over the estates and title of her
late husband. And there were many imponderable and intriguing
aspects to the political scenario there. The Súgán Earl claimed the
estates as the heir of Garrett's disinherited brother. But the Crown had
recognised Garrett as the legal heir. In the field of politics, and given
the financial constraints of the day, recognition of legal title was a
matter of expediency. If the rebellion in Munster got out of control,
Elizabeth might well consider the restoration of James FitzThomas as
the most expedient and least expensive way to end the conflict. The
claim of Eleanor's son, the legal heir, under lock and key in the Tower
of London, could easily be ignored. On the other hand, if O'Neill
could be convinced that her son could, if free, more effectively unite
the Geraldine factions in rebellion against the Crown, then her
aspirations for her son's restoration might be better realised by
supporting the rebellion. And the rumours were flying of a plot by
O'Neill to free the young heir from the Tower. It was said that O'Neill
had employed the services of some of the Munster aristocracy, loyal
to the late Earl of Desmond and with access to his son in the Tower,
to effect his escape. The Privy Council acted on the rumour and
apprehended Maurice FitzGibbon, the eldest son of the White Knight,
and confined him to the Gatehouse in Westminster. It would certainly
have been a dramatic coup if O'Neill could miraculously produce the
almost forgotten heir of Desmond and restore him as the leader of the
rebellion in Munster. With her penchant for politics and her
obsession to have her son restored, Eleanor was irresistibly drawn
towards the complicated web of intrigue and subterfuge that
tantalisingly held out such a hope.

On his return from court in the late summer of 1598, Donogh
joined his wife in Munster. Their presence there amidst the intrigue

and turmoil sounded the alarm-bells in Dublin Castle. The Irish administration anxiously protested to the English Privy Council:

> We understand that O'Connor Sligo ... is aryvid in Mounster and remayneth here with his wife the Countess of Desmond. We cold have wished that he had have staid longer in England consideringe the general unsoundness of the Irishry here and how apt they are to run with each other into disloyaltie.[7]

But in the event O'Neill settled for what was attainable in Munster and backed the claims of the Súgán Earl as the most expedient way to extend the rebellion in Munster. Meanwhile in Sligo, O'Donnell took advantage of Clifford's inability, through lack of supplies and a sufficient army, to extend his control over Sligo. He captured and established his headquarters in Donogh's castle of Ballymote and re-established his MacWilliam nominee in Mayo, while Tibbott-ne-Long was forced to flee and live on his ship anchored off the Mayo coast. Donogh and Eleanor, on their return home, settled at Collooney to await developments.

Since the death of Lord Burgh in October 1597 Ireland had been without a Lord Deputy, and Elizabeth deliberated long over the appointment of a successor. The situation required a strong, steady, trustworthy military leader. But in an ill-advised and impetuous personal decision, of the type which revealed her frequently flawed judgement, the Queen conferred the even more prestigious position of Lord Lieutenant on her current favourite, the temperamental second Earl of Essex. The young, headstrong earl considered the post simply as a means to enhance his reputation at court and to display his courage before an infatuated sovereign. On 15 April 1599 he arrived in Dublin with an army of 14,000 soldiers to confront the rebels, who were said to have a force of over 20,000. Accompanied by Eleanor, Donogh hurried to Dublin to renew acquaintance with the Lord Lieutenant, who had befriended him at court and whose father Eleanor had reason to trust in the past. Donogh accompanied Essex on a hosting through Munster and then returned to Sligo to attempt to hold his ground against O'Donnell. Eleanor remained on in Dublin, where she succeeded in obtaining husbands for two of her daughters. Margaret, her eldest, married Dermot mac An Dubhaltaigh O'Connor Don, a mercenary leader of some repute from Co. Roscommon. Katherine, her third daughter, became the wife of her cousin Maurice Lord Roche. It was a considerable achievement on Eleanor's part to find suitable partners for her daughters, given the political taint on their pedigree and their distinct lack of a dowry or marriage portion, which in sixteenth-century Ireland was considered an essential part of the marriage contract.

On Donogh's return to Sligo he was promptly besieged at Collooney by O'Donnell, who sought to expel him as a supporter of the Crown from the last remaining fortress which commanded the pass into Connaught from Donegal. It was also vital to English interests in Connaught that O'Connor should retain possession of the castle. Consequently Essex ordered Sir Conyers Clifford to relieve him, and sent an urgent request to O'Connor's brother-in-law, Tibbott-ne-Long, to bring ordnance and supplies in support by sea to Sligo. Clifford, the Earl of Clanrickard, O'Connor Don and an army of 2,000 soldiers marched towards Collooney. On 5 August 1599 they attempted to cross the Curlew mountains but were defeated with heavy losses by O'Donnell's forces. Clifford was killed in the battle, and his corpse was decapitated. O'Donnell came before Collooney castle, where the siege was still in progress, and displayed to Donogh the head of his friend. O'Donnell promised that if Donogh surrendered the castle, he would restore him to his chieftaincy and provide him with cattle and supplies. It was subsequently reported to Essex that O'Connor Sligo submitted to O'Donnell because he, being 'under the tyranny of the other, will think any bargain good for him if it bring assurance of life and recovery of lands'.[8] But Donogh had little option but to surrender to O'Donnell. The Crown had proved unable to protect him, and in his present difficult situation discretion appeared the better part of valour.

Unfortunately Donogh's submission had not allayed the suspicions of the Ulster chieftains that both Eleanor and he were in league with the Crown. Eleanor's preference in the troubled field of Munster politics naturally favoured the side which proposed to advance her son's prospects; up to the present time O'Donnell in particular seemed more inclined to back the cause of the Súgán Earl. There was, of course, no love lost between Donogh and O'Donnell. The hostility between them was deep-rooted and of long duration. 'I have never slept quietly since you came into Ireland', O'Donnell was reported to have said to Donogh, 'for fear of you and your draughts.'[9] O'Connor's every move was monitored by O'Donnell, and it was only with extreme difficulty and great stealth that he managed to maintain contact with Eleanor in Dublin. He secretly conveyed letters to her by way of his trusted servants James Crean and Mulroney Oge. 'I thought good to write these few lines to you', he explained to her in September 1599, 'to let you understand that I received no answer of the last letters I sent you by Mulroney Oge.'[10] He informed her that he was being closely guarded by O'Donnell, who at a meeting with O'Neill at Lifford had with great reluctance allowed his ally to have temporary custody of Donogh. During his sojourn with O'Neill he had become godfather to the Ulster leader's young son, Shane. But despite the attempts of the Ulster chieftains to cajole or intimidate him into aligning himself with them, Donogh would give no commitment. His preference continued to be for the Crown. But the English administration in Ireland had become unable to extend the necessary support and protection to him and the many minor Gaelic chieftains, who appeared to be unwillingly falling one by one under the dominating influence of O'Neill and O'Donnell. Donogh had little option but to try to keep his head and play for time. Through his secret correspondence with Eleanor, however, the Crown could be made aware of his true allegiance. To indicate his restricted position, he pointedly sent her four blank sheets signed with his name which he asked her to deliver to the Lord Lieutenant and Council. He urged her to hurry to him at the first opportunity so that, as he stated, 'I might confer with you of matters that I dare not write, fearing the way'.[11]

As reports of her husband's capitulation circulated in Dublin, Eleanor requested permission from the Council to go to him, 'under pretence', as the ever-suspicious officials recorded, 'to give him advice and to hold him sound in heart to the state'.[12] Permission was refused, and the Council instead proposed 'to let slip the bishop his uncle who hath been always fast to the state'.[13] The bishop in question was the unscrupulous chameleon of intrigue and double-dealing, Miler Magrath, the Archbishop of Cashel. Despite the suspicions of the Council, there was little reason for Eleanor's loyalties to incline, at his juncture, towards O'Neill and O'Donnell. In advancing his own cause in Munster, O'Neill seemed determined to espouse the cause of the Súgán Earl at the expense of her son. And there is no evidence to suggest that, as FitzMaurice had at least claimed to do three decades earlier, James FitzThomas sought to preserve the earldom in trust for the lawful heir. On the contrary, he unequivocally asserted his right to the title and estates, which he claimed 'of long time hath been wrongfully detained from me and my father who by right of succession was lawful heir to the earldom of Desmond'.[14] At the same time the Dublin administration was taking no chances whereby the Countess of Desmond could, intentionally or otherwise, be drawn further into the intrigue. Eleanor refused to be deterred in her quest for the restoration of herself and her family, and amid the panic and war of words she slipped out of Dublin and made her way north to her husband to see for herself if the situation there could be turned to their advantage.

The Earl of Essex spent twenty-one weeks in Ireland, and under his ineffectual leadership the power of the Crown reached its nadir, while the Gaelic confederacy grew from strength to strength. Totally unopposed, O'Neill toured Munster and propounded the more lofty aims of the rebellion as a struggle to the death for the liberty of all Ireland from the English Crown. Meanwhile his ally, O'Donnell, ran riot in Connaught and compelled the vacillating chieftains there to support his cause. From England, the Queen berated Essex and ordered him to confront the rebel O'Neill in Ulster. But apart from meeting in private with the rebel chief—an incident which was later to be used to discredit him in England—Essex achieved little. His many enemies at court made the most of Essex's indiscretions as they plied the Queen in his absence with rumours about his supposed disloyalty and intrigue with O'Neill in Ireland. On hearing of this, the impetuous Essex deserted his post and fled to the side of his Gloriana to defend himself. But there was no favouritism with Elizabeth where money and the security of the realm was concerned. She promptly imprisoned her errant protégé and finally set her mind to the task with which she had temporised for so long. The reconquest of Ireland could no longer be postponed.

The new formula for success centred on two people: Charles Blount, Lord Mountjoy, a straightforward, determined military man, who succeeded the ill-chosen Essex as Lord Deputy, and Sir George Carew, a wily political manipulator, who was appointed Lord President of Munster. Both arrived in Ireland in the early months of 1600. The military abilities of the one, combined with the deviousness of the other, were finally to bring Gaelic Ireland to its knees. Mountjoy contended that the total destruction, both economically and militarily, of O'Neill's lordship was the only way to overcome him. Carew's job was to loosen O'Neill's grip on Munster by destroying the Desmond alliance there. With this end in view, he was to bring his Machiavellian capacity for intrigue and subterfuge to bear on the complex political situation in the province. And he had rich and fruitful pastures in which to sow the seeds of discord and dissension. The pawn he chose to use in the game of deception and strategy was the young man who as yet lay unsuspectingly entombed and forgotten behind the forbidding walls of the Tower of London.

Many schemes presented themselves to the unscrupulous mind of Carew. He cleverly set about exploiting every facet of the unstable and divided Gaelic society by pandering to the greed, fear and ambition of the principal actors. 'We hold it a very good piece of policy', he stated, 'to make them cut one another's throats, without which this kingdom will never be quiet.'[15] First he attempted to involve Eleanor in a plot against James FitzThomas, the Súgán Earl, though he hastily abandoned this plan when it was rumoured that Eleanor and her husband were in league with O'Donnell in Connaught. Carew next turned his attention to Eleanor's daughter, Margaret, the wife of the mercenary leader, Dermot O'Connor Don. Dermot commanded an army of over 1,500 men in Munster, supposedly in the pay of O'Neill. Carew learned of Margaret's opposition to the Súgán Earl and of her determination that her brother should be restored to the title and estates of his father. Carew enlisted her help in a plot whereby her husband, for the sum of £1,000, would capture FitzThomas and deliver him to Carew. To further sow dissension among the confederates, Carew was to write a letter to FitzThomas to make it appear that he had conspired with him to kill Dermot O'Connor. This letter was then given to Dermot and was represented as having been intercepted on its way from Carew to James FitzThomas. Dermot subsequently captured FitzThomas, ostensibly in O'Neill's name, displayed the fraudulent letter, secured his prisoner at Castle Lishin, near Charleville, and secretly alerted Carew. But before Carew could take custody of the prisoner, a large force of rebels under the command of Piers Lacey rescued FitzThomas, and when the plot was discovered Dermot was forced to flee into Connaught. But despite his dramatic escape, the tide of the war seemed to flow against the Súgán Earl, and his supporters gradually deserted him. He had little hope of immediate assistance from O'Neill, who was being harried without respite by Mountjoy in Ulster. After a heavy defeat by the garrison of Kilmallock, like his uncle before him the Súgán Earl took to the woods and mountains of Munster to await the promised aid from Spain. But anxious to destroy completely the Desmond alliance and its usefulness to O'Neill, Carew conceived a crafty project which, if successful, would transfer the allegiance of the Desmond adherents from O'Neill to the Crown. In order to put his plan into operation, Carew produced both his trump and his pawn in the person of Eleanor's son James.

Little had been heard from or about the young Geraldine since 1593, when in a plaintive letter to Sir Robert Cecil he described himself as

an unknowne stranger who though young in years, yet

being old in miserye ... being born the unfortunate son
of a faulty father. I have never since my infancy breathed
out of prison—the only hellish torment to a faithful hart
to be houlden in suspect when it never thought upon
offence.[16]

His long prison confinement had left its mark on the young Desmond
heir. The feebleness of his physical constitution was mirrored in his
timid and shallow personality. There was little fight or vision in the
young man, nor any sense of personal destiny, only a nervous and
ingratiating desire to do his captor's bidding. Carew's proposal was to
restore the legal Geraldine heir to the Desmond title and a small
portion of his father's estate. Not unnaturally, this plan was greeted
with little enthusiasm by the Queen, who had expended so much to
subdue and destroy his father. Cecil, although generally supportive of
the idea, voiced the Queen's fears to Carew. 'Much ado we have had',
he wrote, 'to persuade her to have him sent, because she feareth that
when he shall be there, it is not unlike but he and his cousyn [James
FitzThomas, the Súgán Earl] may be reconciled.'[17] Cecil, however,
used his influence with the Queen, and in the autumn of 1600
preparations were set in train for the return of the forgotten Geraldine
to Munster.

There is no evidence to suggest that Eleanor was involved or even
aware of the preparations and plans for her son's return. She was at
this time in semi-captivity at Ballymote castle, where she lay ill, when
news of her son's arrival in Munster reached her. But the happy
tidings of the fulfilment of her main ambition were tinged with
disappointment. To prevent the formation of a Carew-inspired
conspiracy between her son and her husband, O'Donnell imprisoned
Donogh on Lough Esk. There he was 'so cruelly kept in prison that
were it not for my soul's safety I would wilfully have ended my days
... my legs being almost rotted with the fretting of the irons'.[18]
Eleanor nevertheless looked forward with understandable anticipation
to some communication from her son. But there was no letter or
messenger from him. Carew watched and spied on his every move,
and in any event James seemed incapable or unwilling to undertake
anything contrary to the wishes of his handlers.

It was during this time that Eleanor became further involved in the
current political manoeuvrings by her promotion of a matrimonial
match between her daughter Joan and Hugh O'Donnell. Whether to
effect her husband's release, or to have the Ulster chieftains back her
son rather than the Súgán Earl in Munster at the expense of the

Crown, she agreed to the alliance. She subsequently sent her servant and confidante, Mary MacShee, 'who served her at and ever since the rebellion of her husband and in whom she reposeth her greatest trust',[19] with letters to her daughter Joan with O'Donnell's proposal. She told her daughter that she was to return with Mary MacShee by the way of 'Thomand to Clanrickarde to Tibbott-ne-Long and so to Sligo',[20] thus giving rise to speculation of a wider-based conspiracy. Mary MacShee duly made the journey to Limerick and delivered her mistress's letters to her daughter and to other contacts there. But the wily Carew had Eleanor's servant under surveillance and bided his time to see if his young Geraldine charge would reveal any knowledge of her visit to his sister and the contents of his mother's letter. And Carew was not disappointed for 'at the end of three days the Earl related to the President that such a woman was in Towne',[21] though he insisted that she had brought no message to him from his mother, but only to his sister Joan. Carew arrested Mary MacShee, who under interrogation revealed 'that the especiall cause of her coming was to convey away the said Lady Joane to her mother and from thence to O'Donnell who had promised to consummate a Marriage with her'.[22] Upon examination by Carew, Joan acknowledged the fact, but insisted that she had never intended to yield to her mother's command without the advice and consent of her brother, whom, she vowed, she had been about to acquaint with the details of her mother's letter. To deter further intrigue, Carew had Joan committed under restraint to the house of an alderman in Limerick, while Mary MacShee was made a close prisoner in Limerick jail.

The entire episode, from beginning to end, was testimony to the undercover scheming and deception that shrouded the actions of both sides during the period, with Carew the principal manipulator of every cut and thrust of the political sword-play. The true motivations of Eleanor and the other involved parties are difficult to ascertain, as the surviving records are mainly derived from sources close to Carew, who seemed at times to lose himself in the depth and extent of his own duplicity. In Carew's opinion, the entire episode masked a wider and more devious conspiracy against the Crown, involving not only O'Donnell but also the supposedly loyal lords of Connaught like Donogh O'Connor Sligo and Tibbot-ne-Long Bourke of Mayo. Of Eleanor's part in the affair, Carew reported to the Crown that

> The old craftie Countesse, understanding that this complot was discovered, pretended that her indeavours in seeking to effect this Marriage tended to no other end but

to reduce O'Donnell to be a subject, although indeed there was nothing lesse meant.[23]

Eleanor's son was reported by Carew to have been 'grievously offended with his mother, that would deal in a business of that weight and so nearly tending to his subversion'.[24]

A further incident occurred during this time which would add substance to Carew's theory of the existence of a wider conspiracy. Carew requested Dermot O'Connor Don, who since the abortive plot against the Súgán Earl had remained in Connaught, to return to Munster to support his brother-in-law, the official Earl of Desmond. Carew issued O'Connor with a safe pass out of Connaught. As he moved south with a small armed force, he was apprehended and killed at Gort, Co. Galway, by Tibbott-ne-Long Bourke, who protested that he slew O'Connor as a traitor to the Crown. Carew, however, dismissed his protestations and accused him of conspiracy with O'Neill, O'Donnell and O'Connor Sligo in a bid to extend support for the rebellion in Munster either by compelling the Earl of Desmond to their cause or, failing that, by ensuring that there would be no Gaelic support forthcoming for him or for the Crown in Munster.

Amid the storm of accusations and counter-accusations that followed both incidents, Eleanor never actually met her son during his brief and tragic stay in Munster. In fact she was never to see him alive again. His brief involvement in the affairs of Munster had ended in a sad anticlimax. His initial reception in the province as the lawful Geraldine heir had been encouraging. As Carew had anticipated, the very presence of the young earl seemed sufficient to draw the crowds away from the Súgán Earl. At Youghal and Kilmallock they flocked in their thousands to welcome the rightful heir of Desmond. At Kilmallock particularly he was greeted by a large multitude 'as if they came to see him whom God had sent to be that comfort and delight, their souls and hearts most desired'.[25] And as was reported, 'They welcomed him with all the expression and signs of joy, everyone throwing upon him wheat and salt as a prediction of future peace and plenty.'[26] But when the anglicised Geraldine displayed his religious preference by attending a Protestant service, Carew reported to the Crown that he became an alien overnight among his people and asked to be allowed to return to England. 'So far is his humour and religion different from the Irish as he thinks all time lost which is spent among them,'[27] Carew assured Sir Robert Cecil. After that, his usefulness to the Crown's cause in Munster rapidly receded; and with no further political use for the unfortunate earl, Cecil ordered his return to England, with a promise to find him a suitable bride there and to bestow on him a small allowance. But after a brief sojourn of nine months in semi-captivity in England, James died at the age of thirty in mysterious circumstances in the Tower. Notice of his death was brief. 'I have buried according to your direction my Lord of Desmond,' his doctor reported to Cecil in November 1601. 'His necessary charges for his lodging in my house, my counsel unto him, his physic taken and funeral charges I have in a bill ready to show.'[28] In death as in life, the last Earl of Desmond seemed destined to be a drain on Elizabeth's purse-strings, as bills for the services and necessities provided for him during the last months of his life continued to be submitted to the Crown after his death.

The death of her son grieved Eleanor greatly, as it would any mother, and perhaps her grief was made more bitter by feelings of guilt. From his infancy James had been used by both his parents and by the Crown as a political pawn in a momentous game of survival. He had been abandoned by his parents in order to appease their tormentors, who in turn had turned the child against them, his heritage and his natural environment. There could never be a real and trusting relationship between Eleanor and her son, no matter how much she schemed and sacrificed for his restoration. Her actions for his welfare had been determined both by political circumstances and by her belief that his safety and future political prospects could be guaranteed in the custody of the Crown. Such an attitude towards his upbringing had contributed to his alienation from his parents. She could never hope to be reconciled with and accepted by an offspring who had been reared and educated to abhor and deny all those objectives for which she had suffered and schemed. Perhaps with a little more Desmond fight and pride and a little less subservience, James, like the Earl of Ormond, could have survived the great political transition in Ireland and demonstrated to his English captors that his presence in Munster was vital to their policy in Ireland. But, unlike his father, James had no great passion or pride in his ancestry, and in the final analysis he did not belong to Ireland at all; ironically and tragically, he was more at home in the captivity of his adopted country.

Four of his sisters and his servant, William Power, remained on at Cork and petitioned the English Privy Council for additional subsistence and for 'p'curing Her Majesty's most gracious goodness towards them for their reasonable matching there or here'.[29] Regarding the future of their sister Joan, the Privy Council agreed in August 1601 'to set her at liberty again as she was before, referring the care of her well doing to some of her sisters that they may have an eye over her'.[30]

The final episode in the Crown's long war against O'Neill and O'Donnell, and in the even longer war between Gaelic Ireland and her old enemy, England, drew to a ominous close. While Carew schemed and bullied the Geraldine adherents into gloomy submission in Munster, Mountjoy wreaked havoc against O'Neill and O'Donnell in Ulster. The policy of devastation and spoliation that had been successfully used against the Earl of Desmond two decades earlier seemed likely to succeed again in Ulster. 'Our only way to ruine the rebels', Mountjoy advised, 'must be to make all possible waste of the means for life, but', he added significantly 'if we be not supplied out of England, we shall as well starve ourselves as them.'[31] The policy of destruction was carried on without respite throughout the year 1601 and allowed the Gaelic leaders no time to harvest or to replenish stocks vital to the campaign. At the same time Mountjoy established well-provisoned forts in the areas he subdued and backed the land campaign with a naval operation led by Sir Henry Docwra, who landed behind O'Donnell's lines with an army of 4,000 men at Lough Foyle. There was little O'Neill or O'Donnell could do but grimly hold out and wait for the promised aid from Spain. In Munster the Súgán Earl was captured by his erstwhile ally the White Knight and delivered to Carew. He was sent to the Tower, where he subsequently died 'in his lunacy'[32] in 1607.

Finally on 21 September 1601 an army of 3,800 Spanish soldiers, under the command of Don Juan del Águila, landed at Kinsale and by the end of October had been completely surrounded by Mountjoy and his army. O'Donnell assembled his forces at Ballymote castle and on 2 November set out on a long and heroic march to Kinsale. Eleanor and her husband were still held in confinement by O'Donnell, who left a garrison at Ballymote to deter them from any last-minute action on behalf of the Crown. O'Neill deliberated at length over his position and eventually at the end of November joined his ally at Kinsale, in the knowledge that the coming battle would in effect seal his fate and the fate of Gaelic Ireland, whose cause he claimed to champion. In Mayo Tibbott-ne-Long finally displayed his true allegiance to the side which he hoped would restore him to the power he had forfeited to O'Donnell and his puppet MacWilliam; he gathered his clansmen and hastened south to join Mountjoy's forces. O'Connor Sligo could do little but await the outcome of the decisive battle and, like so many of his kind, be prepared to accept and to seek terms from whichever side emerged the eventual victor. For such chieftains, and indeed for everyone in Ireland, the implications of the coming battle were enormous. For the struggle that was fought out at Kinsale was far more than a mere military engagement with tactical objectives. With O'Neill and O'Donnell rested the hopes that Gaelic Ireland could continue to exist as a real entity. A victory at Kinsale for Mountjoy, on the other hand, would destroy the power and influence of the Gaelic confederacy, remove the fear of foreign intervention, and pave the way for the effective completion of the English conquest. But even if victory had been with the Gaelic confederates at Kinsale, it is doubtful whether the ambitions, jealousy and tribalism inherent in their antique world could ever have been erased and the fierce individuality of the many chieftains and lords moulded into loyalty to one single person or to one political entity. It is noteworthy that, apart from a brief period under the kingship of Brian Boru in the eleventh century, there had never been a unified Ireland.

England's victory at Kinsale at the end of December 1601 put the final touches to the Tudor reconquest of Ireland. O'Neill returned to an Ulster devastated by famine and opened negotiations with the Crown. O'Donnell departed to Spain in the vain hope of reviving Spanish interest and support for the Gaelic cause. Elizabeth, in the last years of her long and eventful reign, had lived to see her ambition in Ireland fulfilled, though at immense cost.

News of the defeat trickled through to Sligo as the remnants of O'Donnell's army, under the leadership of his brother Rory, made their way back to Ulster. Eleanor heard of the defeat of the cause which two decades earlier had wreaked such havoc on her life. The cause of Gaelic Ireland held a strange and fatal attraction for those who allowed themselves to be sucked into conspiracy after conspiracy in its defence. Already rumours of O'Donnell's imminent return with help from Spain kept the fires of resistance aglow in Sligo. Rory O'Donnell, by alleging that the government's policy in Connaught was 'to dispossess the principall men of their lands and livings and to get the same unto her Majestie's hands',[33] managed to induce Donogh O'Connor Sligo and Tibbott-ne-Long Bourke to oppose the advance into Sligo of an army commanded by Sir Oliver Lambert. But Lambert evaded the ambush they had planned for him and reached the town, which he found virtually destroyed. Rory O'Donnell again compelled O'Connor Sligo in August 1602 to help him in the last recorded victory of the campaign against the Crown when they routed a substantial English army at the place of Clifford's defeat three years previously. But the collapse of the cause and fortunes of Gaelic

Samples of signed correspondence from Eleanor to Sir Robert Cecil, Secretary of State.

right honorable as I am, but alwaies most thankfully acknowledge your honorable favo. — For wch I crave pardon in that I presume to be troublesome unto yow in your great and waightie affaires wth that wch I am still afflicted wth. Synce my [illegible] I have continually sustained great troubles and charges in followinge my suites, Albeit that by her Maties gratious letters and my good Lo: yor fathers honorable meanes I have obtained the possession of some small quantitie of Lande wch my Lo: my father bestowed on me in [illegible] of my porcion at the tyme of my marriage, as by the evidence thereof may appeare. The said Land beinge by me putt in trust to my Lo: my brother the Lo: Baron of Donboynes [illegible] at the beginninge of the Desmonds warres before the which my husband was proclaimed, his Lp hathe ever since detained the same from me. Upon the restoringe of me into the possession, It hath pleased the LL. Justices to referre the triall of my right therin to the common Lawe where to be tryed this next Michaelmas terme by a Jury of the Cittizens of Dublin, whome in respect that my brother is more favored in his lande of ffreeholde, and a [illegible] inhabitant to the said Cittie, And that I am taken as a stranger there, and of small habilitie, I feare I shalbe oppressed. In consideracon whereof I humbly beseeche yor honor as yow have alwaies dealt most honorably for me. Soe nowe yt may stande wth yor good pleasure to be a meane that I may speedely have the most honorable the LLs. of the Councells letters in my behalfe unto the LL. Justices and Councell there, bothe to stande favorable unto me and to call backe my said suite, that the hearinge and determininge thereof may be before them at the Councell table or in her Highe Courte of Chancery havinge to that effect in other letters humbly besought my good Lo: yor fathers furtheraunce. And for that I am not hable in regarde of my longe suites and great necessities (havinge not assurance as an house to rest in) to sustaine the great wants of my many poore daughters whom I have hitherto staied from troublinge her Matie hopinge I might have ben hable in some sorte to helpe them, whoe by their and such as seeme to frend them doe much blame me for restraininge them all this tyme from suinge unto her Matie for relief, they nor I havinge none other under god unto whom wee should relie, but onely unto her highnes gratious goodnes. In tender regarde

whereof I most humbly beseeche yor honorable favo and remembraunce as occasion shall serve, bothe of them and me Beseechinge the Almightie God to preserve yor honor. I humbly take leave. Dublin the [illegible] of July 1598

Yor honors most humble

E. Desmond

Eleanor to Sir Robert Cecil, Secretary of State.

Right honorable I do make yo[ur] honor finde by my
maonie importunities the true nature of a miserable
creature, who like to a sicke boddie seeketh all coorses
to recover his impayred healthe, so fareth it w[i]th me
who do not shaddowe it either in mynde or body
(but am the true substaunce it selfe) continuall
call uppon yo[ur] honorable favoure that it woulde
please you to procure soome ease of comforte to
my longe languishinge spent. And since it
hath stoode w[i]th yo[ur] good likinge amongst numbers
of the rest of my presumptions for to take into
yo[ur] hands the mediation unto hir most sacred
Ma[jes]tie of my detts (though in soome discretions
the importuninge thereof might be forborne
I haveinge receaved such a demongstration of
hir highnes so greate inclyminge mercy towards
me and yo[ur] worthines to whom I will acknowledge
to owe much services) yet my creditors troublesom
clamors drieven by these extreamities do so
afflicte me that though I cannot but much be
ashamed to press yo[ur] honor, yet knowinge th[a]t
it is a charge i[tha]t must grine to be concluded
in and maye goe uppon the reckninge of that
accomp[t]e that hir Ma[jes]tie in hir princely clemency
will finde my necessities to require (If I shall be
so happy to be imployed in hir service) I humbly
beeseech yo[ur] hono[ur] to procure hir highnes order
therein, and to pardon my maonie presumptions
in whatsoever wherein I have beene overtroublesom
And so in all humidity I take my leave from
the Tower this x[vii]ith of Februarie
1599.

yo[ur] hono[ur]s in all humble and
dutiefull service

Letter written by Eleanor's son James to Sir Robert Cecil from the Tower of London, 1599.

Right honorable I do holde my selfe so much bound
unto yo[r] favours as what I maye be though
absolutely I must holde it to coome from that
glorious sun wch fills the worlde wth wonderment
yet myne affectionat service to yo[r] honorable nature
wherein I am obliged, shall allwaies present you wth
the fruites of a never unthankefull spirit, in wch
holdinge my selfe assured and yo[r] honor I hope therein
pleased wth my humble indevours becawse I must
not be tied to manie and unto these fewe to whom
I will engage the ernest of my love remayne constantly
respective, amongst a number of my bolde Importunities
wch yo[r] honor hath pleased to pardon I beseech you
to undertake this, in wch I have longe travayled
and wthout yo[r] ayde, do dispaire ever to coome forthe
of. Where I have been longe a sutor unto S[r] John
Fortescue to acquainted his Ma[tie] wth my letts
wch he hath performed and signified his highnes
pleasure unto the Lieutenant that some order
shoulde be taken for the satisfyinge thereof, findinge
the continuall clamor of my poore creditors wch I
protest unto yo[r] honor noth grieve my very soule
and my tedious sicknes to drive an extraordinary
charge unto his highnes wch as yet is unsatisfied
and as yet loosinge the benefite of that happy hearinge
whose princely commiseration gave consent halfe
yeare at leaste agoe that I shoulde be dischardged, onely
order therein wantinge) and delayes puttinge
me still of. I do humbly beseech yo[r] honor to
moove his highnes herein that I maye receave
his bountie for my so weake contentment and
yo[r] honors labor for the freeinge of so much my spes
vexation wth troubles me more. God is my witnes
then my twenty yeares imprisoment. And so reserving
this my humble sute my selfe and whatsoever else
shalbe thought fitt to yo[r] honorable consideration take
for the coomforte of my longe affliction. Take
my leave from the Tower this 23th of December

1599

yo[r] honors in all humble service

Letter written by Eleanor's son James to Sir Robert Cecil from the Tower of London, 1599.

Letter to Sir Robert Cecil signed by Sir Donogh O'Connor Sligo, Eleanor's second husband, 1598.

Ireland was too far advanced to be reversed by a single victory. And at almost sixty years of age Eleanor realised this better than most. She knew only too well the outcome of defeat in rebellion. In late 1602 news of Red Hugh O'Donnell's death in Spain reached Sligo. In Ulster O'Neill made his conditional peace with the Crown to ensure his survival and to salvage his earldom from the wreckage of his defeat. O'Connor Sligo made terms with Lambert, who conducted him to Athlone to meet with Mountjoy. O'Connor Sligo made a good case for pardon before the Lord Deputy, who was aware that he had been made a virtual prisoner by O'Donnell and had no option but to align with the rebels. Anxious also to end the hostilities in Connaught, Mountjoy pardoned him, and in 1604 Donogh O'Connor Sligo received a knighthood.

But peace and pardons aside, the financial fortunes of Eleanor, her family and her husband were still precarious. During the long years of war and turmoil her pension from the Crown had not been regularly paid and her daughters had not received their allowances. Her husband's territory of Carbury, which lay in close proximity to the lordship of O'Donnell, had been wasted by the incursions of O'Donnell and the retaliatory attacks of the Crown. O'Connor Sligo testified as to the condition of Ballymote, the only habitable castle of his estate: 'It is also greatly defaced and the house burnt down by O'Donnell's people. . . . I will, if granted it,' he promised, 'repair the castle and house.'[34] During Donogh's long absence in England the English administration in Connaught, particularly under Bingham, had made great inroads into his estates. The focal point of Crown interest was Sligo castle, which had been taken by Sir John King. Moreover, the rents normally forthcoming from his estates had been rendered negligible by the late unrest. Both Eleanor and her husband were once again near the poverty line. Sir Donogh eventually obtained letters patent to Sligo castle and lands, and it was there he settled with Eleanor and entered into the new war that had begun over the ownership of the land of Ireland.

While English military dominance had been established over Ireland, the ownership of the land still remained largely in Gaelic hands. Under Elizabeth's successor, James I, the battle for possession of the land of Ireland intensified. It was a war waged by lawyers, adventurers, profiteers and officials who, armed with pens, parchment, obscure deeds and money, sought to acquire, by illegal or quasi-legal means, the estates and property of the impoverished native aristocracy. In Sligo Sir James Fullerton, a Scottish spy of James I, had been granted the castle of Ballymote and the valuable lands of Sligo abbey, and the rents payable to Sir Donogh for these properties were distrained from him. Sir Donogh, prodded by Eleanor, entered the fray and lay legal claim to lands not necessarily part of his inheritance and contested the claims of the new planters. Some of his claims were admitted by the Crown, and 'subsidised with government money, Sir Donogh bought from Sir William Taaffe much of the land which the latter had acquired in Sligo'.[35] He successfully instituted legal proceedings in the Courts of Chancery and Exchequer to protect his estates from avaricious entrepreneurs who sought flaws in his titles, and also to have restored the rents and services due to him from dependent septs. He spent the remaining years of his life attempting to put his estate and property on a secure legal footing in English common law. His estate, however, failed to yield sufficient profit, and he was forced to mortgage much land and property, particularly to the merchant families of Galway, who had the means and the money to exploit the reduced circumstances of the old aristocracy on the collapse of the structures of Gaelic society.

While her husband strove to untangle the legal and financial web of his estate, Eleanor, together with her daughters Joan and Ellen, proceeded to England once more to attempt to extract additional maintenance from the new king. Despite her advanced age and the long years of making ends meet and surviving on the meagre subsistence that she had eventually extracted from the English administration, and in the face of the most awesome and persistent misfortunes, her hope had never waned that fate eventually would deal her a kinder hand. She arrived in London in the summer of 1603 and, as she attested, 'for nine months following the court at great cost',[36] petitioned the King and the Privy Council for the restoration of her pension and for some part of her late husband's estate in Munster. She told Sir Robert Cecil that, owing to the destruction wrought by the late rebellion on her second husband's lordship, she was 'destitute of a place of abode both for me and mine'.[37] Her daughters petitioned the King in similar vein and attested 'that the misery of our estate is such as we are ashamed to make it manifest to the world'.[38] They appealed also to Sir Robert Cecil because, as they stated, 'your lordship ever stood the best friend that either our brother or selves have had, we beseech you now to assign us some proportionable living to our estates and calling'.[39] By now Eleanor and her daughters were familiar figures on the outer fringes of court circles, as they hovered irresolutely in the background, without the money, means or political clout to assert their case, but entirely dependent on the pity and charity of Cecil and the other court officials. They followed the royal court from place to place for as long as their meagre means would allow. They lodged in back-street boarding houses and inns and starved themselves of food and necessities in order to appear in some suitable state at court, wherein lay their only chance of alleviating their lowly plight. They could not afford to dwell on the humiliation and degradation of their position, for the alternative—the possibility that they might be denied access to the court to plead their case— was far too frightening and all too real. It was only Eleanor's great sense of hope and her will to survive that took them through the ordeal.

At last, after much hardship, their mission seemed likely to be blessed with success. In 1605 Cecil managed to have Eleanor's pension and arrears sanctioned for payment, and Eleanor contrived to have an advance of one year paid to her, which she used to clear the debts incurred during their prolonged stay in England. She assured Cecil that she had arranged with the Earl of Kildare that he 'will join her in bonds, that if she die within the year, to restore so much thereof as shall not fall due during her life',[40] for, as she informed him, 'I know no other means to rid me hence or bear my charges; otherwise I must stay longer than I meant, and run further in debte, so much as I shall be unable to go at any time.'[41] But the old campaigner would see many more decades and outlive those from whom she now begged and borrowed. Whether out of compassion for her age and position, or whether as a means to rid himself finally of a wily and persistent petitioner whose mental and physical energies defied her years, Cecil granted her demands and instructed the Lord Deputy and Council in Dublin henceforth to deal favourably with the countess and her daughters 'now on their return from England to Ireland and particularly to take order that they be paid from time to time the pension granted them by His Majesty without unnecessary delay'.[42]

While Eleanor had managed to have her material wants alleviated, on her return to Sligo with her daughter Ellen she found Sir Donogh still deeply involved in the legal battle for his estates and property. His competitors ironically accused him of seeking to acquire too large an estate, of having 'a great living and cannot be contented',[43] to which he replied, understandably enough in view of the encroachment on the estates of his family by the self-same accusers, 'I bear the name but they have all the substance.'[44] During 1607 and 1608 Sir Donogh fought a series of lawsuits to defend his estate from avaricious entrepreneurs and ambitious former tributary septs who sought to establish legal claims on the strength of broken or faulty titles to lands in the hereditary possession of his ancestors. The pressures and expenses of each successive case began to take their toll. 'I am since my coming into Ireland', he complained to Cecil, 'tossed and troubled in wronged lawsuits by my continual disturber Sir William Taaffe, with whom is joined Sir Lionel Guest.'[45] But Sir Donogh was fighting a losing battle. His most deadly adversary was the swelling tide of greed and sharp practice that, in its way, was far more insidious and effective as a means of reducing the Gaelic aristocracy than the guns and cannon of the previous century. Against this onslaught, Sir Donogh's determined endeavours, even when aided by Eleanor's diplomatic skill, had no hope of success. On 11 August 1609 the old chieftain died at Sligo castle; as Eleanor informed Cecil, 'The tediousness in withstanding the said causes did so weary and wear him out that in the end the grief finished his life.'[46]

Eleanor had every reason to grieve the death of her sober, well-intentioned second husband. He had been kind and considerate and had striven unceasingly to provide her with a status and lifestyle suitable to her rank. When every back was turned on her in her years of greatest poverty and humiliation, Donogh O'Connor Sligo, whether motivated and encouraged by political or social considerations or simply from a sense of affection for the abandoned countess, offered her his hand and his protection. The inscription Eleanor later had carved over his tomb is a testimony to the deep affection she bore her second husband:

> Is your hand the martial hand that shone in war
> And yours the gentle one that shone in peace
> Turned to ashes . . . ?
> I . . . who with moistened cheeks stretch forth
> My arms in redoubled lamentation
> Will ever be mindful of your death.[47]

And the affection which Sir Donogh bore his wife was more materially demonstrated by the extraordinarily substantial inheritance which he bequeathed to her and which, inadvertently, was to complicate yet further the already tangled legal affairs of his estate. As part of her jointure, Sir Donogh bequeathed to his wife 'thirteene castles, one hundred messuages, ten gardens, four thousand acres of land, one thousand acres of pasture, one thousand acres of wood, one thousand acres of moor and three thousand acres of heath'.[48]

Eleanor was, for a second time, a widow, but this time under less traumatic and calamitous circumstances. In theory she was substantially well-off, but in practice the revenue-raising power of the O'Connor estate had been eroded over the previous decades. It was impossible to extract rents and dues from tenants and tributary septs who were unable or unwilling to pay. Moreover, the land had been plundered by both sides in the late war and had been neglected in the succeeding years when the legal war as to its ownership was under way. The estate required a substantial injection of capital if it was to survive the financial and legal difficulties with which it was threatened. To ease the financial strain which again threatened to overwhelm her, Eleanor embarked on a matchmaking exercise. In an attempt to consolidate control of the O'Connor Sligo estate, she married her daughter Ellen to Sir Donogh's brother and heir, Donal, a widower of thirty-five years of age. Of Sir Donal and his impending marriage to Eleanor's daughter, it was reported to Sir Robert Cecil:

> He speaks English well; he was bred up in the wars in France; the people have a great opinion of him and he is like to prove an honest man if his grafting upon a crabbed stock do not alter his proper nature.[49]

But Eleanor's hopes were destined to be thwarted, for Sir Donal survived his brother by a mere two years. Ellen married secondly Sir Robert Cressey of Cong, a member of the English administration in Connaught. Her marriage jointure, due from the O'Connor Sligo estate on her second marriage, placed added strain on the viability of the estate. Eleanor married off her youngest daughter, Ellis, to Sir Valentine Browne, son and heir of Sir Nicholas Browne of Kerry. She had initially attempted to arrange a marriage between one of her daughters and the heir to the neighbouring O'Connor Don estate, but for political reasons the Crown was opposed to 'two such great families joining together'.[50]

Having finally secured reasonable matches for her daughters, it was not unreasonable that Eleanor should expect to enjoy her remaining years in the peace and tranquillity that had evaded her all her life. But it was not to be, for she was forced to embark on yet another legal battle to protect her right to the lands and property bequeathed to her by Sir Donogh. On the untimely death of her late husband's brother and heir, the O'Connor estate was inherited by his son by a previous marriage who was then a minor. The wardship of the young heir was granted by the King to a certain Sir Faithful

Fortescue. 'Alarmed by the extent to which the property was tied up in marriage jointures, Fortescue initiated an action in the Dublin courts to have the Countess of Desmond's jointure overthrown'[51] because, he claimed, of defects in the wording of the conveyance. During the course of the year 1613 Eleanor made frequent representations to the Irish Privy Council regarding the properties in dispute, which were situated mainly in the area of Sligo town. When the case was eventually scheduled to be heard, she pleaded inability to appear, on the grounds of illness and old age. After a further delay the Council ordered an official investigation into the dispute. The investigators found in her favour and recommended to the Lord Deputy that Eleanor, whom they described as 'growne aged and hath not long to live', should be shown 'as much favour as may be afforded to a lady of her years and quality ... that shee may at length be freed of theise unexpected troubles'.[52] Eleanor played the part of the aged, feeble lady, who at the end of her days found herself the victim of greed and circumstances; as such she successfully evoked the sympathy of the Lord Deputy and Council, who ruled that she should hold the lands for the term of her life and that they would then pass to Charles, the King's ward.

The Council, not unnaturally, presumed and based their judgement on the premise that Eleanor's death was imminent. She long outlived both her opponents and her advocates, however, and retained possession of her jointure to the end of her long life.

Epilogue

Is that Penelope, Elinor, that second chaste Judith,
Indeed buried beneath marble stones?
I, mother Ierne, who with moistened cheecks stretch forth
My arms in redoubled lamentation,
Will ever be mindful of your death.

Inscription on Eleanor's tomb, Sligo abbey

Eleanor resided at Sligo castle for the rest of her life. Her days of petitions and appearances at the English court were over. No more correspondence from her prolific quill appears among the state papers of the day. There are no more allusions to the presence of the 'Lady of Desmond' at the royal court. References to payment of her prized pension, which she had fought so diligently to obtain from the Crown, appear sporadically throughout the state despatches of the early decades of the seventeenth century. She doggedly fought her case in the law-courts and hung on tenaciously to every acre bequeathed to her by Sir Donogh O'Connor Sligo. She stood her ground despite the powerful and resourceful opposition of the new breed of fortune-seekers, entrepreneurs and wealthy merchants who, in the years after Kinsale, flooded into Sligo to take advantage, by way of defective title, bribery and sharp practice, of the impoverishment of the remnants of the old Gaelic aristocracy and, whenever possible, to replace them as the new masters and the owners of the land. It took courage and gumption for an aged widow, entirely on her own, to defend her interests with such success against such able opposition. But her days of penury were at last behind her, and her remaining years were spent in the relative comfort and dignity which had eluded her throughout her early and middle life.

Her ability as a matchmaker for her daughters had paid dividends. Her daughter Joan, for whom she had plotted a marriage with Red Hugh O'Donnell, had married Dermot O'Sullivan Beare of Cork. Her

Eleanor's tomb, Sligo Abbey.

third daughter, Katherine, after the death of her first husband, Lord Roche, had married Donal O'Brien, afterwards Viscount Clare. On the death of her second husband, Sir Robert Cressey of Cong, her daughter Ellen had married her cousin Edmund, who in 1629 had succeeded his grandfather as Baron of Dunboyne; by this marriage Eleanor's unhappy feud with her brother over the disputed estate was at last laid to rest. Her youngest daughter, Ellis, married Sir Valentine Browne of Ross castle, Killarney, and 'thus as the wife of an undertaker's son enjoyed some portion of the vast estates which had been forfeited by her father's rebellion'.[1] Eleanor's only son, James, the 'Tower Earl', left no heir. Soon after his death the title was claimed by her first husband's old antagonist, Black Tom, Earl of Ormond, in right of his mother, Joan, as the daughter and heiress of James, the eleventh Earl of Desmond. When the daughter and heiress of Black Tom was bestowed in marriage on a Scotsman, Sir Richard Preston, by King James I, the claim to the Desmond earldom was revived, and Preston, in right of his wife, was created Earl of Desmond by patent dated 1619. The patent stipulated that if Preston died without male heirs, the earldom should descend to George, the younger son of William Fielding, Earl of Denbeigh, with whom a marriage was then being contemplated by Preston's only daughter and heiress. While the marriage did not in fact take place, the provision of the patent was allowed, and the ancient title passed into the Fielding family, who became the Earls of Denbeigh and Desmond. The spirit of Garrett FitzGerald would surely have rested uneasily had the title which he prized so highly come to rest on the descendants of his rival.

In 1624 Eleanor erected an impressive tomb for her second husband in Sligo abbey. It is an interesting monument built in renaissance style, and is in an excellent state of preservation to this day. Situated in the south wall of the abbey, adjacent to the high altar, it consists of two arched recesses in which are carved two kneeling figures in profile, representing Eleanor and Sir Donogh. 'Sir Donogh is clad in plate armour, his helmet being placed on the ground behind him. His wife is dressed in a loose flowing robe overmantle, with a close-fitting cap on which a coronet is placed. Round her neck is a large ruff and a string of beads which supports a cross of the Greek pattern with expanded ends.'[2] The monument is decorated with heraldic emblems of the O'Connor, Butler and FitzGerald families, together with several symbols of death. Together with Eleanor and her husband is buried her daughter Ellis, who died in 1623. The date of Eleanor's own death is less certain. Some authorities state that she lived until the 1650s. Her will, however, is dated 26 November 1638.

By it she appointed her sons-in-law, Sir Donal O'Brien and Sir Robert Cressey, her executors 'and willed them to pay all her debts, called her stated accounts, and her funeral expenses out of her moveable goods and chattels'.[3] She bequeathed to her daughter Joan a silver ewer and basin, and to her daughter Ellen all the remainder of her goods, including her plate and jewels. She left various legacies to her grandchildren, friends and servants. 'She bequeathed towards the building of a hospital in Sligo £100, and £200 more (both out of her arrears in England) to be laid out in an annuity mortgage, or land, so as to yield £20 a year towards the support of the poor residing in said hospital.'[4] Thus although we do not know the exact year of her death, the evidence of her last will and testament shows that, despite her traumatic life, she lived to the remarkable age of well over ninety years, almost double the average life expectancy of the time.

That she lived so long is a tribute to her courage and indomitable will and her superhuman capacity to withstand so much suffering, loss and deprivation. Her mental ability enabled her to overcome the Machiavellian political practices of her time which brought about the downfall of others greater and more powerful than herself. She endured great personal hardship and tragedy, but with extraordinary resilience had returned time after time to meet and to contend with each successive challenge. She was both a witness of and a participant in a period of almost unparalleled upheaval and destruction which had sucked into its maw an entire civilisation. She had seen a fertile green province scorched to a blackened and wasted heathland. She had seen its population starve to death, their pitiful cries mingling with the sound of war and the clamour for spoil of the victors. She herself had suffered the pangs of hunger and the deprivation of a fugitive's life as she stoically stayed by her outlawed husband in his desperate need. She knew the pain of being forced to part with her children as on countless occasions political necessity tore them from her side. She experienced humiliation and insult, isolation and friendlessness as she pursued her mission for survival alone and without means. But her innate will to survive and adapt to the new order was the spur which impelled her to overcome her adversity and gave her the strength to outlive her opponents. Elizabeth, FitzMaurice, Sidney, Perrot, Drury, Sir John of Desmond, Pelham, Malby, Dr Sanders, Black Tom, Essex, Red Hugh, Cecil, the endless list of great and colourful characters with whom she had shared the stage, had all passed on. Eleanor alone remained as the last surviving participant in as great a tragedy as ever befell a family and a nation.

In the quiet ruins of Sligo abbey today the tomb erected by herself stands as the only reminder of this extraordinary but unsung heroine. In life Eleanor received few bouquets, and her lot in death was total oblivion in written history and even in popular folklore, which has preserved the memory of many of her contemporaries. Yet, hidden away from view in musty archives, her prolific correspondence, the script almost indecipherable on the age-darkened, brittle parchment, bears testimony to the life, aims and ambitions of this extraordinary woman on whom fortune seldom smiled but who steadfastly refused to succumb to the dark shadows that relentlessly clouded her life.

The 'Old' Countess of Desmond. The wife of Thomas FitzGerald, 12th Earl of Desmond.

Appendix
The 'Old' Countess
of Desmond

While the story and contribution of Eleanor Butler, Countess of Desmond, to the affairs of the sixteenth century has received little acknowledgement, the life of another Countess of Desmond, a contemporary of hers, has been extensively recorded by both contemporary and latter-day historians and writers. The countess in question was Katherine FitzGerald, daughter of John FitzGerald, second Lord of Decies in Waterford, and wife of her own second cousin, Thomas FitzGerald, twelfth Earl of Desmond. Her main claim to fame was her great longevity, which resulted in her appellation as the 'Old' Countess of Desmond.

One of the earliest references to this extraordinary woman is contained in Sir Walter Raleigh's *History of the World*. In it he records that while she was married in the reign of Edward IV, she was still alive in 1589. Presuming, as was the custom, that she was married at the age of fifteen, and that the marriage took place in the last year of the king's reign, that would leave her at the remarkable age of 121 years in 1589. But evidence of her continued existence,.well into the seventeenth century, is recorded by many contemporary historians, among them the famous Elizabethan writer and traveller, Fynes Moryson, who died in 1614. In his *Itinerary*, published in 1617, he stated:

> In our time the Irish Countesse of Desmonde lived to the age of about one hundred and forty yrs, being able to go on foot four or five miles to the market towne, and used weekly so to do in her last yeares and not many yeares before she died.[1]

A few decades later, Lord Bacon in his *History of Life and Death* claimed that she lived to be 140 years old and that in the process of her long life she grew two new sets of teeth.

On the death of her husband in 1534, the Old Countess of Desmond settled at Inchiquin castle, a few miles south-west of Youghal, which her husband had assigned to her as part of her jointure for the duration of her life. On her death the castle and lands would automatically revert to the Earls of Desmond. There, it was not unnaturally expected, she would live out her few remaining years. But successive Earls of Desmond came and went and Inchiquin remained in the possession of its elderly chatelaine.

It is likely that she and Eleanor met several times during their long lives, especially during 1575 when the controversial enfeoffment by Garrett of his lands was being effected. By a deed dated 5 April 1575 the Old Countess enfeoffed the castle and lands of Inchiquin to the Earl of Desmond, who in turn enfeoffed them in trust to his servants, Morris Sheehan and David Roche, for thirty-one years. Whether she supported Garrett's rebellion is unknown, but she was witness to the devastation of Munster and the subsequent death and attainder of the earl. In the plantation that followed, Inchiquin castle and lands were part of a Crown grant to Sir Walter Raleigh, who, whether obliged by law or in deference to the great age of its antique resident, allowed the Old Countess to remain undisturbed at Inchiquin. Raleigh expected that her demise would be imminent, but she lived on to see Raleigh depart and Inchiquin pass into the grasping hand of Richard Boyle, Earl of Cork. Boyle was less inclined to tolerate the now seemingly unending occupancy of his new property by an aged tenant who simply refused to die. But she resisted his attempts to dislodge her from her perch, and when Boyle persisted she took matters into her own hands. In 1604, at the phenomenal age of some 136 years, this female Methuselah set out from Co. Cork, with her daughter who was over ninety, for the court of the new king, James I. It was recorded that 'landing in Bristol she came on foot to London', while her daughter 'being decrepid was brought in a little carte, their poverty not allowing better means'.[2] While there is no conclusive evidence as to the outcome of her petition to the King, it does seem likely that the touching and incredible apparition of this ancient woman, who had lived through the reigns of seven monarchs and overlapped with two others, was suitably rewarded. For the Old Countess returned to Inchiquin, where her long life was abruptly brought to an end later in 1604 by a bizarre accident. Sir Robert Sidney recorded the circumstances of her death:

She might have lived much longer hade she not mette with a kind of violent death, for she must needs climb a nutt tree to gather nuts, soe falling down, she hurt her thighe, which brought a fever, and that brought death.[3]

So ended the incredible life of the Old Countess of Desmond, although another account places her death ten years later, in 1614. A portrait of a woman which once hung in Muckross abbey, Co. Kerry, purports to be of her, painted during her visit to the court of King James in 1604.

Whether she met her death in 1604 or in 1614, the Old Countess of Desmond has entered the legends and annals of Ireland and Britain, where she has long continued to be considered as an inspiration and example in the records of human longevity.

Older far than my grand-dam, indeed, aye, as old
As that Countess of Desmond of whom we are told
That she lived to much more than a hundred and ten,
And was killed by a fall from a cherry tree, then
What a frisky old girl.[4]

1 : The Family and Connections of Eleanor, Countess of Desmo

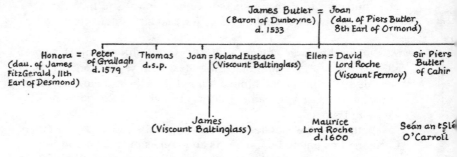

James Butler = Joan
(Baron of Dunboyne) (dau. of Piers Butler,
d. 1533   8th Earl of Ormond)

Honora = Peter   Thomas   Joan = Roland Eustace   Ellen = David   Sir Piers
(dau. of James of Grallagh d.s.p.   (Viscount Baltinglass)   Lord Roche   Butler
FitzGerald, 11th d. 1579   (Viscount Fermoy)   of Cahir
Earl of Desmond)

James   Maurice   Seán an tSlé
(Viscount Baltinglass)   Lord Roche   O'Carroll
d. 1600

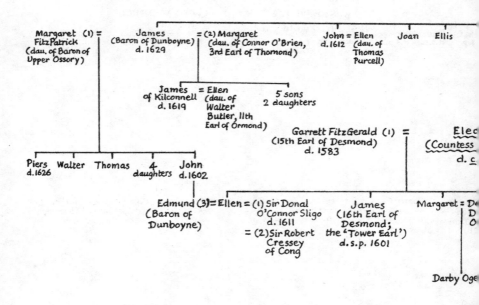

Margaret (1) =   James   = (2) Margaret   John = Ellen   Joan   Ellis
FitzPatrick   (Baron of Dunboyne) (dau. of Connor O'Brien,   d. 1612 (dau. of
(dau. of Baron of d. 1629   3rd Earl of Thomond)   Thomas
Upper Ossory)   Purcell)

James   = Ellen   5 sons
of Kilconnell (dau. of   2 daughters
d. 1619   Walter
Butler, 11th
Earl of Ormond)

Garrett FitzGerald (1) =   Eleo
(15th Earl of Desmond)   (Countess
d. 1583   d. c

Piers Walter Thomas   4   John
d. 1626   daughters d. 1602

Edmund (3)= Ellen = (1) Sir Donal   James   Margaret = D
(Baron of   O'Connor Sligo   (16th Earl of   D
Dunboyne)   d. 1611   Desmond;   O
= (2) Sir Robert   the 'Tower Earl')
Cressey   d.s.p. 1601
of Cong

Darby Oge

The author is indebted to Dr K.W. Nicholls, of University College, Cork,
for his assistance and his kind permission to use his research material in
the compilation of this genealogy.

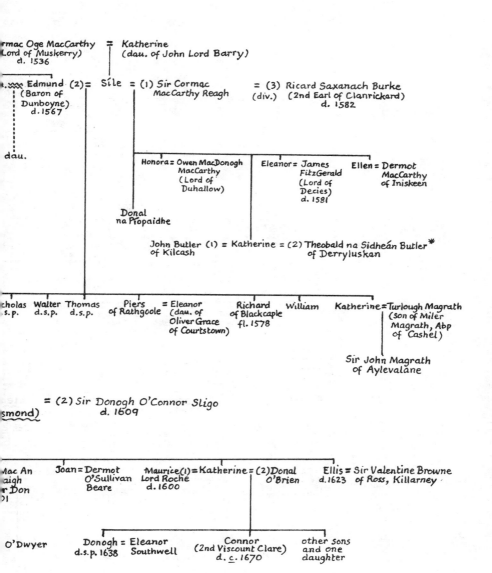

...rmac Oge MacCarthy (Lord of Muskerry) d. 1536 = Katherine (dau. of John Lord Barry)

...xxx Edmund (2)= Síle = (1) Sir Cormac MacCarthy Reagh   = (3) Ricard Saxanach Burke (div.) (2nd Earl of Clanrickard) d. 1582
(Baron of Dunboyne) d. 1567

dau.

Honora = Owen MacDonogh MacCarthy (Lord of Duhallow)   Eleanor = James FitzGerald (Lord of Decies) d. 1581   Ellen = Dermot MacCarthy of Iniskeen

Donal na Propaidhe

John Butler (1) = Katherine = (2) Theobald na Sidheán Butler * of Kilcash   of Derryluskan

...cholas s.p.   Walter d.s.p.   Thomas d.s.p.   Piers of Rathgoole = Eleanor (dau. of Oliver Grace of Courtstown)   Richard of Blackcaple fl. 1578   William   Katherine = Turlough Magrath (son of Miler Magrath, Abp of Cashel)

Sir John Magrath of Aylevalane

= (2) Sir Donogh O'Connor Sligo d. 1609
...smond)

...Mac An ...aigh ...r Don ...1   Joan = Dermot O'Sullivan Beare   Maurice(1) = Katherine = (2) Donal Lord Roche   O'Brien d. 1600   Ellis = Sir Valentine Browne d. 1623 of Ross, Killarney

O'Dwyer   Donogh = Eleanor d.s.p. 1638 Southwell   Connor (2nd Viscount Clare) d. c. 1670   other sons and one daughter

* Tibbot na Sidheán's father was John Butler, a brother of James Butler, Baron of Dunboyne. Tibbot married secondly Katherine Burke, widow of James FitzMaurice FitzGerald (d.1579).

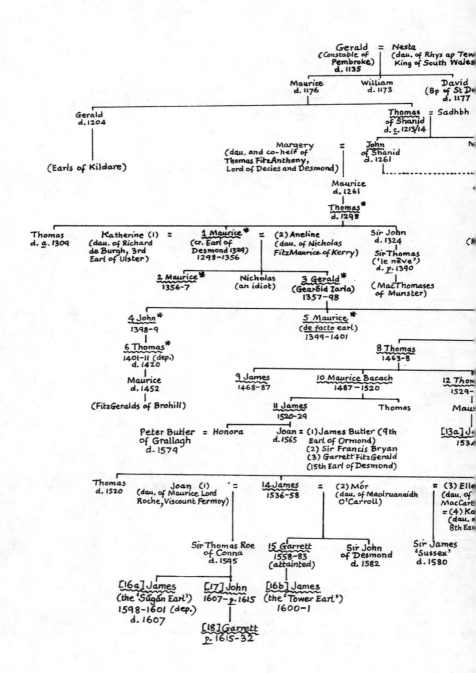

2 : FitzGeralds, Earls of Desmond, 1329–1632, and their antecedents

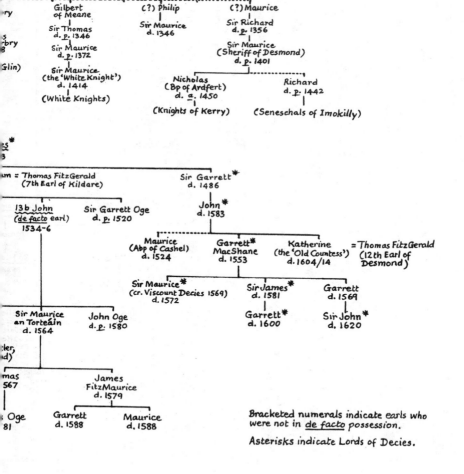

Bracketed numerals indicate earls who were not in *de facto* possession.

Asterisks indicate Lords of Decies.

3: Butlers, Earls and Dukes of Ormond, 1328–1745, and their antecedents

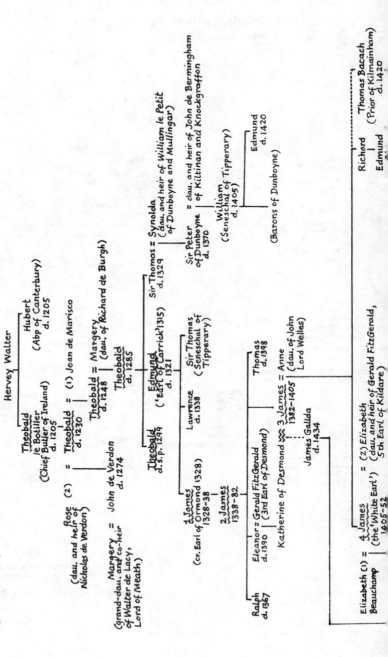

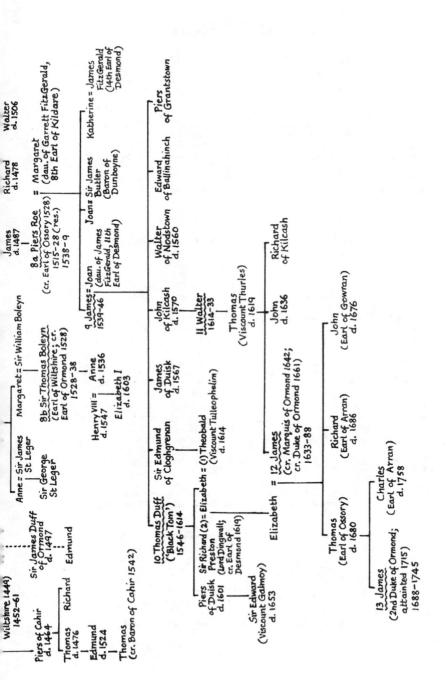

References

CHAPTER 1
1. Maher, *Romantic Slievnamon*, 48.
2. *Cal. S.P. Ire., 1601–3*, 251.
3. Canny, *Elizabethan Conquest*, 22.
4. Nicholls, *Gaelic and Gaelicised Ireland*, 8.
5. Beckett, *Making of Modern Ireland*, 14.
6. Nicholls, *Gaelic and Gaelicised Ireland*, 83.
7. Ibid., 73.
8. Ibid., 78.
9. Joyce, *Social History of Ancient Ireland*, II, 120.
10. Butler, 'Peter Butler of Grallagh Castle', *Butler Soc. Jn.*, I, 3 (1970), 197.

CHAPTER 2
1. Smith, *Elizabethan Epic*, 90.
2. 'The Housekeeping of Irish Chiefs', *Dublin University Magazine*, LIII (1959), 463.
3. *Annals of the Four Masters*, V, 1561.
4. N.L.I., MS 2289.
5. *Unpubl. Geraldine Docs*, I, 505.
6. Ibid.
7. N.L.I., MS 2289.
8. Ibid.
9. *Unpubl. Geraldine Docs*, I, 20.
10. Ibid.
11. Cox, *Hibernia Anglicana*, II, 392.
12. Nicholls, *Gaelic and Gaelicised Ireland*, 164.
13. Berleth, *Twilight Lords*, 76.
14. *Cal. Carew MSS*, I, 417.
15. Ibid., 416.
16. MacCurtain, 'The Fall of the House of Desmond', *Kerry Arch. & Hist. Soc. Jn.*, VIII (1975) 89.
17. Ibid.
18. *Annals of the Four Masters*, V, 1579.
19. Bagwell, *Tudors*, II, 48.
20. Ibid.
21. *Unpubl. Geraldine Docs*, II, 506.
22. Berleth, *Twilight Lords*, 81.

CHAPTER 3
1. Berleth, *Twilight Lords*, 80.
2. FitzGerald, *Geraldines*, appx.
3. *Unpubl. Geraldine Docs*, I, 42.
4. Ibid., 56.

5. FitzGerald, *Geraldines*, 64.
6. *New Hist. Ire.*, III, 87.
7. *Unpubl. Geraldine Docs*, I, 61.
8. *Sidney State Papers*, 34.
9. Ibid.
10. Canny, *Elizabethan Conquest*, 32.
11. *Sidney State Papers*, 67.
12. *Cal. Carew MSS*, III, lvii.
13. Bagwell, *Tudors*, II, 114.
14. *Cal. Pepys MSS*, 47.
15. Ibid.
16. Wright, *History of Ireland*, 419.
17. Ibid., 422.
18. Gaughan, *Knights of Glin*, 29.
19. *New Hist. Ire.*, III, 88.
20. *Cal. Cecil MSS*, I, 349.
21. FitzGerald, *Geraldines*, 102.
22. *Unpubl. Geraldine Docs*, I, 23.
23. Ibid., II, 517.
24. Countess of Desmond to Munster Commissioners, 11 Jan. 1568 (S.P., 63/23/16 ii).
25. Ibid.
26. Munster Commissioners to Countess of Desmond, 13 Jan. 1568 (S.P., 63/23/16 iv).
27. L'Estrange, *Conna and Desmond*, 46.
28. *Cal. Cecil MSS*, I, 355.
29. S.P., various entries.
30. Desmond to Thomas FitzGerald, 10 May 1568 (S.P., 63/26/39).
31. *Unpubl. Geraldine Docs*, II, 515.
32. Bagwell, *Tudors*, II, 137.
33. Ibid., 138.
34. Canny, *Elizabethan Conquest*, 67.
35. FitzGerald, *Geraldines*, 259.
36. Bagwell, *Tudors*, II, 151.
37. *New Hist. Ire.*, III, 92.
38. Bagwell, *Tudors*, II, 154.
39. *New Hist. Ire.*, III, 93.
40. Bagwell, *Tudors*, II, 151.
41. *New Hist. Ire.*, III, 89.

CHAPTER 4
1. FitzGerald, *Geraldines*, 262.
2. Ibid., 263.
3. Black, *Reign of Elizabeth*, 477.
4. *Unpubl. Geraldine Docs*, II, 484.
5. *Cal. Carew MSS*, V, 415.

6. *Unpubl. Geraldine Docs*, II, 415.
7. Ibid.
8. Ibid., 485.
9. Desmond to Cecil, 5 July 1570 (S.P., 63/30/69).
10. *Sidney State Papers*, 130.
11. St Leger to Privy Council, 17 Oct. 1570 (S.P., 63/30/87).
12. Ibid.
13. *Cal. Pat. Rolls Ire., Eliz.*, 546.
14. *New Hist. Ire.*, III, 99.
15. Berleth, *Twilight Lords*, 40.
16. St Leger to Burghley, 6 June 1571 (S.P., 63/32/54).
17. Ibid.
18. *Unpubl. Geraldine Docs*, I, 28.
19. Ibid., 62.
20. Ibid.
21. N.L.I., MS 2289.
22. *Unpubl. Geraldine Docs*, II, 485.
23. Ibid.
24. *New Hist. Ire.*, III, 91.
25. Lambeth Palace Library, MS 616.
26. Bagwell, *Tudors*, III, 210.
27. Ibid.
28. Ibid., 234.
29. *Cal. Carew MSS*, V, 430.
30. Bagwell, *Tudors*, II, 238.
31. Wright, *History of Ireland*, 437.
32. *Unpubl. Geraldine Docs*, II, 485.

CHAPTER 5
1. *New Hist. Ire.*, III, 99.
2. Bagwell, *Tudors*, II, 248.
3. Ibid., 251.
4. Desmond to Lord Deputy and Council, 25 Nov. 1573 (S.P., 63/43/6 i).
5. Bagwell, *Tudors*, II, 487.
6. Justice Walshe to Lord Deputy, 24 Nov. 1573 (S.P., 63/43/6 iii).
7. Bagwell, *Tudors*, II, 253.
8. Desmond to Lord Deputy and Council, 25 Nov. 1573 (S.P., 63/43/6 i).
9. Ibid.
10. Bagwell, *Tudors*, II, 263.
11. Ibid.
12. *Cal. Carew MSS*, I, 463.
13. Ibid.
14. *Cal. S.P. Ire., 1574–85*, 169.
15. Lord Deputy to Burghley, 18 Apr. 1574 (S.P., 63/45/72).
16. *Cal. S.P. Ire., 1574–85*, 27.
17. Ibid.
18. *Cal. Carew MSS*, I, 473.
19. Bagwell, *Tudors*, II, 281.
20. Ibid.
21. *Cal. Carew MSS*, I, 475.
22. *Cal. Pat. Rolls Ire., Eliz.*, 109.
23. *Cal. Carew MSS*, I, 480.

24. Ibid., 482.
25. Bagwell, *Tudors*, II, 284.
26. Countess of Desmond to the Queen, 12 Sept. 1574 (S.P., 63/47/55).
27. Ibid.
28. Ibid.
29. FitzGerald, *Geraldines*, 274.
30. *Cal. S.P. Ire., 1574–85*, 482.
31. *Unpubl. Geraldine Docs*, I, 25.
32. Ibid.
33. *Cal. S.P. Ire., 1574–85*, 65.
34. *Cal. Carew MSS*, II, 21.
35. Ibid., 22.

CHAPTER 6
1. Canny, *Elizabethan Conquest*, 154.
2. *New Hist. Ire.*, III, 91.
3. Canny, *Elizabethan Conquest*, 3.
4. *New Hist. Ire.*, III, 100-1.
5. Wright, *History of Ireland*, 446.
6. MacCarthy, *Florence MacCarthy Mór*, 2.
7. Bagwell, *Tudors*, II, 314.
8. Wright, *History of Ireland*, 447.
9. Ibid.
10. Ibid., 448.
11. *Cal. S.P. Ire., 1574–85*, xxxv.
12. Perrot, *Chronicle of Ireland*, 141.
13. Ibid., 142.
14. *New Hist. Ire.*, III, 102.
15. *Cal. De L'Isle and Dudley MSS*, II, 60.
16. Ibid., 66.
17. *Cal. S.P. Ire., 1574–85*, xli.
18. Lord Deputy to Privy Council, 20 Feb. 1578 (S.P., 63/60/14).
19. Ibid.
20. Ibid.
21. *Cal. S.P. Ire., 1574–85*, xlii.
22. Chambers, *Granuaile*, 93.
23. S.P., 63/19/56.
24. Countess of Desmond to the Queen, 30 Sept. 1578 (S.P., 63/62/23).
25. Ibid.
26. *Cal. Carew MSS*, II, 140.
27. *Walsingham Letter-Book*, 161.
28. Ibid.
29. Ibid.
30. Lord Chancellor Gerrard to Burghley, 3 Jan. 1579 (S.P., 63/65/3).
31. Ibid.
32. Bagwell, *Tudors*, II, 365.
33. O'Faolain, *The Great O'Neill*, 76.
34. Curtis, *History of Ireland*, 198.
35. *New Hist. Ire.*, III, 104.
36. FitzGerald, *Geraldines*, 279.
37. Nicholls, *Gaelic and Gaelicised Ireland*, 73.
38. *Cal. S.P. Ire., 1574–85*, lvi.
39. Ibid.
40. Ibid.

41. Bagwell, *Tudors* III, 21.
42. Ibid., 22.
43. *Walsingham Letter-Book*, 135.
44. *Annals of the Four Masters*, III, 3784.
45. *Unpubl. Geraldine Docs*, I, 30.
46. *Walsingham Letter-Book*, 168.
47. Ibid.
48. Ibid., 169.
49. Ibid.
50. Benvenuta, 'The Geraldine War – Rebellion or Crusade?', *Ir. Cath. Hist. Comm. Proc.* (1963–8), 17.
51. *Walsingham Letter-Book*, 195.
52. Desmond to Privy Council, 10 Oct. 1579 (S.P., 63/69/51).
53. *Walsingham Letter-Book*, 195.
54. *Cal. S.P. Ire., 1574–85*, 190.
55. Ibid.
56. *Walsingham Letter-Book*, 202.
57. Desmond to Privy Council, 10 Oct. 1579 (S.P., 63/69/51).
58. Desmond to Ormond, 10 Oct. 1579 (S.P., 63/69/50).
59. Archbishop Loftus and Sir Henry Wallop to Privy Council, 31 Oct. 1579 (S.P., 63/67/76).
60. Perrot, *Chronicle of Ireland*, 162.
61. *Cal. Carew MSS*, II, 162.
62. *Unpubl. Geraldine Docs*, I, 32.
63. Ibid.
64. Perrot, *Chronicle of Ireland*, 164.
65. *Cal. Carew MSS*, III, xvii.

CHAPTER 7
1. Smith, *Elizabethan Epic*, 143.
2. *Cal. Carew MSS*, III, 164.
3. Ibid., 265.
4. Ibid.
5. Ibid., II, 207.
6. Ibid.
7. Pelham to Walsingham, 16 Feb. 1580 (S.P., 63/71/209).
8. Ibid.
9. Ibid.
10. *Cal. Carew MSS*, II, 190.
11. Cox, *Hibernia Anglicana*, II, 361.
12. *Walsingham Letter-Book*, 249.
13. *Cal. Carew MSS*, II, 225.
14. Berleth, *Twilight Lords*, 125.
15. *Cal. Carew MSS*, II, 236.
16. Pelham to the Queen, 1 Apr. 1580 (S.P., 63/73/28).
17. Pelham to Walsingham, 5 Apr. 1580 (S.P., 63/73/33).
18. Pelham to Wallop, 21 June 1580 (S.P., 63/73/68 i).
19. Countess of Desmond to Privy Council, 28 June 1580 (S.P., 63/73/67).

20. Wright, *History of Ireland*, 470.
21. Captain Golde to Walsingham, 17 Sept. 1580 (S.P., 63/70/51 i).
22. *Cal. Carew MSS*, II, 292.
23. Fenton to Walsingham, 8 Aug. 1580 (S.P., 63/75/27).
24. *Cal. Carew MSS*, II, 297.
25. St Leger to Burghley, 9 Oct. 1580 (S.P., 63/77/24).
26. Perrot, *Chronicle of Ireland*, 170.
27. Malby to Walsingham, 24 Oct. 1580 (S.P., 63/77/52).
28. Bagwell, *Tudors*, III, 64.
29. Ibid., 69.
30. Perrot, *Chronicle of Ireland*, 172.
31. *Annals of the Four Masters*, V, 1761.
32. St Leger to Burghley, 15 May 1581 (S.P., 63/83/25).
33. Countess of Desmond to Lord General and Council of Munster, 29 Apr. 1581 (S.P., 63/83/6 ii).
34. Ibid.
35. Ibid.
36. Spenser, *Poetical Works*, ed. Smith and de Selincourt, 3.
37. Lord Deputy and Council to Lord General and Council of Munster, 10 May 1581 (S.P., 63/83/6 iii).
38. Ibid.
39. Ibid.
40. Ibid.
41. St Leger to Burghley, 15 May 1581 (S.P., 63/83/25).
42. *Annals of the Four Masters*, V, 1779.
43. *Cal. S.P. Ire., 1574–85*, 339.
44. Perrot, *Chronicle of Ireland*, 178.
45. Lord Deputy to Privy Council, 22 June 1582 (S.P., 63/93/45).
46. Walsingham to Lord Deputy, 25 June 1582 (S.P., 63/93/53).
47. Ibid.
48. Countess of Desmond to Burghley, 28 Aug. 1582 (S.P., 63/94/104).
49. Countess of Desmond to Lord Deputy, 28 Aug. 1582 (S.P., 63/94/104 i).
50. FitzGerald, *Geraldines*, 289.
51. Ibid.
52. O'Faolain, *The Great O'Neill*, 81.
53. Captain Norris to Lords Justices Loftus and Wallop, 24 Sept. 1582 (S.P., 63/96/3 i).
54. *Cal. S.P. Ire.*, 1574–85, 268.
55. Ibid.
56. *Annals of the Four Masters*, V, 1783.
57. *Cal. Carew MSS*, II, 364.
58. Desmond to Ormond, 5 June 1583 (S.P., 63/102/87 i).
59. Captain Golde to Burghley, 13 Apr. 1583 (S.P., 63/101/25).

60. *Cal. S.P. Ire., 1574–85*, 287.
61. Ormond to Burghley, 18 June 1583 (S.P., 63/102/88).
62. *Annals of the Four Masters*, V, 1793.
63. Bagwell, *Tudors*, III, 113.
64. Ormond to Burghley, 28 Nov. 1583 (S.P., 63/105/83).
65. Perrot, *Chronicle of Ireland*, 182.
66. Ibid.
67. O'Faolain, *The Great O'Neill*, 83.

CHAPTER 8
1. *New Hist. Ire.*, III, 111.
2. *Cal. Pat. Rolls Ire., Eliz.*, lxv.
3. Ibid.
4. Ormond to Burghley, 28 Nov. 1583 (S.P., 63/105/83).
5. Ormond to Lords Justices Loftus and Wallop, 16 Dec. 1583 (S.P., 63/106/13).
6. Ibid.
7. *Cal. S.P. Ire., 1574–83*, 484.
8. *Cal. Pat. Rolls Ire., Eliz.*, 94.
9. Ormond to Burghley, 26 June 1584 (S.P., 63/107/48).
10. *Unpubl. Geraldine Docs*, II, 67.
11. Ibid.
12. Lord Deputy to the Queen, 24 Oct. 1584 (S.P., 63/112/35).
13. Bagwell, *Tudors*, III, 123.
14. *New Hist. Ire.*, III, 112.
15. Lord Deputy to the Queen, 24 Oct. 1584 (S.P., 63/112/35).
16. Ibid.
17. *Unpubl. Geraldine Docs*, II, 68.
18. Ibid.
19. *New Hist. Ire.*, III, 113.
20. *Unpubl. Geraldine Docs*, III, 552.
21. Ibid.
22. Ibid., 553.
23. Ibid.
24. Ibid.
25. Ibid.
26. Ibid., 535.
27. Ibid.
28. *New Hist. Ire.*, III, 113.
29. Archbishop Loftus to Burghley, 18 June 1585 (S.P., 63/112/89).
30. Countess of Desmond to Burghley, 4 Sept. 1585 (S.P., 63/112/90).
31. Countess of Desmond to Burghley, 10 Feb. 1586 (S.P., 63/113/68).
32. *Cal. Pat. Rolls Ire. Eliz.*, 108.
33. Smith, *Elizabethan Epic*, 177.
34. Ibid., 175.
35. Ibid., 176.
36. Ibid., 181.
37. Ibid.

38. Archbishop Loftus to Burghley, 10 May 1586 (S.P., 63/124/8).
39. *Unpubl. Geraldine Docs*, II, 69.
40. *Cal. Pat. Rolls Ire., Eliz.*, 116.
41. Ibid., 70.
42. Ibid., 72.
43. Smith, *Elizabethan Epic*, 182.
44. *Unpubl. Geraldine Docs*, II, 72.
45. Spenser, *Poetical Works*, ed. Smith and de Selincourt, 3.
46. Smith, *Elizabethan Epic*, 203.
47. *Cal. Pat. Rolls Ire., Eliz.*, 186.
48. N.L.I., MS D.10028.
49. Ibid.
50. B.L., Lansdowne MS 65.
51. *Unpubl. Geraldine Docs*, appx, 567.
52. O'Dowd, 'Landownership in the Sligo Area, 1585–1641', 85.
53. Wood-Martin, *History of Sligo*, I, 323.
54. *Cal. S.P. Ire., 1596–7*, 325.
55. *Cal. Pat. Rolls Ire., Eliz.*, 479.
56. Ibid.
57. O'Dowd, 'Landownership in the Sligo Area, 1585–1641'. 111.
58. *Cal. Cecil MSS*, VII, 282.
59. Ibid.
60. *Cal. Pat. Rolls Ire., Eliz.*, 479.
61. *Cal. Cecil MSS*, VII, 378.

CHAPTER 9
1. *New Hist. Ire.*, III, 123.
2. *Cal. Cecil MSS*, VIII, 248.
3. O'Faolain, *The Great O'Neill*, 203.
4. Ibid., 205.
5. Bagwell, *Tudors*, III, 303.
6. Ibid.
7. Lords Justices Loftus and Gardiner to the Privy Council, 31 Oct. 1598 (S.P., 63/202/3/135).
8. *Cal. S.P. Ire., 1599–1600*, 172.
9. Ibid., 158.
10. Ibid.
11. Ibid.
12. Ibid., 172.
13. Ibid.
14. *Cal. Salisbury MSS*, X, 67.
15. *Cal. S.P. Ire., 1600–1*, 424.
16. *Unpubl. Geraldine Docs*, II, 489.
17. Ibid., 492.
18. *Cal. S.P. Ire., 1601–3*, 572.
19. *Cal. Carew MSS*, II, 490.
20. Ibid.
21. *Pacata Hibernia*, 108.
22. Ibid.
23. Ibid., 109.
24. Ibid.
25. Bagwell, *Tudors*, III, 383.
26. Ibid.

27. *Cal. Carew MSS*, IV, 33.
28. *Cal. Salisbury MSS*, II, 491.
29. *Unpubl. Geraldine Docs*, II, 497.
30. Ibid.
31. Moryson, *Itinerary*, IV, 390.
32. Bagwell, *Tudors*, III, 391.
33. Moryson, *Itinerary*, IV, 214.
34. 'History of Ballymote Castle', *R.S.A.I. Jn.*, LVII (1927), 98.
35. O'Dowd , 'Landownership in the Sligo Area, 1585–1642', 240.
36. *Cal. Salisbury MSS*, XVI, 371.
37. Ibid.
38. Ibid., XV, 373.
39. Ibid.
40. Ibid., XVII, 587.
41. Ibid.
42. *Cal. S.P. Ire.*, *1603–6*, 568.
43. *Cal. Salisbury MSS*, XVIII, 291.
44. Ibid.
45. Ibid., XX, 136.
46. *Cal. S.P. Ire.*, *1608–10*, 760.

47. National Monuments Commission, *Sligo Abbey*.
48. Wood-Martin, *History of Sligo*, II, 12.
49. *Cal. S.P. Ire.*, *1608–10*, 298.
50. *Cal. S.P. Ire.*, *1606–8*, 197.
51. O'Dowd, 'Landownership in the Sligo Area, 1585–1641', 244.
52. Wood-Martin, *History of Sligo*, III, 11.

EPILOGUE
1. Bagwell, *Tudors*, III, 384.
2. National Monuments Commission, *Sligo Abbey*.
3. Wood-Martin, *History of Sligo*, I, 257.
4. Ibid.

APPENDIX
1. Rowan, *Olde Countesse of Desmonde*, 5.
2. Ibid., 12.
3. Ibid., 21.
4. Ibid.

Bibliography

1. MANUSCRIPT SOURCES

British Library
Cotton Titus MSS, BXIII, BXVIII, Papers on Irish affairs, 1559–1602.
Lansdowne MS 65.

Hatfield House, Hertfordshire
Cecil Papers, 50/83; 51/30, 101; 55/15; 62/25, 86; 68/38; 75/46; 179/96.

Lambeth Palace Library
MS 616, ff. 157, 163, 165 (N.L.I. microfilm p1701).

National Library of Ireland
MSS 2163, 2288–9, 2788, D. 2541, D. 2604, D. 2648, D. 2679, D. 10028.
State Papers relating to Ireland (microfilm; originals in Public Record Office, London): 63/19/56; 63/23/16, 16 ii, 16 iv, 32 viii, 32 ix; 63/26/29, 39; 63/30/69, 87; 63/32/54; 63/34/33 i; 63/43/6 i, 6 iii; 63/45/72; 63/47/55; 63/60/14; 63/61/53; 63/62/23, 24; 63/65/9, 58; 63/65/3, 4; 63/67/76; 63/69/50, 51, 76; 63/70/35, 51 i; 63/71/46, 209; 63/73/28, 33, 67, 68 i; 63/75/27; 63/76/51 i; 63/77/24, 52, 53; 63/80/39; 63/83/6 i, 6 ii, 6 iii, 25; 63/87/7; 63/93/45, 53; 63/94/104, 104 i; 63/96/3 i; 63/101/11, 25 ; 63/102/86, 87 i, 88; 63/103/14; 63/105/83; 63/106/13; 63/107/48; 63/109/59; 63/112/35, 68, 89, 90; 63/113/68; 63/124/8; 63/150/39; 63/202/3/135; 63/207/1/32.

Glin, Co. Limerick
Papers and records in the keeping of the Knight of Glin.

Kiltinan, Co. Tipperary
Papers and records in the keeping of Mrs M. Ogden White.

2. CONTEMPORARY SOURCES

Annála Ríoghachta Éireann: Annals of the Kingdom of Ireland by the Four Masters, from the earliest period to the year 1616, ed. and trans. J. O'Donovan, 7 vols (Dublin 1851).

Annals of Loch Cé: A Chronicle of Irish Affairs, 1014–1590, ed. W. M. Hennessy, 2 vols (London 1871).

Carney, J., ed., *Poems on the Butlers of Ormond, Cahir and Dunboyne, 1400–1650* (Dublin 1945).

Cox, Sir R., *Hibernia Anglicana*, 2 vols (London 1689–90).

Davies, Sir J., *A Discovery of the True Causes Why Ireland Was Never Entirely Subdued until the Beginning of His Majesty's Happy Reign* (London 1612); facsimile reprint (Shannon 1969).

Derricke, J., *The Image of Irelande* (London 1581).

Holinshed, R., *Chronicles of England, Scotland and Ireland*, ed. J. Johnson, 6 vols (London 1807–8).

Moryson, F., *An Itinerary* (London 1617); 4 vols (Glasgow 1907–8).

O'Cleary, L., *The Life of Hugh Roe O'Donnell, Prince of Tirconail, 1586–1602* (Dublin 1893).

O'Daly, D., *Initium, Incrementa et Exitus Familiae Geraldinorum ac Persecutionis Haereticorum Descriptio* (Lisbon 1655); trans. C. P. Meehan (Dublin 1878).

O'Sullivan Beare, P., *Ireland under Elizabeth, being portion of the History of Catholic Ireland by Don Philip O'Sullivan Beare*, ed. M. J. Byrne (Dublin 1903).

Perrot, J., *The Chronicle of Ireland, 1584–1608*, ed. H. Wood (Dublin 1933).

Spenser, E., *A View of the Present State of Ireland . . . in 1596*, ed. W. L. Renwick (Oxford 1970).

[Stafford, T.], *Pacata Hibernia* (London 1633); ed. S. H. O'Grady (London 1896).

Unpublished Geraldine Documents, ed. S. Hayman, 4 pts (Dublin 1870–81).

The Walsingham Letter-Book, or Register of Ireland, May 1578 to December 1579, ed. E. Hogan and N. MacNeill (Dublin 1959).

3. CALENDARS AND PRINTED MANUSCRIPT SOURCES

Calendar of the Carew Manuscripts, ed. J. S. Brewer and W. Bullen, 6 vols (London 1867–73).

Calendar of the Cecil Manuscripts, 8 vols (London 1883–99).

Compossicion Booke of Conought, ed. A. M. Freeman (Dublin 1936).

Calendar of the De L'Isle and Dudley Manuscripts, 6 vols (London 1925–66).

Calendar of Fiants of the Reign of Elizabeth (Appendix to 12th – 18th Reports of the Deputy Keeper of the Public Records of Ireland) (Dublin 1877–94).

Calendar of Ormond Deeds, ed. E. Curtis, Vols II-VI (Dublin 1934–70).

Calendar of the Patent and Close Rolls of Chancery in Ireland, Henry VIII to 18th Elizabeth, ed. J. C. Morrin (Dublin 1861).

Calendar of the Patent and Close Rolls of Chancery in Ireland, Elizabeth, 19 year to end of reign, ed. J. C. Morrin (Dublin 1862).

Irish Patent Rolls of James I: Facsimile of the Irish Record Commission's Calendar, foreword by M. C. Griffith (Dublin 1966).

Calendar of the Pepys Manuscripts (Dublin 1911).

Calendar of the Manuscripts of the Marquis of Salisbury, 23 vols (London 1883–1973).

Sidney State Papers, 1565–70, ed. T. Ó Laidhin (Dublin 1962).

Calendar of the State Papers relating to Ireland, 24 vols (London 1860–1912).

4. SECONDARY SOURCES: BOOKS

Anthologia Hibernica, Vol. I (Dublin 1793).

Bagwell, R., *Ireland under the Tudors*, 3 vols (London 1885–90).

— — — — *Ireland under the Stuarts*, 3 vols (London 1909–16).

Beckett, J. C., *The Making of Modern Ireland, 1603–1923* (London 1966).

Berleth, R., *The Twilight Lords* (London 1979).

Black, J. B., *The Reign of Elizabeth, 1558–1603* (Oxford 1959).

Burke, Sir B., *Genealogical History of the Dormant, Abeyant and Extinct Peerages of the British Empire* (London 1883).

Canny, N., *The Elizabethan Conquest of Ireland: A Pattern Established, 1565–76* (Hassocks 1976).

Chambers, A., *Granuaile: The Life and Times of Grace O'Malley (c. 1530–1603)* (Dublin 1979).

———— *Chieftain to Knight: Tibbott-ne-Long Bourke, First Viscount Mayo (1567–1629)* (Dublin 1983).

Clare, W., ed., 'The Testamentary Records of the Butler Families in Ireland' in *Genealogical Abstracts* (Peterborough 1932).

Cogan, A., *The Ecclesiastical History of the Diocese of Meath, Ancient and Modern*, Vol. I (Dublin 1874).

Curtis, E., *A History of Ireland* (London 1936).

Dunboyne, Lord, *Butler Family History* (Kilkenny n.d.).

Falls, C., *Elizabeth's Irish Wars* (London 1950).

FitzGerald, B., *The Geraldines: An Experiment in Irish Government, 1169–1601* (London 1951).

Gaughan, J. A., *The Knights of Glin: A Geraldine Family* (Dublin 1978).

Joyce, P. W., *Social History of Ancient Ireland*, Vols I-II (Dublin 1913).

Knox, H. T., *History of the County Mayo* (Dublin 1908).

Leask, H. G., *Irish Castles and Castellated Houses* (Dundalk 1972).

L'Estrange, A. G., *Conna and Desmond* (Dublin 1897).

Lodge, J., *Peerage of Ireland*, Vol. VI (Dublin 1789).

McCalmont, R. F., *Memoirs of the Binghams* (London 1915).

MacCarthy, D., *The Life and Letters of Florence MacCarthy Mór* (Cork 1975).

McClintock, H. F., *Handbook on Old Irish Dress* (Dundalk 1958).

———— *Irish and Highland Dress* (Dundalk 1950).

MacCurtain, M., *Tudor and Stuart Ireland* (Dublin 1972).

McGurk, J. J., *The Fall of the Noble House of Desmond, 1579–85*.

Maher, J., ed., *Romantic Slievenamon in History, Folklore and Song* (Tipperary 1955).

Moody, T. W., and Martin, F. X., *The Course of Irish History* (Cork 1967).

Morley, H., ed., *Ireland under Elizabeth and James I* (London 1890).

National Monuments Commission, *Mainistir Shligigh (Sligo Abbey)* (Dublin n.d.).

New History of Ireland, Vol. III: *Early Modern Ireland, 1534–1691*, ed. T. W. Moody, F. X. Martin and F. J. Byrne (Oxford 1976).

Nicholls, K. W., *Gaelic and Gaelicised Ireland in the Middle Ages* (Dublin 1972).

———— *Land Law and Society in Sixteenth-Century Ireland* (Dublin 1976).

O'Brien, B., *Munster at War* (Cork 1971).

O'Dowd, M., 'Landownership in the Sligo Area, 1585–1641' (M.A. thesis, University College, Dublin, 1979).

O'Faolain, S., *The Great O'Neill* (London 1950).

Ronayne, C. O'L., *History of the Earls of Desmond* (London 1929).

Rowan, A. B., *The Olde Countesse of Desmonde* (Dublin 1860).

Sainthill, R., *The Old Countess of Desmond* (Dublin 1861).

Smith, L. B., *The Elizabethan Epic* (London 1966).

Spenser, E., *Poetical Works*, ed. J. C. Smith and E. de Selincourt (London 1912).

Tower of London, Official Handbook (London 1984).

Wood-Martin, W. G., *History of Sligo, County and Town*, 3 vols (Dublin 1882).

Wright, T., *The History of Ireland from the Earliest Period of the Irish Annals to the Present Time* (London n.d.).

5. SECONDARY SOURCES: JOURNALS AND ARTICLES

Butler Society Journal, I, 3 (1970): Butler, T., 'Peter Butler of Grallagh Castle'.
———— I, 5 (1973–4): Butler, G., 'The Battle of Affane'.
Clonmel Historical and Archaeological Journal, I (1968).
Cork Historical and Archaeological Society, Journal, 2nd series, III, 28 (1897): Butler, W., 'The Division of South Munster under the Tudors'.
———— 2nd series, XXVI (1920).
Dublin University Magazine, LIII (1959): 'The Housekeeping of Irish Chiefs'.
Irish Catholic Historical Committee, Proceedings (1962): Mooney, C., 'The Irish Church in the Sixteenth Century'.
———— (1963–8): Benvenuta, Sister M., 'The Geraldine War – Rebellion or Crusade?'.
Irish Genealogist, II, 3–6 (1945–8): Ward, M., 'The Barony of Dunboyne'.
Irish Geography, V, 3 (1966).
Irish Monthly, LIV (1926).
Kerry Archaeological and Historical Society, Journal, II (1969): Culhane, T. F., 'Traditions of Glin and its Neighbourhood'.
———— VIII (1975): MacCurtain, M., 'The Fall of the House of Desmond'.
Limerick Field Club Journal, I, 2 (1897).
Meath Archaeological and Historical Society, Records, VI, 2 (1976): Ward, M., 'Townland Names in the Barony of Dunboyne'.
Royal Historical and Archaeological Association of Ireland, Journal, 4th series, V (1878–9).
Royal Society of Antiquaries of Ireland, Journal, XXXIII (1903): Westropp, T. J., 'Notes on Askeaton, Co. Limerick'.
———— XXXVII (1907): Westropp, T. J., 'The Principal Ancient Castles of the County Limerick'.
———— XXXIX (1909).
———— LVII (1927): 'History of Ballymote Castle'.

Index